Victims and Warriors

Violence, History, and Memory in Amazonia

CASEY HIGH

UNIVERSITY OF ILLINOIS PRESS

Urbana, Chicago, and Springfield

Library of Congress Cataloging-in-Publication Data
High, Casey, 1977–
Victims and warriors: violence, history,
and memory in Amazonia / Casey High.
pages cm. — (Interpretations of culture in the
new millennium)
Includes bibliographical references and index.
ISBN 978-0-252-03905-8 (cloth : alk. paper)
ISBN 978-0-252-08067-8 (pbk. : alk. paper)
ISBN 978-0-252-09702-7 (ebook)
1. Huao Indians—Ecuador—Ethnic identity.
2. Huao Indians—Ecuador—Social conditions.
3. Huao Indians—Wars.
4. Violence—Ecuador.
5. Ethnic relations—Ecuador.
I. Title.
F3722.1.H83H55   2015
305.8009866—dc23   2014033693

Victims and Warriors

INTERPRETATIONS OF CULTURE
IN THE NEW MILLENNIUM

Norman E. Whitten Jr.,
General Editor

*A list of books in the series
appears at the end of the book.*

For my parents, Fred and Sue, Amowa and Ñai

Contents

List of Illustrations

Acknowledgments

This book was made possible by the kindness, support, and intellectual engagement of a seemingly endless list of people at different times and in very different places. First and foremost I would like to thank all of my Waorani friends and acquaintances, whom I occasionally refer to somewhat awkwardly in the following pages as my "hosts." These are the kind and, above all, patient people in the villages of Toñampari, Kiwado, and elsewhere who have opened their homes and lives to me over the years. The tolerance, humor, and care I encountered in these places made my fieldwork not only possible but also enjoyable. I especially thank Amowa and Ñai, my Waorani parents, for sharing their home with me during my fieldwork. Their friendship and generosity, and their many children, have given me abundantly fond and entertaining memories of my time in Toñampari. This book also owes much to many other people whose conversations, concern for my well-being, and tolerance for my often ill-informed questions continue to make my research possible: Koba, Gakamo, Toka, Sarita, Timo, Ramona, Kemperi, Uboye, Ana, Manuela, Wareka, Jorge, Wira, Gemea, Apa, Paa, Alicia, Nanto, Moipa, Yato, Awanka, Iteka, Rosa, Jaime, Cesar, Gaia, Taremo, Abraham, Juan, and the late Dayuma.

I would also like to thank my friends at the Waorani political office in Puyo for supporting my fieldwork and for arranging my travel to Waorani villages. Special thanks to Manuela Ima, whose gift packages and radio communications from the city made the remote location of much of my fieldwork less daunting. In this book I reluctantly use pseudonyms to conceal the identities of most Waorani individuals because narratives of violence and "othering" appear in much of the writing. I hope this would not disappoint them too much.

The research upon which the book is based was funded by grants from the Wenner-Gren Foundation, the Fulbright Commission, the Economic and Social Research Council (ESRC), the Centre national de la recherche scientifique (CNRS), and the Central Research Fund of the University of London. I would like to thank all of these institutions for helping make my research possible.

In addition to the Waorani political office, I owe thanks to a number of institutions in Ecuador and elsewhere that have supported my research in various ways. The Honors College of Washington State University provided an undergraduate study-abroad scholarship and much encouragement for my first full year in Ecuador, where the Centro de Investigaciones del Medio Ambiente y Salud (CIMAS) in Quito supported my initial trip to Toñampari. Thanks to Jose Juncosa, my subsequent fieldwork was sponsored in Ecuador by Editorial Abya-Yala. I thank also the schoolteachers in Toñampari, especially Juan Carlos Armijos, who allowed me to participate in their classes and conversations. In Quito, linguist Connie Dickinson has provided valuable support in training me and several of my Waorani friends to film, transcribe, and translate video recordings. This work, which is part of a collaborative project to document the Waorani language, has helped me significantly in my analysis of Waorani narratives.

Many people have helped me rethink the ideas presented in this book by commenting on earlier drafts or being part of conversations that have contributed to the book. These include Magnus Course, Anne-Christine Taylor, Mary-Elizabeth Reeve, Laura Rival, Jason Sumich, Amit Desai, Girish Daswani, Maurice Bloch, the late Olivia Harris, Mette High, Eve Zucker, Maya Mayblin, Giovanni da Col, Liana Chua, Harry Walker, Ann Kelly, Marc Brightman, Vanessa Grotti, Marcelo Fiorini, and Stephen Nugent. Past and present colleagues at the London School of Economics, Goldsmiths, CNRS, and the University of Edinburgh have contributed a great deal to my thinking and writing through their comments and suggestions in seminar presentations. Throughout the process of writing this book, I have been particularly fortunate to have the enthusiastic support of the series editor, Norman Whitten. As both a leading scholar on Amazonian Ecuador and a committed editor, his critical comments, advice, and support have been invaluable. Special thanks are due to my former PhD supervisors, Peter Gow, Rita Astuti, and the late Olivia Harris, for their inspiration and guidance. All of these people have influenced my thinking about the Waorani and anthropology a great deal, even if my efforts fall short of the suggestions they have made for revising the pages that follow.

Above all, I thank my parents, Fred and Sue, who never cease to offer me faithful support in every way for even the most outlandish projects and paths I have taken up over the years.

Chapter 4 appeared in 2013 as "Lost and Found: Contesting Isolation and Cultivating Contact in Amazonian Ecuador." *Hau: Journal of Ethnographic Theory* 3, no. 3: 195–221.

Introduction

In September 2005 I made a trip to Amazonian Ecuador to visit the Waorani village of Toñampari. A few days after arriving, I joined my old friend Toka and his family on a fishing trip a few hours downriver from his village to visit his parents' house. It was on the final night of my stay that several children in the house gathered around my friend's elderly father, Awanka, listening to him tell stories. Awanka, who is known for his skill in storytelling, spoke about past times when many babies died as a result of witchcraft, leading to a cycle of revenge killings with which his own generation is associated today. He warned the children that they should be careful not to speak to a shaman at night when his body is inhabited by his adopted jaguar-spirit (*meñi*). He said that if the children were even to joke with the jaguar-spirit as it speaks through the shaman's voice, telling it to scare people, a jaguar might kill the people they named. Even after a shaman dies, explained Awanka, his or her orphaned jaguar-spirit continues to live and kill people out of sadness and anger for its adopted parent.

During my fieldwork, old people like Awanka often told me how their relatives and ancestors became victims of violence, be it from shamans, spear-killing raids, or the shotguns of outsiders. In this case, he was explicitly warning his grandchildren about their behavior in reference to violent conflicts that occurred in the past. It is stories like this one, and people like Awanka, that attracted my interest in the meanings past killings hold for the Waorani today and, more particularly, the multiple ways they evoke the past in their homes, during treks in the forest, and on visits to urban areas in Amazonian Ecuador.

This book is about how Waorani people experience and remember past violence and the role these memories have in the context of ongoing social, political, and economic changes in Amazonia today. It is principally an ethnography of how Waorani people of different genders and generations remember violence in ways that evoke indigenous understandings of social difference and shared experience in the context of social transformation. However, it is equally an account of how my Waorani hosts reflect on and engage with *kowori*—a word they use to refer to non-Waorani people, whether other indigenous groups, missionaries, Ecuadorian mestizos, or an increasingly diverse range of non-indigenous people who have become part of their lived world.

Like many indigenous Amazonian societies studied by anthropologists, most Waorani people live in small villages in a remote part of the Amazonian rain forest. The location and scale of everyday social life in places like these has tempted some ethnographers to confine their analysis primarily to relations within and between indigenous communities. Although much of my fieldwork has involved living in relatively remote villages, Waorani sociality and cultural imagination also concern people and events that extend well beyond the ethnic reserve on which most Waorani people live. Understanding contemporary violence and social memory demands that we consider social and cultural processes that cannot be characterized simply in terms of the "local" or the "indigenous." This recognition of translocal and intercultural relations does not, however, diminish the importance of ethnography. One of the strengths of contemporary anthropology is an increasing attention to how culturally specific practices and ideas are embedded in wider historical transformations and increasingly global imagery.[1] Indigenous Amazonian people relate to these intercultural dynamics in ways that allow us to reconsider the key themes of violence, history, and memory in anthropology.

For centuries outsiders have imagined Amazonia as a place of violence, whether in colonial European accounts of "Amazon warriors," contemporary ideas about "wild Indians" in South America, or famous studies of "tribal warfare." Although much of this image can be attributed to enduring stereotypes about Amazonia, at certain times anthropologists too have conceptualized violence as a purely localized or even primordial aspect of Amazonian culture. Understanding the experiences of Waorani people today requires a different approach to the anthropology of violence, one that draws on interethnic relations, the history of Christian missionaries in Amazonian Ecuador, and even popular film imagery. This allows us to consider the cultural meanings and political force of violence in terms of indigenous cosmology and a much wider set of relations that are part of Waorani experience. I examine violence not simply in terms of "tribal warfare" or "revenge killing" but as a symbolic practice through which Waorani people today understand themselves, their ancestors, and kowori people.

In recent years anthropologists have described how Amazonian cosmology and sociality depart in significant ways from conventional Western understandings of "nature" (Descola 1992, 1994), "society" (Viveiros de Castro 1992) and "culture" (Viveiros de Castro 1998a, 2011). Only recently, however, have we begun to consider how these ideas relate to contemporary political and economic processes that extend beyond the "local" or the "indigenous." Here I consider not only what Waorani people themselves say about violence but also what happens to memories of violence in the context of social transformations such as urban migration, indigenous political activism, and interethnic marriages with former "enemies." Much of this discussion concerns relations of "alterity"—or how indigenous Amazonian people understand their past and present relations with people they define as "others" of various kinds (Viveiros de Castro 1992; Vilaça 2010; Fausto 2012; Ewart 2013) When Waorani elders talk about the period just prior to mission settlement in the 1960s, they often describe how their relatives were killed by other Waorani groups (*warani*) or by kowori outsiders. Waorani understandings of self and other are changing not just because they now experience relations with an increasingly differentiated group of kowori but also because many Waorani today live in villages that incorporate former "enemy" Waorani. Their memories of violence, rather than revealing violence as a primordial or unchanging feature of Waorani culture, illuminate their ongoing engagements with a diverse landscape of other people, both within their villages and beyond.

Many of the practices, ideas, and relations anthropologists attribute to a given culture or society can be best understood in terms of their transformation. Although most of this book focuses on how Waorani people remember and comment on past events, written historical sources also reveal how the interethnic relations I observed in my fieldwork were reportedly different in previous decades. However, rather than speculating about what "Waorani society" was like in the past or assimilating indigenous perspectives to conventional Western ideas of history, my central concern is the meanings past violence holds for Waorani people today in their homes and in their relations with an expanding constellation of kowori people. Whether asserting the bonds of kinship or calling for revenge killings, Waorani ways of remembering evoke relations of difference and mutual experience that challenge our own ideas of history, tradition, and identity. More than a question of historical accuracy or cultural continuity, these memories are a moral practice that calls for a certain kind of relations in the future.

Waorani Ethnography in Historical Perspective

The Waorani people I describe here live on a vast reserve in eastern Ecuador and speak an indigenous language (*Wao-terero*) that is unrelated to other South American languages (Peeke 1979; Klein and Stark 1985). Their

MAP 1. Ecuador

4

economy is based primarily on hunting, gathering, and gardening on their official ethnic reserve of more than one million acres between the Napo and Curaray Rivers. Most Waorani today live in one of more than thirty villages, many of which have airstrips and schools that provide key links to the broader national society. While the past four or five decades have marked a dramatic transition from highly dispersed and relatively nomadic households to larger and more permanent settlements, their long treks in the forest, residential movement between villages, and temporary migration for employment with oil companies operating within the reserve continue to constitute a mobile way of life for the Waorani.

Despite being a population of only around twenty-five hundred people, the Waorani have for many years held a prominent place in popular imagination in Ecuador and beyond. For much of the twentieth century they were known for their violence, isolation, and assumed resistance to contact with outsiders. Until recently, they were most often referred to by other Ecuadorians as *aucas*, a derogatory term meaning "wild" or "savage."[2] Much like indigenous societies assumed to be inherently violent elsewhere in Amazonia at various historical moments (Muratorio 1994; Taussig 1987), the Waorani came to be defined by their violent encounters with outsiders. This reputation for violence and general "wildness" has made them a target of attention from explorers, missionaries, tourists, and researchers.

MAP 2. The Waorani territory in Amazonian Ecuador

Their reputation for violence brought the Waorani international fame in 1956, when five North American missionaries were killed on the banks of the Curaray River during an attempt to make what was assumed to be "first contact." This event, referred to as the "Palm Beach" killings in subsequent missionary writings, was to become one of the defining moments in twentieth-century missionary lore. The Waorani became not only an icon of Amazonian "savagery" and violence but also the target of one of the most intensive and highly publicized evangelical mission campaigns in the world by the Summer Institute of Linguistics (SIL)/Wycliffe Bible Translators in the 1960s (Stoll 1982). The resulting missionary literature describes how, with the establishment of the now legendary "*auca* mission," the Waorani converted to Christianity and all but completely abandoned internal revenge killings and violence toward outsiders.

Anthropological and missionary writings have emphasized Waorani isolation from other indigenous groups and their famous spear-killing raids prior to their "pacification" in the 1960s. The earliest ethnographic accounts describe a society on the verge of disappearance prior to mission settlement, primarily as a result of an intense cycle of internal revenge killings (Yost 1981). While the cause of this violence has been debated from ethnopsychological (Robarchek and Robarchek 1998), historical (Cipolletti 2002), and sociobiological (Beckerman and Yost 2007) perspectives, it is clear that Waorani people envisioned their conflicts with kowori outsiders as a relationship of predation. Still today, older adults describe how they once feared that all kowori people were cannibals intent on killing and eating them. This is part of a broader Waorani logic that locates personhood in the position of the victim or "prey" to outside aggression (Rival 2002). Oral histories and commentaries about contemporary relations with kowori tend to emphasize Waorani victimhood in the face of powerful outsiders, even after the dramatic decrease in violence since mission settlement. As in previous times, the household (*nanicabo*) and a tightly knit endogamous group of closely related households (*waomoni*) remain the primary units of social organization, even in large villages with as many as two hundred residents.[3] And yet in recent decades missionaries, local schools, oil development, and tourism have made relations between Waorani and kowori people more frequent and varied.

One of the key changes after missionary settlement in the 1960s has been the emergence of interethnic marriages between Waorani and neighboring indigenous Quichua (Runa) people in relatively permanent communities. These villages were established in the aftermath of the joint resettlement efforts of SIL missionaries, the oil industry, and the Ecuadorian government. In recent years rural schools in many of these villages have become the central link between Waorani communities and the Ecuadorian state (Rival 1996). Interethnic marriages between Waorani and Quichua people, as well as those between former enemy Waorani groups, have for the most part replaced raiding as the primary mode of inter-group relations (Robarchek and Robarchek 1996). Celebrated by missionaries as the miraculous conversion to Christianity of "the world's most savage tribe" (Wallis 1960), this changing process in which former enemies became affines brought together members of numerous Waorani groups at larger settlements.

As described elsewhere in Amazonia (Turner 1991; Jackson 1995; Graham 2005), Waorani people have become increasingly aware of themselves as one of several indigenous "ethnic" groups in Ecuador. This political consciousness has coincided with their struggle to have their traditional lands recognized by the government as an official Waorani ethnic reserve. It is also partly the result of Waorani political involvement in the national indigenous movement and the relations of friendship, employment, and affinity they have established in recent years with various kowori people. However, the strict distinction they draw between *Wao* (singular of Waorani) and kowori remains a potent identifier of an internal "we" and outside "others." My occasional reference to "Waorani people" or "Waorani society" should not be taken to suggest that there is a coherent social whole to which all Waorani subscribe but refers instead to this distinction my Waorani interlocutors make between themselves and non-Waorani people. This is not the only way in which they distinguish other people, as the term *warani,* for example, is used to denote other Waorani not seen as particularly close relations and even enemies (see Rival 2002, 55). Another key relational context is that between household groups (*nanicabo*), as household autonomy remains an important value even in large villages like Toñampari, where people embrace the notion of living together in a wider *comunidad* (community). It is for this reason that I use the term "intergroup relations" at times in reference to relations between Waorani groups and at other times to describe interethnic relations between Waorani and neighboring indigenous people, such as Quichuas.

The settlement of most Waorani in villages coincided with a renewed international interest in oil development in and around their territory. Since the 1960s dozens of multinational companies and their subsidiaries have conducted oil exploration and production within the reserve, a trend that, if anything, is increasing at present. In the 1990s many Waorani became active in protesting oil development and particularly the destructive oil roads and the resulting colonization of indigenous lands that came in its wake. This relationship between Waorani communities and the oil industry led to the establishment of an official Waorani political office, the Organization of Waorani Nationalities of Amazonian Ecuador (ONHAE) in 1990.[4] With the establishment of organizations like ONHAE, Waorani people today engage with regional and national indigenous politics in a country noted for its strong indigenous movement (Whitten 1996, 2003; Becker 2008; Roitman 2009). Indigenous political activism and the legal recognition of an official territorial reserve have contributed to a sense of Waorani solidarity as a wider ethnic group. However, this comes in the aftermath of strong internal divisions that in some cases continue within and between Waorani communities. Their entry into wider indigenous politics in Ecuador has also coincided with a growing international interest in indigenous Amazonian people as natural stewards and protectors of the rain forest (Conklin 1997, 2002). The presence of international NGOs and a growing "eco-tourism" industry are bringing the Waorani face to face with foreigners who have their own imaginations and expectations of Amazonian peoples.

While this book is centrally about the Waorani who hosted me during my fieldwork, their relations with Quichua-speaking people form a major part of my analysis of intergroup relations and their transformation (High 2006; Reeve and High 2012). Quichua-speaking people constitute the dominant indigenous group in Ecuador in terms of both population and political power. They have a prominent place in Waorani social life today, at least in part because Quichua villages are found along the borders of the reserve and because Quichua people have for years been at the forefront of the regional indigenous movement. As a source of violent conflict in the past and in much of Waorani discourse still today, the transformation of Quichuas from enemies to affines is a key example of the shifting relations of alterity in which Waorani are engaged. During my fieldwork I have often listened to the perspectives of Quichua women and men who live in the Waorani villages and kindly welcomed me into their homes. However, the chapters that follow should in no way be seen as any real attempt to write Quichua ethnography, a task that has been taken up extensively elsewhere (Whitten 1976, 1978; Whitten and Whitten 2008; Muratorio 1991; Macdonald 1999; Reeve 2002; Uzendoski 2005; Kohn 2013). However, I do attempt to bring about a better understanding of the Waorani as part of a wider system of intergroup relations in the region, of which Quichua-speaking people are a key part.

Between History and Memory

The forms of violence I explore in this book should be understood in terms of a complex intersection of history and memory in Amazonia. Owing to the relatively small scale of its indigenous population and relative lack of scholarly attention until the 1970s, the Amazon was until recently assumed to have little in the way of history at all. However, anthropologists, historians, and archaeologists today recognize the dramatic social and ecological effects of colonialism and other historical processes that transformed the social landscape of Amazonia long before the arrival of anthropologists (see, for example, Roosevelt 1994; Lathrap 1970; Whitehead 1993; Balée 1995; Denevan 1976; and Heckenberger 2005). It has become clear that Amazonian societies should no longer be seen through the lens of an anthropology that ignores the dynamic processes by which culture is constituted and transformed.[5] This historical approach is particularly important when considering the current position of the Waorani, who inhabit a region that suffered colonial mission settlements followed by relative abandonment and the infamous rubber boom at the end of the nineteenth century. These processes surely had an influence on the prevalence of violence and isolation for which the Waorani became known during much of the twentieth century.

As important as this historical context is for understanding past and present Amazonian societies, I am centrally concerned with the meanings past violence has for Waorani people today, or what Maurice Bloch calls "the presence of the past in the present" (1998, 118). Such an approach evokes the much-debated distinction between "history" and "memory." Western understandings of history tend to be based on a notion of "historicism" that implies a sense of disconnection between the past and the present. Eric Hirsch and Charles Stewart (2005) describe this view of history as "a factual representation (usually written) of the past, intentionally researched and composed according to rational principles. Alongside—perhaps beneath—this set of suppositions lies the naturalized assumption that 'history' belongs to the domain of the past. The past is separate from the present and this separation allows the recognition of history as an object" (263). Rather than criticizing this concept of history—or the undeniably important uses of historical methods in anthropology—my aim is to contribute to a historical anthropology of violence that focuses on how Waorani people relate the past to the present in ways that do not appear to follow conventional definitions of "history" (Gow 2001). Waorani understandings of violence

elude the kind of historical thinking that situates the practices of indigenous Amazonian people as either "tradition" or "modernity." Instead of
separating the past from the present in these familiar ways, or interpreting
violence as an artifact of evolutionary or colonial history, I approach Waorani acts of remembering as a social practice that connects past events to
future possibilities. In recent years anthropologists have adopted relational
approaches to the past, describing oral narratives and embodied performances as forms of "historicity" (Sahlins 1985; Whitehead 2003), or more
frequently "memory" (Berliner 2005a). The diversity in Waorani ways of
remembering violence can tell us much about how my hosts conceptualize
their current relationships both within their communities and with kowori
people. Thinking about this process in terms of memory does not mean
that conventional Western understandings of history are completely foreign
or useless to Waorani people—far from it. Popular historical representations of Amazonian violence have become part of Waorani social memory,
particularly for young men. At the same time, conceptualizing memory
as a social practice moves us beyond the notion of the past as a separate,
finished domain, and demands that we consider narratives of violence as
part of the cultural dynamics of everyday life.

The scale and diversity of scholarship on memory in the social sciences
require a more specific explanation of how I use the concept. Much writing
on memory draws on Halbwachs's (1950) observation that narratives of the
past are given meaning and coherence in the present as part of "collective
memory." Beyond describing how the past is shared, transmitted, and contested in diverse ways, studies of "social" or "cultural" memory tend to focus
on memory as a kind of persistence or storage of the past.[6] David Berliner
describes how this concept of memory risks encompassing the notion of
culture itself, as it is often used to describe how "lasting traces of the past
persist within us, as the transmission and persistence of cultural elements
through the generations" (Berliner 2005a, 201). The apparent success of
memory as an anthropological concept, whether as a form of cultural persistence or "living history" (Battaglia 1992), appears to be closely related to
concerns with cultural continuity (Berliner 2005a).[7] What becomes implicit
here is that whereas "history" is about demonstrating change and transformation, "memory" comes to represent forms of cultural continuity and
identity that can be observed in the present.

While memory has only recently become a major anthropological theme
in Amazonia (Fausto and Heckenberger 2007), questions of cultural continuity appear to be at the heart of regional ethnography. In the aftermath of

colonial devastation and the ongoing marginalization of indigenous people, anthropological studies of continuity and creativity present a sense of indigenous agency, often in the face of powerful outsiders. It is striking that even studies of social transformation tend to adopt a Lévi-Straussian approach to structural continuity through change (Gow 2001; Ewart 2013; Viveiros de Castro 2011). While I share this inspiration to understand indigenous agency and Amazonian cultural features in the following chapters, Waorani understandings of the past challenge the idea that memory is centrally about cultural perseverance or a kind of historical evidence. Waorani social memory involves practices that link personal experiences and autobiographical narratives of the past to wider cultural symbols and social relations in the present.

In conceptualizing memory as a "moral practice," Michael Lambek describes how "memory . . . is more intersubjective and dialogical than exclusively individual, more act (remembering) than object, and more ongoing engagement than passive absorption and playback" (1996, 239). Understood as a moral (and thus relational) practice in the present, acts of remembrance become an important object of ethnographic inquiry. This relational approach to memory allows for rethinking a range of contexts in which Waorani people evoke past violence in the present. How, for example, might Waorani narratives and images of the past help us better understand generational changes and the way Waorani people relate to Quichuas and mestizos in urban areas? And how do Waorani people remember violent encounters that have come to define their "history" for outsiders?

In response to questions like these, anthropologists have recently begun to explore how memories of violence are transmitted from one generation to the next in processes of social and political transformation (Berliner 2005b; Argenti 2007; Argenti and Schramm 2009; High 2009a). Approaching memory as a creative cultural process in these contexts allows for moving beyond the tendency to read "history" as change and "memory" as an artifact of continuity in cultural transmission. Nor should we read Waorani forms of social memory as simply a local version of history. Whether they refer to aspects of continuity or change, Waorani acts of remembering are part of an ongoing commentary on everyday interpersonal relations in which social life is defined and contested. As Lambek suggests, "Memory is significant less as the trace of the past than as the kernel of the future" (1996, 244). In this way, many Waorani memories of violence are a fundamentally social process rather than a form of trauma in which individuals objectively retrieve actual experiences of the past.

Since no single narrative genre can be said to define the entirety of so-cial memory in any society (Bloch 1998), thinking about memory in this way requires looking further than just oral narratives, or even language, to understand the multiple meanings and uses of the past. The past is often evoked in nonverbal symbolic forms, such as material objects and bodies (Connerton 1989; Stoller 1995), which can be potent markers of political identity, social disruption, or protest (Argenti 2007; Shaw 2002). In part because Amazonian bodies, and particularly embodied images of warrior-hood, resonate so strongly in national and global imaginations, violent im-agery has become an important part of Waorani memory, ethnic identity, and cultural performance.

Imagining Amazonian Violence

Since the late 1960s anthropology students and much of the wider world have learned about indigenous Amazonian people by reading Napoleon Chagnon's famous and controversial ethnography of Yanomami warfare, *Yanomamö: The Fierce People* (1968). As his book became one of the most widely read ethnographies, Amazonian culture came to be imagined by many in terms of blood feuds and indigenous warfare. Chagnon's ethnog-raphy, although rich in details about other aspects of social life and cosmol-ogy, did little to temper enduring stereotypes about Amazonia as a place of primitive violence and "wildness" (Ramos 1987). Just as early European explorers and later cultural ecologists viewed the rain forest as a harsh and unforgiving environment, with the publication of *The Fierce People* and the subsequent documentary film, *The Ax Fight* (Asch and Chagnon 1975), Amazonia's indigenous population only seemed to live up to Western imaginings of an exotic "other."

With the explosion of ethnographic and historical research in Amazo-nia since the 1970s, few anthropologists today would consider Chagnon's description of Yanomami violence to be characteristic of past or present Amazonian societies. And yet Chagnon's representation of the Yanomami and heated debates about the ethical dimensions of his fieldwork have left a significant mark on Amazonian ethnography. In part as a response to Chag-non's evolutionary arguments about indigenous warfare, anthropologists have since challenged primordialist interpretations of violence in Ama-zonia and elsewhere, arguing that "indigenous warfare" can be explained as a result of the political and economic consequences of colonialism and state formation (Ferguson and Whitehead 1991; Ferguson 1995).[8] Alongside this historical turn in Amazonian anthropology, which tends to explain seemingly negative aspects of indigenous culture as a product of "Western contact" (Viveiros de Castro 1996), there has been an increasing recognition of the less "violent" aspects of Amazonian societies, such as the emphasis many indigenous people place on creating and maintaining peaceful relations in everyday life (Overing and Passes 2000).[9]

This attention to Amazonian models of morality and group solidarity, often referred to as the "moral economy of intimacy" (Viveiros de Castro 1996), has challenged past representations of Amazonian violence. Viveiros de Castro coined this phrase to describe a general model of Amazonian sociality emphasizing the egalitarian aspects of everyday life within and between groups. In contrast to age-old stereotypes about "fierce" and "violent" Amazonian societies, these ethnographers focus on how peaceful internal relations reflect a moral philosophy characterized by sharing, reciprocal generosity, and the creation of solidarity and consanguinity through everyday conviviality (Gow 1989, 1991; Santos-Granero 1991; Belaunde 1992, 2000; Rival 1998a; Overing and Passes 2000; McCallum 2001; Londoño Sulkin 2005). For these authors, Amazonian sociality tends to be premised on efforts to establish the "good life" in everyday intersubjective relations rather than attempts to create rules or hierarchical structures (Overing and Passes 2000).

This body of scholarship represents some of the most ethnographically grounded work on contemporary Amazonia. However, we should avoid simply trading one stereotypical image of a "violent" Amazonia for an image of inherently "peaceful" societies. As Santos-Granero notes, no anthropologist today would support the idea that Amazonian people "are quintessentially violent or quintessentially pacific" (2000, 268).[10] Despite the increasingly critical and reflexive stance anthropology takes against such essentialisms, it appears that one result of Chagnon's controversial work has been a decreasing interest or willingness to study contemporary violence in Amazonia. It is striking that the most widely discussed work on Amazonian violence today concerns the notion of "ontological predation" in indigenous cosmologies (Viveiros de Castro 1992; Fausto 2007, 2012).[11] These studies explain historical practices such as headhunting (Taylor 1993), cannibalism (Viveiros de Castro 1992; Conklin 2001), and early encounters between missionaries and indigenous people (Vilaça 2010; Viveiros de Castro 2011) in terms of symbolic forms of alterity that appear to be at the core of indigenous cosmology. They make a convincing case that predation and "other-becoming" constitute the basis of symbolic exchange across sociopolitical boundaries in much of Amazonia. Yet it remains to be seen how contemporary conflicts between indigenous people, as well as their relations with newcomers to the region, can be understood in terms of this cosmological order.[12]

Violence in Amazonia should be understood in terms of both indigenous cosmology and the dramatic social, political, and economic changes that indigenous people face today. If, for example, "predation" is an important aspect of Waorani cosmology, such an ontological premise should shed some light on the particular ways that Waorani people remember violence and understand their current conflicts with kowori people. To this end, previous work on Amazonian cosmology is an important reference point in this process. However, so too are missionary discourses, popular imagery of "wild Indians," and the complex web of relations and cultural imaginations in which Waorani people engage. In studying situations like these ethnographically, it becomes difficult—and misleading—to separate "indigenous cosmology" from processes often associated with "modernity" or "globalization." To describe violence in Amazonia today as a "traditional" or "modern" phenomenon is beside the point. My intention is instead to present an ethnography of violence and social memory that links indigenous cosmology to wider intercultural relations without simply reproducing popular representations of Amazonian violence, which have themselves become part of the lived experiences of Waorani people.

Meeting the Waorani

This book is part of an ongoing relationship forged between a range of different Waorani people and myself over the past fifteen years or so since I first visited their communities. Although my analysis is based on my experience as a researcher, my fieldwork, and the writing this process inspires, it constitutes more than simply "Waorani ethnography." It is equally a product of my own personal and social positioning within (and at times uncomfortably between) Waorani friends, households, and villages.

I first came to Ecuador in 1994 to work on a volunteer public-health project in a rural Andean community, but it wasn't until my second stay in Ecuador in 1997 that I became interested in working with the Waorani. As an undergraduate student in anthropology from the United States, I had enrolled in a study-abroad program in Quito, Ecuador's capital. At the time there was growing media coverage of the Waorani and their conflicts with

Maxus, a U.S.-based oil company operating on their lands. Public protests by the Waorani came in the context of a country whose indigenous peoples have gained an increasing political presence in recent years, particularly since the famous *levantamiento* (indigenous uprising) in 1990 and subsequent "March for Land and Life" in 1992, which saw tens of thousands of indigenous people march from Amazonian Ecuador to the capital (Whitten, Whitten, and Chango 2008).

As an anthropology student interested in development issues and the rights of indigenous people, I began seeking the advice of various academics in Quito as to how I might go about visiting the areas affected by oil development within the Waorani reserve. Without the necessary local contacts, I was in no position to simply turn up in a remote village and expect local people to host me. Fortunately, by the mid-1990s the Waorani political organization had established its office in the city of Puyo, several hours southeast of Quito by bus in the province of Pastaza. Although at this time the office was manned by just two representatives and appeared still to be developing a definite structure, Juan, the ONHAE *presidente*, listened to me describe my interest in oil development and Waorani "culture" and kindly agreed to arrange for my stay with a family he knew in one of the villages.

The following month I returned to Puyo, where I met again with the ONHAE representatives and was introduced to Timo, a young man whose family would host me during my stay in the village of Toñampari. Reaching the village would require a thirty-minute flight from the nearby airport and military post in the town of Shell. My nervous anticipation of what lay before me in the upcoming months intensified as the three-passenger Cessna floated above the thick canopy of rain forest and approached a seemingly tiny clearing in the forest that served as the village airstrip.

As in most small Amazonian villages equipped with airstrips, the arrival of a plane is met with dozens of local residents who wait at the end of the grassy clearing in anticipation of relatives, friends, or the occasional gift package from the city. I of course was none of these and felt foolish stepping out of the plane until a man named Toka emerged from the crowd and explained to me in Spanish that I would be staying with his family. Toka took me to his parents' house, where I had the good fortune to spend the following months struggling to make sense of Waorani language and learning next to nothing about "oil development." The kind ONHAE *presidente*, rather than sending me to one of the oil areas accessible by road that now line much of the northern boundary of the Waorani territory, had sent me

FIGURE 1. Living well: a family shares a meal of monkey and manioc

to his home village to stay with his relatives. Although my original plans had been foiled, my stay in Toñampari gave me the first glimpse of what has become the subject of the present book. Despite my almost complete ignorance of their language and customs at that time, my initial hosts tolerated my presence and appeared eager to incorporate me into their daily activities. I quickly found myself stumbling through the forest on hunting and fishing trips and treks to visit other households with my patient hosts.

Despite the inevitable excitement I felt in my initial days living with a Waorani family, before long I settled into the slow and seemingly uneventful pace by which my new friends appeared to live their lives. At this point fed more on images and expectations of what Amazonian people are like than by any reasonable logic, I soon began to wonder how anthropologists have been so successful at recording detailed accounts of cosmologies, rituals, myths, and other themes that make for good chapter headings in anthropology books. In contrast to the stereotyped warnings Ecuadorians gave me in the capital about the supposed dangers of living with "*aucas*," I was struck by how uneventful, relaxed, and even boring everyday life was in a Waorani household. Part of this was of course a product of my own background and ignorance about local social values. However, I have since come to see much of this seemingly "boring" everyday life as the realization of something very important to the Waorani people with whom I lived. For them, this relaxed and seemingly uneventful atmosphere is one of the fundamental aspects of what they call "living well" (*waponi kiwimonipa*, "we live well"). This notion of "living well" is a value that Waorani people contrast explicitly to "living badly" (*wiwa kiwinanipa*), which is associated with past violence, scarcity of food, and a range of behaviors they associate with kowori people.

Much of social life within the home and between Waorani households is oriented according to this moral value, which involves a variety of practices aimed at establishing peaceful sociality and avoiding potential conflicts. Here I am not suggesting an ideal image of a perfectly happy and "peaceful" society. The revenge killings that feature in many Waorani oral histories have not completely disappeared from their communities, and violence continues to have a prominent place in Waorani understandings of the world. Furthermore, Waorani people continue to have regular conflicts with oil companies and Quichua communities, whom they see as threatening the borders of their territory.

Locating Toñampari

After my initial stay in Toñampari I returned to my university studies with very different ideas about Waorani people, anthropology, and many of the problems that preoccupied me previously. Waorani were no longer, in my mind, an exotic people whose culture could be defined by their violent reputation and fierce resistance to oil companies. Rather than focusing only on their public confrontations with oil development that had resonated so strongly with my own personal agendas, I became more interested in the ways Waorani people conceptualize and negotiate changing relations in the households and communities where they live. How, for example, do they incorporate spouses and other people from groups they previously defined as "enemies?" How do they engage locally with an official political organization based in the regional capital that represents them to the Ecuadorian state and the wider public? What role do images and stories about past violence have in all of this? These were some of the questions I had in mind as I planned my return to Toñampari to begin a much longer period of fieldwork.

It was not until October 2002 that I finally returned to the Waorani territory. Having been away for more than four years, I decided to begin the project in Toñampari, where I intended to find my old friends who hosted me before. Located in the western part of the Waorani reserve on the north bank of the Curaray River, Toñampari is considered by many to be the Waorani "capital," given its size and relatively sustained links to regional cities, particularly Puyo. Without attempting to exaggerate the village's relative cosmopolitanism, it represents a key point of interaction between the city and remote Waorani lands, located about thirty minutes east of Puyo and thirty minutes west of the Peruvian border by small aircraft. Despite the apparent remoteness of the location to the occasional visitor, a number of other villages lay within one to two days' walk from Toñampari in nearly all directions. One village can be reached in as little as one or two hours' walk west along the Curaray, while a long day's walk to the north brings one to the oil roads, connecting the territory with the regional city of Tena. This journey and the alternative two-day hike to the Quichua town of Arajuno are also paths used to visit what my Waorani friends refer to as *kowori onko*, the "home of the kowori."

Today, flights from Shell-Mera airport, one of the primary means of transportation to and from the city, are increasingly regular. During my fieldwork there were often multiple flights in the same week, some of which were contracted by ONHAE representatives for official visits or by people returning with goods from the city after a period of work at *la compañia*, the oil companies. Toñampari is also occasionally visited by the Mission Aviation Fellowship (MAF) airline *Alas de Socorro*, an organization of North American missionary pilots based in Shell who provide emergency flights for seriously ill patients in Amazonian Ecuador. Given its location, increasing means of transport, and the possibility of temporary employment by oil companies elsewhere in the territory, Toñampari residents generally have more sustained relations with people and institutions from afar than do other Waorani.

FIGURE 2. A sandy bank of the Curaray River near Toñampari

I was particularly attracted to carrying out fieldwork in Toñampari as a result of the long-standing presence of Quichua people. As I discuss in chapter 5, many Quichuas have moved to the village from surrounding areas after marrying a Waorani spouse. This strong Quichua presence allowed me to explore how Waorani interact with and talk about people from a neighboring indigenous group with whom they have a long and ongoing history of violent conflict. Furthermore, the size of Toñampari provided the opportunity to study a situation in which members of different Waorani groups interact with one another on a regular basis. Given that most ONHAE officials are from Toñampari or went to school there, these young leaders make regular visits to the village for festivals, political speeches, and other public events. I was therefore able to observe the indigenous leadership at the local level as well as listen to how villagers interpret and evaluate their practices.

Despite Toñampari's size and translocal links, a typical day in the village reflects anything but a hub of activity as people go about their everyday tasks, such as gardening, hunting, and fishing in the vast surrounding forest. Although the local population reached approximately two hundred at one point during my fieldwork, relatively few are to be found in the village at any given time. Visits to the city, hunting trips, visits to other villages (often for communal feasts), and tending distant gardens generally leave everyday life in Toñampari and other villages very quiet and uneventful. Toñampari also appears smaller and more insular than it actually is due to the general lack of integration, organization, and other features that local schoolteachers and politicians from the city associate with a *comunidad*. With the exception of the local school, much of the social interaction in daily life occurs within relatively small clusters of two or three households. This is not to say that local people do not have a sense of identity and pride as residents of the same community, but rather that many adults in the "community" have rather sporadic if not distrustful relations with one another. This likely reflects a long-standing custom of living in atomized and autonomous longhouses (Rival 2002), as well as the presence of *warani* (nonrelatives) and various *kowori* (non-Waorani) people who now inhabit the same village.

Fieldwork and Methodological Considerations

I returned to Toñampari in 2002 only to find that my previous host family had migrated to the far northeast of the territory to work in the oil block opened by Maxus years before. Even the grandparents had deserted their previous location, moving farther east to exploit more abundant game and company handouts along the oil roads. By good fortune, however, I was invited to live with close relatives of my previous hosts in a nearby home, a Waorani family with whom I lived long after my friends returned to To-ñampari from the oil area. Although I stayed in other households in To-ñampari and in other villages during the course of my fieldwork, it was this household with which I became identified—and remain in many ways still today. Of the roughly two years I lived in Waorani villages, the majority of my fieldwork was spent in Toñampari with this family. Given my interest in intergroup relations, my choice of location was important. While the core household with whom I lived consisted of two Waorani parents and most of their ten children, I also spent a considerable amount of time, as both guest and resident, with a family consisting of a Waorani man, his Quichua wife, and their children. This allowed me to see how a kowori person is incorporated into a Waorani group as an affine, and to compare Wao-Quichua households to those without a Quichua resident.

I also made occasional visits to several other Waorani villages, especially those located in the western part of the reserve. These visits, which ranged from one day to a week, were often inspired by my Waorani friends wanting to attend an *eëme* (party/feast) in another village. In addition, I made a number of short trips to the Yasuní National Park, an ecological reserve within which there are several Waorani villages and intense oil production by the Repsol-YPF consortium. Because of problems I encountered attempting to secure permission from the latter, which closely regulates visits to the area with the support of the Ecuadorian military, I was unable to carry out any extended periods of research in the Yasuní. In 2004 I spent approximately two months in Kiwaro, a village located a couple of days east of Toñampari. Reluctant to base virtually all of my field research on one particular village, I was attracted to Kiwaro as a point of comparison to Toñampari, given its smaller size and the relatively small number of interethnic marriages.

My fieldwork inevitably brought me into ever-closer relations with Waorani politicians and their organizational office in Puyo, which sometimes aided me in finding flights "*adentro*" (to the inside). Although some of my writing is based in part on my observations in Puyo, including the various Waorani political offices that have been established in the city, this book is not intended as an in-depth study of ONHAE itself—a topic that has been considered specifically elsewhere (Zeigler-Otero 2004). I instead focus on what my Waorani hosts in Toñampari and other villages say about formal indigenous politics in the city and how they engage with these ever-changing institutions.

I found fieldwork among the Waorani to be difficult for many of the same reasons I found living with Waorani people so enjoyable. Most foreigners I know who visit a Waorani village comment on the friendly hospitality, informality, and sense of humor they encountered. Few would describe Waorani as stubborn or dogmatic, as they tend to respect the autonomy of individuals, even those whose behavior they find silly or morally questionable. This general lack of overt coercion or obvious power structures had a major influence on my fieldwork. Whereas my Waorani friends were often eager to have me participate in their daily work, such as cutting gardens, fishing, or clearing weeds from the airstrip, they rarely made explicit demands on my behavior. As will become clear in the following chapters, they grant each other a considerable degree of autonomy in much the same way, often expecting people to follow their own agendas and seldom explicitly challenging those of others. This seemingly anarchic informality allowed me a considerable degree of freedom, especially at the beginning of fieldwork. However, I suspect that this lack of dogma and hierarchy may explain why this book makes little attempt to construct an elaborate or complete "Waorani cosmology" or social structure. Waorani people often approached my questions in one of two ways. On more than one occasion my questions, such as "What happens to people after they die?" were met with the response "I don't know, what do you think?" Alternatively, they responded to more abstract questions with the humor characteristic of Waorani. On one occasion, as I sat in the river with one of my host brothers under a bright, starry sky, I asked him if any of the stars in the sky had any particular meaning for Waorani people. He pointed to one star and responded, "That one is Timo's asshole!"[13] before bursting into laughter.

I am not suggesting that Waorani people do not share an underlying ideology or system of cultural assumptions about the world. In fact, I hope that my ethnography here does suggest a set of ideas, practices, and meanings that are particular to the Waorani. However, it became clear to me early on in fieldwork that my direct questioning was not likely to go far toward uncovering such revelations. I mention this because much of what I have learned about Waorani sociality and cosmology has come from listening to and observing how my friends and hosts reacted to and commented on particular situations—many of which I was involved as both participant and observer. It was only later, toward the end of my fieldwork, that I felt my direct questions about particular topics became more fruitful in the anthropological endeavor. Part of this may have been the result of initial language difficulties. I suspect, however, that only later in the fieldwork did I have the sufficient knowledge or experience even to ask the relevant questions. It is clear to me now that much of what forms my ethnography comes not just from how Waorani people answered my questions but from the stories and conversations that they themselves initiated with each other and with me over the course of my fieldwork.

This is not to ignore my own presence or its influence on the stories and conversations on which this book is based. The ways in which my specific place in Waorani social life affected the nature of my fieldwork became particularly clear in 2003, when my girlfriend visited me in Toñampari from Denmark. Up to this point in my fieldwork, I was unambiguously associated with young men in the village. Upon her arrival, my social position changed from that of an immature bachelor to that of an established, albeit incompetent, adult. I slowly saw many of my teenage male friends withdraw from our previous everyday interactions and joking characteristic of Waorani youth. At the same time, elders became more interested in incorporating both of us into the expected roles of adulthood. For me, this meant more fishing trips and work clearing gardens. For my girlfriend, this meant collecting firewood, planting gardens, and making manioc beer with other women. This allowed, or perhaps demanded, a different perspective on the social relations surrounding us than I had previously. It was at this point in my fieldwork that adults from other households began visiting our home to converse and share many of the stories I describe in the following chapters. I should note that even after gaining the new status of a married man (*nanogue*), I always sensed that young teenage women were much less comfortable speaking with me than were their male counterparts. While older women were often just as eager as the men to share their stories and everyday conversation, there remains a general lack of young women's perspectives in the following chapters. While I give relatively equal weight to men's and women's perspectives in my analysis of historical narratives, this disparity emerges in my discussion of interethnic marriages between Waorani and Quichua people in chapter 5.

Notes on Language

My conversations with Waorani people occurred in both Spanish and Wao-terero, a remarkably understudied indigenous language spoken almost exclusively by the Waorani and some of their affines from other indigenous groups. Linguists describe Wao-terero as an "isolate" insofar as there is, as of yet, insufficient evidence to link the language to any other in Amazonia or elsewhere (Klein and Stark 1985). With few study tools other than a preliminary grammar written by an SIL linguist in the 1970s (Peeke 1973, 1979), I embarked on the journey of learning Wao-terero in the field. This was vital to my research since, at the time of my main fieldwork, many older men and women spoke almost no Spanish, and many middle-aged adults spoke Spanish only minimally. Teenagers, especially those who studied in schools and have lived in the city, tend to speak Spanish relatively well. Although I have made considerable progress in learning the Waorani language, much of my fieldwork with young adults was in Spanish. My daily conversational exchanges occurred primarily in Wao-terero, while many longer, more detailed conversations and narratives were sometimes in Spanish. Learning Wao-terero was part of my attempt to understand and translate what often appeared to me as incommensurable differences between their world and my own. Rather than interpreting Waorani culture as "an illusory version of our own" (Viveiros de Castro 2004, 4), my partial knowledge of the language has at once limited and enabled my insights into how Waorani people conceive of difference and remember violence.

The Presentation of this Book

The first two chapters explore the conjunctures between Waorani memories of violence and what missionaries, anthropologists, and other kowori have described as Waorani "history." In chapter 1, I begin by examining the kinds of social memory that emerge in the autobiographical narratives of Waorani elders. Their stories about past revenge killings and becoming "civilized" not only describe a time of intense violence but also voice indigenous understandings of what it means to be Waorani and kowori in the context of social transformation. By relating the emphasis on victimhood in Waorani narratives to imagery of Christian martyrdom in missionary writings and a recent Hollywood film about the Palm Beach killings in 1956, I point to how indigenous forms of social memory are closely linked to intercultural processes that transcend the spatial and temporal dimensions of ethnographic fieldwork.

Chapter 2 describes how young people talk about and perform past violence in ways that contradict the "victim's point of view" often expressed in stories told by elders. Despite the ideal of peaceful relations in Waorani villages today, colonial imagery of Amazonian "warriorhood" has in certain contexts come to define their relations with kowori people. The warrior performances of Waorani youth in local school events and state-sponsored folklore festivals reveal the generational and embodied dimensions of memory in urban intercultural encounters. While this imagery reproduces colonial representations of the "wild" Amazonian warrior in the national imagination, the symbolic transition from "victim" to "killer" performed in these contexts also conveys Waorani strength and autonomy in relation to powerful outsiders.

Chapter 3 looks more specifically at the gendered dimensions of alterity and Waorani understandings of what it means to be "like the ancient ones" (*durani bai*). Despite a strongly egalitarian ethos, Waorani women and men experience the generational changes that have come with oil work, urban migration, and other social transformations in different ways. As young men struggle to demonstrate the abilities for which male elders and ancestors are remembered, they embrace the Amazonian warrior of colonial imagination and violent imagery in popular cinema in expressing a form of masculinity they associate with "the ancient ones." Rather than leading to pronounced gender antagonisms between women and men, these generational changes reflect Waorani understandings of gendered agency that associate women with the production of interiority and men with relations of exteriority.

Chapter 4 takes us from the historical and symbolic construction of violence to the revenge killings that occurred at the time of my fieldwork. In 2003 a group of Waorani men led an attack against their "uncontacted" Taromenani neighbors, killing some twenty-five people and fueling debates about the rights of indigenous people living in "voluntary isolation." In the aftermath of the killings, many Waorani came to see spatially distant people as kinsmen who became disconnected from Waorani in past times. Described as kin of victims, the Taromenani are understood by Waorani as dangerous enemies, a source of desired relations, and a potent image of indigenous strength and autonomy. The Taromenani massacre reveals a complex intersection of Waorani cosmology and ongoing processes of economic development in Amazonia, including oil roads and the rapid influx of colonists and illegal loggers.

Chapter 5 focuses more specifically on the dynamics of kinship and marriage in Toñampari and what it means for Waorani people to live in a community that incorporates kowori people into household and village life. For many Waorani, Quichua people are highly desired marriage partners and the primary source of shamanic curing. At the same time, they describe Quichuas as morally different from themselves, as "enemies" who invade Waorani lands and practice powerful assault sorcery. This seemingly paradoxical relationship illustrates the symbolic importance of affinity in transforming intergroup relations in Amazonia and contributes to my broader aim of destabilizing strict divisions between "violence" and "peace," "victims" and "perpetrators" through ethnographic and historical analysis.

Chapter 6 extends my analysis of Waorani-Quichua relations in the previous chapter to consider the theme of shamanism and witchcraft. Like the idea of "civilization" in Waorani oral narratives, in Toñampari today the notion of *comunidad* ("community") is associated with living in close proximity to neighbors, incorporating various kowori people, and avoiding potential conflicts in everyday life. For many Waorani, the suppression of shamanic practices is part of this effort to live as a community. In describing indigenous understandings of shamanism and the historical role of shamans in mediating intercultural relations in Amazonia, I illustrate how previous work on this subject tends to neglect the "dark" aspects of shamanic practices that Waorani often fear today.

The final chapter brings together several strands of my wider argument that memories of violence are as much about establishing a sense of mutual experience and kinship as they are the basis of alterity and revenge. Located at the intersection of indigenous cosmology, intercultural relations, and ongoing social transformations, these memories construe the relationships between past and present in ways that challenge dominant ideas about tradition, modernity, and indigenous peoples as historical objects. The chapter also considers recent events that have crucial consequences for the future of Waorani communities, such as changes in Ecuadorian national politics, proposals to halt oil development in the Yasuní National Park, and the escalation of violence between Waorani and Taromenani people.

CHAPTER 1

Civilized Victims

I was born on Fish River.
Afterwards we lived well on Palm River.
We saw the high hills far off clearly.
We saw far downriver.

My big brother was Wawae.
My father was Tyaento, my mother Akawo.
Nampa my brother was a small child.
Oba my sister was still younger.
My big sister was Onaenga, my other sister, Gimari.
My mother's relatives were many.
My uncles were Wamoñi and Gikita.

Moipa and Itaeka did not do well.
Fleeing and hiding we came, far, far downriver.
We went by canoe, then we went back.

When did they spear? They speared at night.
My father escaped into the water.
They dug a grave for him and he was caused to die.
But he didn't die right away.
I didn't see it. They spoke and I heard.
My relative said, "I buried him."

Moipa and Itaeka speared.
Where did they go, did they say?
On a small stream upriver we returned.
We didn't see them.
We drank the water of maeñika fruit.
It rained, we got wet.
The jaguar growled, the monkeys called.
We climbed the trees when the Jaguar came.

Then we fled.
We came at night in the moonlight.
We speared gyaegyae fish.

We were planting peanuts on Palm River.
The outsiders came with guns and shot.
Their dogs barked.
We went in the water, then fled on the other side . . .

—Ethel Wallis, *The Dayuma Story*

In this chapter I begin to explore the links between historical representations of the Waorani and indigenous forms of social memory that define Waorani people as victims or "prey" to violence. The story above was told in the late 1950s by Dayuma, a well-known Waorani elder who became a key figure in relations between her people and Christian evangelical missionaries in the years that followed. During much of my fieldwork she lived in Toñampari, where I came to know her well. While her story is unique insofar as she was among the first Waorani to live with kowori people in the twentieth century, her account of her father's death is also part of a shared cultural narrative that is central to Waorani understandings of the past.

While historical accounts often present the Waorani as fiercely isolationist, intercultural relations are an important part of Waorani understandings of sociality and personhood. Indigenous perspectives on the past reveal how Waorani relate to kowori people in ways that both engage and challenge historical representations of Amazonian people. Understanding this process requires looking at how missionaries and filmmakers have represented Waorani violence and how this imagery has become part of the lived world of indigenous people. These translocal connections can be seen in the oral narratives elders like Dayuma tell about past violence and their conversion to Christianity, and in embodied performances of violence in urban contexts, described in chapter 3. In this chapter I explore how the narrative of violence and subsequent self-sacrifice presented in scores of missionary books written about the Waorani shed light on the intersections between missionary and Waorani ideas about past violence. Anthropologists have long since appreciated the value of historical sources in contextualizing ethnography. The present case demonstrates how historical missionary writings and popular cinema allow for rethinking Waorani memories in terms of experiences that transcend the spatial and cultural boundaries of their communities.

My aim in comparing missionary narratives to the stories of indigenous people is not to establish a more accurate or definitive "history" of Waorani violence, nor is it simply to criticize Christian-inspired representations of Waorani history. It is instead to explore the shared and contrasting ways in which Waorani and kowori people represent past violence. Although missionaries and my Waorani hosts engage narratives of violence for different purposes, both draw strongly on imagery of victimhood that has been described as lying at the core of Waorani sociality and cosmology (Rival 2000, 2002). The interconnections between indigenous perspectives on past violence and the trope of martyrdom in Christian representations of the Waorani since the 1950s point to the relational character of Waorani memory and its transmission in the context of social transformation (Argenti and Schramm 2009).

The Making of Waorani History

Waorani history presents an immediate paradox: despite the symbolic weight of "wild" *aucas* in the national imagination and beyond, there remains a profound lack of specific and reliable historical references to the Waorani prior to the twentieth century. This is in spite of a rich regional historiography that describes diverse and interconnected indigenous societies, many of which disappeared or merged with others as a result of the epidemics and violence that characterized colonial expansion into Western Amazonia.[1] It is clear that these events led to new social formations and intercultural relations through processes of "ethnogenesis" (Whitten 1976b; Hill 1996). Some authors, such as Cabodevilla (1999) and Rival (2002), reject the notion that the Waorani are descendants of a larger precolonial ethnic group, such as the Abijiras, Aushiris, Avishiris, or another of the myriad names attributed to the indigenous peoples encountered in the region by explorers in past centuries. Rival in particular argues that they "survived the vicissitudes of history" by maintaining their independence at the headwaters of the Tiputini River before expanding into their current territory after the collapse of the Zaparoan population in the nineteenth century (2002, 40). The Tiputini, an area where at present the Repsol-YPF consortium is carrying out intensive oil development near Waorani communities, is located several days' walk northeast from Toñampari and the Curaray River.

It is difficult to pinpoint with any degree of certainty the exact reasons for the Waorani's relative isolation in the decades leading up to missionary contact in the 1950s. Taylor (1999) speculates that they are the descendants of larger groups from the Napo River who were dispossessed during the colonial period. Her ethnohistorical research emphasizes interactional links between indigenous societies in the region and the powerful effects of colonialism in reshaping the social composition of the western margins of Amazonia. Taylor points out that from the sixteenth century to the nineteenth century many of the intricate trade networks in the region broke down with the arrival of European influences, leading to the more fragmented picture of the region's social landscape we see today.

Muratorio describes the initial period of epidemics and abuses brought by Europeans as the "ethnocidal simplification of the Amazon's rich ethnic variety" (1991, 42). As the banks of major rivers were abandoned by indigenous people and larger-scale residential units dispersed, a pattern of relatively isolated domestic units followed as "crisis tactics" in the face of colonial control, leading to new and more localized forms of social organization. This, according to Taylor, would have led to increased autonomy and mobility precisely in the area where we would expect to find the Waorani or their ancestors at that time. In this process trade was suspended and multitribal polities were replaced by the more informal egalitarian political systems that we find in groups like the Waorani today. Cipolletti (2002) presents a similar hypothesis linking the origins of contemporary Waorani to violent measures taken by Jesuit missions as they attempted to settle various indigenous peoples in the mid-eighteenth century. Those who fled from the Jesuits sought refuge in the most remote areas between major rivers, where they defended themselves against invaders and other indigenous groups. She suggests that the mixing of these small groups around the Pastaza River and elsewhere led to the ethnogenesis of the Waorani (115). Later, in the nineteenth century, the Waorani and their neighbors endured the violent incursions of slave raiders who abducted indigenous peoples for labor in the famous rubber boom (Taussig 1987). Processes like these surely contributed to the relative isolation and violence associated with Waorani people during much of the twentieth century.

Given the general lack of reliable historical information about the Waorani prior to the twentieth century, much of the writing of "Waorani history" has taken shape in the context of Christian missionaries who wrote about their lives on the mission settlement in the 1960s.[2] These writings emphasize how "contact" and "pacification" led to what has been described as the "the world's most savage tribe" converting to Christianity and abandoning their legacy of spear-killing (Wallis 1960). And yet, the history of Waorani violence and the "*auca* mission" resonates far beyond the experiences of Christian missionaries. The links between this history and popular imagery of Amazonian violence became clear in January 2006, when a feature film, *End of the Spear* (Hanon 2006), opened in more than a thousand cinemas across the United States. It depicted Waorani spear-killings that were emblematic of Western stereotypes of Amazonian violence and "wildness," focusing particularly on the killing of five North American missionaries in 1956. The film's release coincided with the fiftieth anniversary of these famous "Palm Beach" killings, which became a widely publicized story of missionary martyrdom among Christians in the United States and Europe.

The Palm Beach killings depicted in the film made the Waorani a powerful symbol within the evangelical world and beyond. In the 1950s there were no more than about five hundred Waorani, many of whom were involved in an intense cycle of interhousehold revenge killing. They were also well known in the region for their ongoing conflicts with other indigenous groups and oil companies, whose work camps were often attacked or looted while oil exploration was being conducted on Waorani lands (Cabodevilla 1999). This reputation for violence and self-isolation made them a key target of North American missionary work, and in the 1950s missionaries began dropping gifts from airplanes over remote Waorani longhouses in hopes of establishing peaceful contact.

In January 1956, five missionaries made a long-anticipated attempt to contact and proselytize a Waorani group living near the Curaray River. Only days after landing a small airplane on an exposed riverbank known to the missionaries as "Palm Beach," they were speared and killed by Waorani. News of the Palm Beach killings soon reached the American public in an article with photographs in *Life* magazine, titled "'Go Ye and Preach the Gospel': Five Do and Die" (1956). As this event received increasing international attention, the campaign to establish the "auca mission" intensified. In the years that followed, a widow (Elisabeth Elliot) and a sister (Rachel Saint) of two of the deceased missionaries entered the Waorani territory and eventually established Tiweno, the first mission settlement.

Rachel Saint, inspired by her brother Nathan Saint's death at Palm Beach, was closely involved with the Waorani until her death in 1994, living much of her life in Tiweno and later in Toñampari. At the time of the Palm Beach killings she was conducting interviews and linguistic research with Dayuma, who had fled from her Waorani relatives to live on a frontier hacienda in the 1940s following the killings she described in the narrative above. The relationship between these two women became a key platform for establishing the mission at Tiweno. Dayuma, who lived in the village of To-

FIGURE 3. Dayuma at her house in Toñampari

ñampari until her death in 2014, had a key role in aiding the missionaries
to establish themselves among her relatives in the Waorani territory. Her
life story subsequently became the topic of missionary books published in
the United States. The front cover of the most famous of these books, *The
Dayuma Story* (Wallis 1960), claims to tell "the breathtaking story of the
Ecuadorian Indian girl who escaped from—and returned to—the world's
most murderous tribe."

By the 1970s the missionaries had attracted the vast majority of Waorani
to live in a single village at Tiweno, where many ceased spear-killing and
came to live in close proximity to people they regarded as "enemies" (Robarchek and Robarchek 1996, 1998; Stoll 1982; Yost 1981). Dayuma and Saint

facilitated relations between Waorani groups, other indigenous communities, the Ecuadorian authorities, and petroleum companies, which sought to develop oil resources on Waorani lands. Like Dayuma herself, by the 1970s many Waorani at the mission had converted to Christianity, and there were an increasing number of marriages between Waorani and Quichua people who came to live in Tiweno (Yost 1981). In this way Dayuma's narrative is not only one of personal tragedy, but it is also a story that maps the ways Waorani people came to establish enduring relations with kowori—non-Waorani people.

It should be no surprise that the stories Waorani people like Dayuma tell about these events, and past violence more generally, depart in significant ways from the historical accounts of missionary books and the recent film. And yet the missionary narrative of martyrdom in the Palm Beach killings that has been influential in the United States and Europe for decades is also part of Waorani social memory. The following sections explore how Waorani remember the violent deaths of their close kin and the missionaries who came to have a key presence in their lives for decades. Their oral narratives of past events reveal indigenous understandings of violence and social transformation that, in some contexts, incorporate evangelical representations of Waorani history.

Remembering Violence

When I first visited Toñampari and lived with Waorani people, I was not primarily interested in studying how my hosts remembered violence in the distant past. However, even before I was able to understand their language, it became clear that a great deal of Waorani storytelling concerned past killings. In telling me about their deceased relatives and ancestors, my hosts would mimic the body motions involved in killing with spears. Elders often tell these tales in the evening around the cooking fire, as younger people sit quietly and listen to accounts of people and events, many of which they know only through these stories. Waorani also evoked the past while on treks in forest when they identify particular rivers, streams, ridges, and other places in the landscape where their relatives were killed.[3] What is most impressive about these tales, apart from the tragic events themselves, is the amount of detail in their telling. They often describe the precise place where a victim was killed, what was going on within the home, what the victim was eating, drinking, or thinking, whether or not the person was awake, and in some cases even what he or she was dreaming before or at the time of the attack.[4] Along with this detail, which often reveals deception and surprise at the expense of the victims, orators make extensive use of sounds they associate with violent struggle. They often use onomatopoeic words and ideophones that describe or mimic different sounds, such as people brushing up against leaves in the forest or the sound of spears entering a person's body.[5] In some cases they report the dialogue that occurred between the killers and victims during the actual struggle.

I heard these stories told by a number of different Waorani people. While many stories were told by men, women also describe the violence suffered by their families in the past. Although most young people know about the people involved in these events, especially when the subjects of the stories are their own family members, they usually lack the detailed knowledge that adults exhibit in their own storytelling. This has much to do with differences in age and practice in telling stories, but the older generations also have much more personal experience with the violence they narrate. Many adults have witnessed or taken part in the killings they describe, and even stories about events that are temporally distant from the teller almost always involve people they consider close kin. Elders demonstrate a remarkable ability to describe even the most obscure details of events that they could not possibly have witnessed themselves. Their speculations about the thoughts, dreams, and words of victims who died many years ago suggest not only that these stories have a powerful presence in Waorani social life but also that a considerable degree of creativity goes into their performance.

During my fieldwork I rarely recorded these narratives as they were told or even asked people to tell them to me. However, my questions about genealogy and life history were often met with tragic tales of how siblings, parents, or grandparents were speared in the past. Stories were sometimes told in the Waorani language and at other times in Spanish when directed at me specifically. In other cases I simply overheard stories as part of a wider household audience. Listening to Waorani oral narratives, it became clear to me that there was an exchange of valued knowledge in these situations beyond merely learning who killed whom in the past. As anthropologists have described elsewhere, stories about the past have an important role in constructing moral identities in relation to specific audiences (E. Basso 1987, 1995; K. Basso 1996; Cruikshank 1998; Oakdale 2004). Like other forms of social memory, they constitute a relational—and often dialogical—practice whereby individual speakers comment on and negotiate their present position in relation to the past (Briggs 1993; Oakdale 2005; Course 2007; Uzendoski and Calapucha-Tapuy 2012). In this way, I approach Waorani

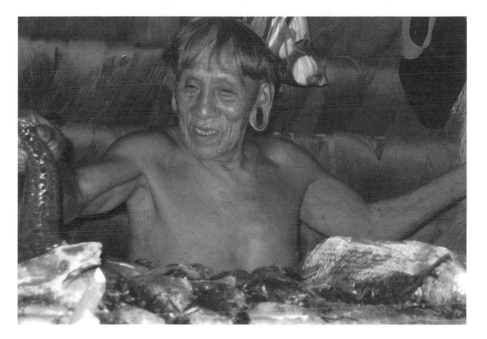

FIGURE 4. An elder smokes fish

accounts of past victimhood as a social and moral process rather than the objective retrieval of traumatic past experiences (Lambek 1996).

I generally accept that the events described in these narratives did in fact occur. However, rather than attempting to determine any real "history" in the sense of an actual sequence of events as they objectively occurred, my concern is with the meanings and uses representations of the past have for Waorani people today. Rival suggests that the Waorani, like many indigenous peoples of Amazonia, do not draw a strong contrast between mythic and historical narratives (2002, 46). The forms of social memory that emerge in these stories are presented by the narrators as real in describing specific people from no more than two or three ascending generations, as opposed to other types of narrative, such as myth, that generally are not presented as events that actually happened to known people. While the relationship between myth and history is the subject of ongoing debate in anthropology (Hill 1988; Turner 1988; Gow 2001), there is little confusion among Waorani people about the difference between the comic follies of mythical characters and the seriousness and anguish they describe in stories about past spear-killings.

Becoming Victims

When I asked my hosts why there was so much killing between Waorani in the past, elders often answered that men killed because they were "angry" (*pii*). They described this anger as sometimes becoming uncontrollable after a close relative is killed or suffers assault sorcery by another group. This concern with anger and revenge remains an important part of how Waorani people understand violence today. They often explained, with much sadness, the deplorable nature and lack of justification for spear-killings. Past killings are commonly referred to in morally charged terms, such as *ononki* (unjustified/deceptive), *wene* (bad/evil), or *wiwa* (bad/ugly). While the term *ononki* can refer casually to a mistake someone has made, perhaps simply going the wrong way on a path, in some contexts it is used to describe unprovoked violence or an act of deception. The word *wene* is also used with a degree of moral charge, as Waorani people sometimes translate it as the Spanish word *diablo* ("devil"). They use words like these not just to describe how their relatives were killed in the past but also to convey a sense of victimhood. While the word "victim" does not have an exact equivalent in the Waorani language, since most deaths are attributed in some way to human action, attaching the suffix *wori* (meaning "deceased") to the name of kin often conveys a sense of unjustified violence. However, I use the term "victimhood" in reference to the dominant theme of moral transgression and suffering at the hands of kowori and rival Waorani groups, as well as the particular perspective that Waorani people evoke in their stories about past violence.

Older Waorani adults have diverse and highly personal experiences of past violence. And yet their stories are also part of a shared symbolic understanding of what it means to be Waorani. One story that I heard on a number of occasions during my fieldwork illustrates how the victim's point of view is evoked in Waorani memory. It was told to me by Gaba, the father of the family with whom I lived for much of my fieldwork. A reserved man in his fifties, Gaba is well known in Toñampari for his skill in hunting peccaries, toucans, and other animals and game birds, as well as for his generosity in sharing meat with neighbors and teachers at the local school. Gaba is also renowned for his knowledge of myths and his ability to tell stories about the lives of the *pikenani*—Waorani elders.

On several occasions Gaba told me about the tragic events surrounding his family history as I sat with him around the cooking fire in the evenings, alongside his wife and children. He described growing up with his parents and siblings along the Keremeneno River, about two days' walk east from Gaba's house in Toñampari. Sometime in the 1950s, when Gaba was a young boy, his longhouse was attacked by an enemy group from downriver. Although his father and most of the rest of his group were killed, Gaba's mother managed to escape into the forest carrying him to safety. Gaba's older sister was abducted by the attacking group and became a wife of Minkaye, one of the men involved in the raid. After Gaba's fortunate escape with his mother, they faced great hardships while living by themselves in the forest with nowhere to go. His mother later took him to the recently established mission settlement, where they lived with the evangelical missionaries and other Waorani. After his mother died of polio at the mission settlement when Gaba was still a child, he grew up on the mission and later became an evangelical pastor.[6]

At different times within his home and in the presence of his family, Gaba described several events in what is outlined above as an autobiographical narrative. He often focused on his father as a victim of violence and the hunger he himself later suffered without anyone to bring him meat. I have since learned that this story, along with Gaba's experience of being an orphan with few close kin, is an important part of his social positioning in the village where he lives. In describing how his father was killed in the violence that took the lives of many of his generation, Gaba evokes his own sense of suffering and loss in these events. In this context Gaba, his kin, and other Waorani voice a form of social memory that is at the very heart of contemporary social life in Toñampari.

The cultural importance of victimhood in framing past violence becomes particularly clear when stories are reproduced from one generation to the next (High 2009a). One well-known story among the family with whom I lived concerns the death of an ancestor called Iniwa. It was first told to me by Ompure, a very old woman, as I attempted to piece together a genealogy of her family. She and her husband were among the families who founded Toñampari in the 1970s after leaving Tiweno, where overpopulation and disease had by then led many families to abandon the mission. Today they move regularly between their son's house in the village and the Tiputini area, where they visit relatives and regularly demand food and other gifts from the oil company. In telling me about her family history as we sat in her son's house, Ompure launched into a lengthy story about *Iniwa-wori* ("dead Iniwa"), her maternal grandfather. After naming his wives and children, she focused on his death at the hands of enemies. Iniwa was involved in an ongoing conflict with another Waorani group when he decided to build an enormous longhouse with the aim of bringing together the warring factions for a communal feast (*eëme*). Iniwa was working to place palm leaves on the roof of the house when his enemies attacked, spearing him from below. Ompure explained in detail how the struggle ensued, demonstrating with her hands where the spears entered Iniwa's body and reenacting the motions of his killers in this unusual attack waged from below.

Ompure emphasized that, at the time of the attack, her grandfather was seeking to rebuild alliances with his enemies, situating him unambiguously as a victim of violence and betrayal. Communal feasts are special events that involve one household inviting others to share in abundant food, drink, singing, dancing, sexual liaisons, and rituals to mark out marriage arrangements. The description of Iniwa working on a new house for a planned feast evokes the sense of victimhood in which she situates her family. Upon my questioning her further about Iniwa, Ompure admitted that he had killed enemies before. However, this clearly was not relevant to the story she wanted to tell.

I later heard a separate account of Iniwa from Ompure's daughter, the mother of the family with whom I was living. In this case I asked her directly about her great-grandfather. She had much less to say about Iniwa than her mother did, but before long she too was describing and mimicking with hand motions how he was speared while working on his rooftop. Ompure's daughter did not appear to know the story well, perhaps lacked the ability or confidence to fully tell it, or simply did not want to take the time to explain it to an imperfect speaker of her language. However, her short account did identify the betrayal in Iniwa's death, which appeared to be what gives this story the moral charge it has for her family. Situations like these illustrate how memories of the past are transmitted from one generation to the next in culturally particular ways. In remembering events that occurred long before she was born, people like Ompure are not simply involved in a technical process of recording or retrieving historical "facts" from the stories they hear from elders. As Bloch argues, "Episodes of the distant past are 'remembered' in ways which are strikingly similar to those which people have experienced within their lifetime" (1998, 125). Beyond reproducing accounts of past killings, narratives like Ompure's engender what Graham describes as "a subjective sense of continuity" in which people "create and reaffirm their links to those who have performed them in the past" (1995, 6). In this way, narratives of violence constitute an expressive form in which Waorani people position themselves and their kin as victims. While elders who explained events like these to me from the victim's point of view certainly could have told stories about the enemies their ancestors killed, this is not the perspective they generally took in their accounts of past violence. The ways people like Ompure and her daughter narrated events point to how violence is a form of social memory in which Waorani people locate themselves not only in relation to the past but also in ongoing processes of social transformation.

Victims and Martyrs

Narratives of the past, whether in autobiographies, myths, songs, or other expressive forms, define and comment on the present in many ways. In a seminal study of indigenous Amazonian oral history, Basso observed: "The rhetoric of conflict that is developed within . . . stories about the past becomes merged with the rhetoric of conventional ideology in the practice of contemporary life" (1995, 304). In a similar way, the stories that elders like Gaba and Ompure tell about violence present a view of the past that is part of indigenous understandings of what it means to be a Waorani person. Rival (2002) suggests that this "victim's point of view" constitutes a shared Waorani identity as "prey" to aggressive outsiders. When discussing past conflicts with kowori "outsiders," elders explain that they, until recently, assumed all non-Waorani people to be cannibals (Yost 1981; Robarchek and Robarchek 1998). This sense of being "prey" emerges not only in the stories Waorani people tell about past killings but also in their descriptions of suffering unfair treatment in everyday life. This includes complaints about assault sorcery, greed, and theft they attribute to other indigenous groups, oil companies, and other sources external to the household. Positioning oneself as a victim is related to the assumption, common to many Amazonian societies, that death and misfortune are always to some extent the result of human agencies rather than "natural" causes (Taylor 1996).

Waorani self-identification as paradigmatic victims appears to reflect a more general emphasis on "predation" in indigenous Amazonian cosmologies (Fausto 2007, 2012; Vilaça 2010; Conklin 2001; Viveiros de Castro 1998a). Fausto, for example, describes how "in Amazonia, predation is the main mode of determining the point of view in any relation between entities possessing agency and intention" (2001, 305). Whereas in many Amazonian societies personhood is produced through the symbolic incorporation of "prey" in hunting and warfare, Waorani people offer a contrast to this model of alterity by insisting on their own position as victims of violence. As Rival suggests, "[Waorani] lore values the killed, not the killer" (2005, 297). In this way, part of being a Waorani person involves seeing and experiencing the world from the point of view of "prey"—rather than that of predators.

The Waorani present an interesting case for the comparative study of predation in Amazonian sociocosmologies. However, more than simply constituting an "indigenous" model of alterity, their narratives of victimhood also reveal the convergence or "conjuncture" (Sahlins 1985) between indigenous models of predation and the teachings of Christian missionaries in the 1960s. Waorani social memory today incorporates imagery of Christian martyrdom represented in the historical writings of missionaries and in the film *End of the Spear* (Hanon 2006). Watching this film and reading the missionary texts on which it is based, it is difficult to ignore the antithesis between Amazonian violence and Christian self-sacrifice presented in this image of Waorani history. Rather than reifying this proposed contrast between "indigenous violence" and missionary compassion, Waorani people appear to integrate the stories of individual missionaries and their narrative of martyrdom into their own ways of remembering the past and defining what it means to be a Waorani person.

The film *End of the Spear* primarily concerns a series of Waorani spear-killings leading up to and including the deaths of the missionaries at Palm Beach. Although it claims to be based on a true story, it is clearly not meant to be a documentary and is shot within the conventions of a Hollywood production.[7] It largely follows an evangelical narrative of how American Christians sacrificed their lives so that the "word of God" would reach Ecuador's remaining "savage Indians," thus ending a timeless cycle of indigenous violence.

The main protagonist of the story presented in the film is "Mincayani," a Waorani man who participated in the Palm Beach killings before later renouncing violence and converting to Christianity. His film character appears to combine the actions associated with a number of Waorani men, including Minkaye, one of the well-known elders who participated in the Palm Beach killings. This man also took part in the raid that killed Gaba's father described above and still lives today with his wife (Gaba's sister) in a Waorani village along the Curaray River. The other key characters in the film are Nathan Saint, the pilot who died with the four other missionaries in 1956, and his son, Steve Saint, who returns to live with the Waorani years later and discovers that Mincayani was his father's killer. Steve Saint, who was a consultant for the film and appears in an interview at the end, also authored a book by the same title, *End of the Spear* (2005).

Consistent with previous missionary writings, the film depicts a violent Amazonian society unable to escape a pattern of revenge killing until the Christian martyrs and their surviving relatives teach the Waorani to follow the Bible. This transformation is achieved in two ways. First, we see the missionaries choosing not to fire their guns when attacked, a sacrifice made clear by Nathan Saint's dying words in which he tells his killer (Mincayani) that he is his friend. Second, in the film the Palm Beach killers are inspired by seeing that instead of taking revenge, the relatives of the dead missionaries seek to live among them. The missionary narrative becomes less subtle as the film progresses, culminating with Mincayani taking Steve Saint to the Palm Beach site in the 1990s to describe how he killed Saint's father decades before. As Mincayani narrates the story, the film replays the fatal spearing and shows a light forming above Nathan Saint as he lies on the beach with a spear in his body, indicating the martyr's ascension to Heaven. The film concludes with Mincayani's insisting that his victim's son spear him, and with Steve Saint's refusing and thus forgiving his father's killer.

In their descriptions of the intensity of pre-contact spear-killings and the Palm Beach killings, Waorani people tell a story that is in some ways consistent with that of the film. There is one exception, however, which illustrates the centrality of victimhood in Waorani social memory. In contrast to the film narrative, which presents the missionaries as martyrs who chose to die themselves rather than to fire their guns on their attackers, Waorani describe how Dayuma's brother Nampa was fatally wounded in the head by a gunshot fired by one of the missionaries during the struggle.[8] Although my hosts often criticized the actions of the Waorani killers involved, it is striking that even this story is ultimately cast in terms of Waorani victimhood. Another telling aspect of this narrative is that, even for the few remaining Waorani evangelical Christians today, Palm Beach is a less commonly told story than the frequent accounts of how their kin were killed by other Waorani in the past. Their stories of internal raids appear to have greater salience for them in presenting an unambiguous image of Waorani as victims.

This insistence on victimhood also surfaced in an official denouncement of the film, published on the Internet by the Waorani political organization (ONHAE) soon after the opening of the film. The announcement stated:

> As the legal representative body of the Waorani Nation we give to you our formal denouncement against those who have taken advantage of our

innocence and produced a film by the name of "END OF SPEARS" [*sic*], the same one which speaks of our Waorani history and that was filmed in Panama by actors who were looking to imitate us. [2006][9]

Despite the organization's rejection of the history depicted in the film, the story of Christian martyrdom introduced by missionaries through biblical teachings in the 1960s still resonates strongly in Waorani communities and can be found in many of their own historical narratives. While in the film relatives of the martyred missionaries teach Waorani killers to forgive, the Waorani accepted subsequent missionaries at least partly because they were close kin of the Palm Beach victims (see Rival 2002). Seeing that these kowori were not intent on attacking or eating them, the Waorani identified the missionaries as members of a victim group much like themselves. In chapter 4 I describe how, in the aftermath of recent intergroup violence, some Waorani people defined the victims of an attack as their kin on the basis of a shared position as victims. Both in this case and in that of missionaries in the past, a shared identification as victims of violence denotes the possibility of establishing relations with unknown people. Just as the term *kowori* previously referred to the semi-human status of "cannibal outsiders," being the kin of victims appears to denote a certain sense of personhood. It is this understanding of victimhood as a marker of potential sociality, rather than the Palm Beach attack itself, that has made particular missionaries an important part of Waorani history. This is because, in the eyes of many Waorani people who joined the mission settlement, the missionaries shared the same history of losing close kin to violence.

The Time of "Civilization"

In some ways Waorani narratives of violence, like oral traditions described elsewhere in Amazonia, tend to draw out social boundaries between one's own group and others (Hendricks 1993; Basso 1995). This can be seen in stories about ancestors who were killed by other Waorani or who encountered dangerous kowori in the past. And yet this same narrative genre allows us to begin considering how kowori and other "enemies" are incorporated into indigenous notions of personhood and group identity. Despite the relatively small number of Waorani Christians today, Waorani people evoke imagery of missionaries and their evangelical teachings in stories about how their own kin became victims of violence. The place of missionaries in Waorani understandings of past violence emerges in the stories my hosts tell about what they call the time of *civilización* ("civiliza-tion"), which refers to the period between the 1960s and 1980s when the majority of Waorani people came to live with Dayuma, Rachel Saint, and other missionaries at the mission settlement of Tiweno. Although a wealth of historical material exists from the writings of missionaries who lived in Tiweno and observed Waorani converting to Christianity, less attention has been given to the prominent place of Waorani concepts of civilización in contemporary autobiographical narratives.

The notion of civilización constitutes an important point of reference in Waorani narratives despite the fact that, thirty years after the official closure of the mission, few Waorani today call themselves *cristianos* ("Christians") or take serious interest in biblical teachings.[10] The idea of having become *civilizado* ("civilized") is a central theme by which Waorani people define their present way of life. Waorani adults today often contrast themselves to their pre-contact ancestors on the basis that they or their parents became "civilized." In the 1980s, many Waorani were attracted to formal schooling because they saw it as an opportunity to become civilizado (Rival 2002), a Spanish term they still use in reference to living in villages and in contrast to revenge killings and conflicts with outsiders.

Waorani narratives of civilization constitute a form of social memory wherein indigenous understandings of predation and imagery of Chris-tian martyrdom are closely intertwined. This link between the trope of victimhood in Waorani oral narrative and missionary representations is particularly clear in the following account of civilization told to me by a middle-aged man in Toñampari:

> My family came from far downriver. There were no missionaries then, and people killed a lot. My father's family speared many people from the upriver group and took my mother away with them when she was a young girl. My father married her. Later, my mother's brother Toña[11] went with the missionaries to find my mother and civilize my father's group. They flew overhead making noise and talking from the airplane with a loudspeaker. Then they landed along the river, and Toña brought my mother's sister to help find my mother. They met my father's group, and Toña and five missionaries stayed with them for two months. They wanted to civilize my father's group so they would no longer kill. But my father's group threatened Toña, thinking that the missionaries wanted to take my mother back to where she came from. They thought Toña was a kowori, so they lied to him. They told Toña to cut down chonta trees to

make spears, and said they were for him to take and sell. But Toña already knew they wanted to kill him, because he had dreamt of a jaguar eating his head. My mother overheard the men planning to kill Toña, and she went to warn him. He was a cristiano, so he was not afraid. Early in the morning, they took Toña to a hill to kill him. They had waited for him there without spears the day before. They told Toña to chop down a tree to make spears. While he was chopping, the other men speared him in the back. With spears in his body, Toña said that he had no problems with the men who had speared him (forgiving them), saying that he was a real Waorani person. He said "don't kill" and "I die so that you should no longer kill." Then they speared him more and Toña cried.

My father did not approve of the other men killing Toña. The others chopped up Toña's body "like meat," thinking he was a kowori. Just before they cut off the head, my father said, "Don't cut up my brother-in-law like an animal!" Then one of the men threatened to kill my father. He wanted to take my father's sister for a wife. My father went home to tell his family about the killing, but they couldn't stop the killers taking his sister away. The next day my father went with his family to the burial site of Toña. Later he went with his brothers to live on the Tiputini River, where I was born. We lived there for five years. My mother wanted to return to her family upriver. My father did not want to go, but didn't want my mother to leave. Later they went to hide next to an airstrip near the river, and the missionaries took them all to a Quichua town by plane. They stayed there, next to Quichuas, for fifteen days. Then they were flown to Tiweno (the mission), and my mother was reunited with her relatives there. Everyone cried because they were so happy, having thought each other were dead. They lived there with Toña's wife, the missionaries, Dayuma, and several other families in one big community. We lived there for four years. We were very happy and we became civilized in Tiweno. But then many diseases came, and more than twenty people died. Dayuma and some others decided to leave and founded Toñampari. My family went too. That's why we live here now.

What becomes clear in this story is a transition from intergroup violence to many Waorani living together in one place. In addition to emphasizing Toña's position as a victim of violence, the narrator describes his family's eventual move to the mission settlement and ultimately their escape from intergroup conflict in terms of "civilization." Accounts like these refer to the process in which missionaries attempted to relocate as many Waorani groups as possible to Tiweno in the 1960s. Although his father's group is implicated in a series of killings, the story represents the narrator's closest kin as victims. His mother was taken captive as her relatives were killed and his father only narrowly escaped being killed after opposing the killing of Toña. Since the man who told this story was a small boy when his family relocated to the mission, it appears that he was both reproducing a historical narrative of victimhood told by members of his family and defining himself as "civilized."

The story incorporates a clearly biblical perspective on the apparent martyrdom of Toña, who forgives his killers after being speared and conveys his sense of self-sacrifice in saying to them, "I die so that you should no longer kill." It suggests that the missionary narrative of martyrdom continues to be significant for the Waorani, even decades after the closure of the mission settlement (High 2009b). Perhaps the imagery of martyrdom is unusually direct in this particular story because the narrator spent much of his youth growing up on the mission. However, the notion of forgiving or not avenging past killings is part of how many Waorani adults envision the process they call civilización. They appear to value narratives of becoming civilizado and cristiano precisely because they refer to the conditions by which the most intense period of past revenge killings was transcended and enemy groups began living in closer proximity at the mission settlement.

Dayuma's Story

In addition to incorporating imagery of Christian martyrdom, Waorani accounts of "civilization" establish a sense of shared history with kowori people. The presence of missionaries surely had a profound impact on Waorani social organization and cosmology. However, it is also evident in the autobiographies of Dayuma and other elders that Waorani people remember key missionary figures in terms of the narrative of victimhood and civilization that I have described.

In June 2009 I recorded an interview with Dayuma in Toñampari, not far from the locations where her relatives and the missionaries were killed in past times. Since the time when I first met her in 1998, Dayuma shared fragments of her remarkable life history with me on several occasions. As the oldest person in her community, she often spoke of her deceased relatives, international travels at the height of her fame in the 1960s, and the missionaries with whom she shared much of her life. On this occasion, she spoke for nearly an hour, mostly in the Waorani language, about her past experiences. What follow are short excerpts from our conversation that bear certain resemblances with her narrative recorded in *The Dayuma Story* more than fifty years before:[12]

> Long ago they speared my father dead, you understand?
> They speared my father dead long ago, but I did not see it myself
> We went and hid on the other side,
> Then we heard that they speared my father
> I ran away, all the way to the outsiders' house
> But nobody was there
> We went far away, but we found no outsiders
> We were worried, so we returned
> When we returned, Wamoñe had been speared in the leg
> Despite so much killing they survived, only my father died . . .

Casey: *What about your mother?*

> Yes, my mother Akawo only recently died in Tiweno
> She died of sickness
> My father was speared dead and so was my brother Wawe
> Other Waorani people killed Wamoñe for no reason at all, that's how he died
> They speared him all over
> Then, after he was dead, they speared him in the head and in the eyes, again and again
> My mother told me that he was lying there dead, she said they speared him in the head

> Not long ago my mother Akawo died in Tiweno
> My brothers and Nemo died, they cut her with a machete
> My sister Onenka . . .
> At night the wind was blowing so much, the branches were breaking from the trees . . .
> One went right through my sister's eye, like this (gesturing with her hands)
> She died . . . two of my sisters died, but two survived and are still alive today
> I came to Tiweno and we lived very well until Gimare's child had a painful birth
> She died while giving birth, but her child Tomás and her other child survived
> My sister Oba became sick and died of measles
> So now I am alone, an old woman

I live all alone, but there are many children of Oba and Gimare
Her (Gimare's) husband already died but Oba's husband Yowe still lives

Casey: *Was Nemo (missionary Rachel Saint) like your sister?*

Nemo was like my sister, and I lived loving her very much
She used to go to Quito and brought me food
She brought rice, noodles, oatmeal . . .
Now Nemo is gone, and there is nobody to bring me food
Nemo was very good
She brought medicine for everyone when they were sick

When they found out that Nemo died . . .
They no longer listened to god's words since Nemo was gone
She was a great preacher
Now they live badly
They get drunk and fight

Don Pedro, Eduardo, captain Nathan (missionaries) . . . five of them died
They died because Nenkiwi was angry and speared them
When they buried Gimare, they became angry among themselves and
    wanted to kill
They grabbed his (Nenkiwi's) spear and broke it
Then they went and killed the outsiders
I am angry because they secretly speared and killed them while I was
    away in Quito
If I wouldn't have gone to Quito, I would have heard them calling . . .
I would have returned
If the outsiders would have lived, they would have made a big runway
We would have lived very well
I am angry because they did this very bad thing
Babe (missionary Steve Saint), Nathan's son, used to live here
But he doesn't come anymore
He used to come a lot, but he doesn't come anymore

In Dayuma's 2009 story the missionaries who were killed in 1956 appear as part of the same narrative of victimhood and loss by which Waorani elders describe their own kin being killed in the past. Like other narratives of victimhood that I have described, Dayuma's account laments the severing of past and potential relations and sources of support. At the end of her story, Dayuma speculated that, had Waorani people not killed the missionaries, they would have built a "big runway" for airplanes, providing further links with the outside world. This is followed by Dayuma's regretting how living missionaries and their kin no longer visit her village. Similarly, Dayuma lamented the absence of Rachel Saint much in the same way she describes her own family. A common theme in stories like these is how past violence deprived a person of his or her potential kinship relations, whether these were deceased relatives or missionaries like Rachel Saint who were incorporated into Waorani households. Like in Gaba's story about the hunger he suffered upon the death of his father, Dayuma described the absence of her "sister" and other kin who used to bring her food. This imagery of scarcity and group depletion evokes a strong contrast to the Waorani ideal of abundance and "living well" with many kin. It also contradicts the emphasis on expanding potential sources of sociality in narratives of "civilization."

In missionary writings like *The Dayuma Story*, Dayuma's acceptance of Christianity through Rachel Saint's teachings is presented as having a pivotal role in the mission at Tiweno. Part of what appears to have made this narrative so compelling for Christian readers is how the missionaries, particularly Rachel Saint and Elizabeth Elliot, joined Dayuma to establish a mission among some of the same Waorani who had previously killed their close relatives at Palm Beach. Whereas for Christians in the United States this became a powerful narrative of Christian martyrdom and compassion, the notion that Saint and Elliott's close kin were victims of violence appears to have also resonated strongly with many Waorani. The missionaries enter Waorani narratives as people whose kin were speared "wrongly" (*ononki*), just like their own relatives. In contrast to stories about aggressive kowori outsiders, these missionaries are described in line with Waorani understandings of personhood and sociality: they are remembered as members of the convivial group, generous providers of food and, perhaps most important, kin of people who were killed violently. In this way, for elders like Dayuma, kowori missionaries have become part of a social memory that defines what it means to be Waorani.

Conclusion

The stories presented in this chapter illustrate that intercultural relations and kowori people are an important part of Waorani social memory. Remembering their relatives who were speared by enemies, the invasions of kowori "cannibals," or the process of "civilization," Waorani elders establish a strong sense of being victims in the face of violent outsiders. And yet specific kowori missionaries are incorporated into this narrative of victimhood, as is the Christian imagery of martyrdom that has become prominent in historical representations of the Waorani. These stories appear to contain within them a historical "structure of the conjuncture" (Sahlins 1985) between indigenous Amazonian forms of ontological predation and Christian understandings of compassionate self-sacrifice presented in books like *The Dayuma Story* and the film *End of the Spear*. They point to how Amazonian cosmology relates to sociopolitical processes that extend beyond the spatial boundaries of indigenous communities and the temporal dimensions of ethnographic fieldwork (see, for example, Whitten 2008).

For anthropologists, historical encounters like these between indigenous people and Westerners provide an opportunity to explore how new "others" have been incorporated into Amazonian cosmology and sociality (Albert and Ramos 2000; Vilaça 2010; Viveiros de Castro 2011). My interest in these encounters, however, is not primarily "historical" in the sense of attempting to uncover the true origins of ideas that emerge in Waorani stories or the practices that I observed in my fieldwork. Waorani stories about violence, victimhood, and "civilization" are specific genres of social memory that people evoke in their everyday relations with each other and with their kowori neighbors that tell us at least as much about Waorani understandings of the present as they do about the past.

Memories of the past also imply a certain vision of what might be possible or desirable in the future (Basso 1995, 25). The following chapter describes Waorani ways of remembering violence that assert a sense of indigenous agency and autonomy in the face of powerful contemporary outsiders. Gendered and generational experiences reveal a diversity of perspectives within Waorani social memory, some of which challenge the victim's point of view in stories told by elders. What is at issue here is not whether Waorani notions of victimhood should be seen as an "authentic" expression of indigenous Amazonian cosmology. As with all practices and ideas that we encounter in ethnographic fieldwork, "indigenous" conceptualizations of violence are produced within diverse and changing sociocultural environments. What is at stake is how indigenous Amazonian forms of memory and alterity can be understood in the context of ongoing intercultural relations.

CHAPTER 2

Becoming Warriors

The oral histories discussed in the previous chapter bring violence into focus both as a marker of social difference and a way in which kowori are incorporated into indigenous forms of sociality. However, the victim's point of view and the process of "civilization" described by older adults are only part of Waorani social memory. Understanding the diversity of indigenous representations of the past requires a shift in focus from the language of elders to the embodied performances of young people in urban intercultural encounters. In this chapter I explore specific situations where people remember their ancestors not as quintessential "victims" but as the "wild" Amazonian warriors of colonial imagination. The experiences of young Waorani in urban areas and the kinds of remembering and forgetting that emerge in their public performances reveal gendered and generational aspects of memory that draw on deeply rooted historical imagery of Amazonian people in Ecuador. In contrast to the oral histories of elders that refer to specific people and events, they project a generalized image of Waorani people as a symbol of Amazonian warriorhood. The ways memory is embodied and (re)created in urban Amazonia reveal the multiple perspectives and unified cultural logic within seemingly contradictory representations of the past. In this context, indigenous uses of violent imagery and emergent notions of "culture" are as much about forgetting as they are about remembering the past.[1]

From Victims to Killers

Not long after hearing Gaba describe his father's death, I joined his son Taremo on a trip to a neighboring village, located one day's travel downriver from Toñampari by canoe. Upon arriving we visited the home of Taremo's paternal aunt, the same sister of Gaba who was abducted as a young girl in the raid in the 1950s described to me by Gaba. The woman still lives with her husband Minkaye, the man who killed her father and most of the rest of her family some fifty years before. In describing this woman to me, Taremo referred to her household in the Waorani language as *girinani* (extended kin) and in Spanish as *familia* (family). Late that evening, as we were eating fish in the home of some of Minkaye's relatives, an old woman began telling Taremo the story of his grandfather's death. She described the event from the perspective of the attacking group, insisting that her male kin only decided to attack because they were afraid that the other group would ambush them as they fished and hunted along the river. She continued, saying that the killing was mistaken (*ononki*), as the attackers did not realize that among the victims were people they identified as familia (*girinani*). In this account, it was explained that the killers feared Taremo's ancestors because they did not know who they actually were and wanted to continue hunting and fishing safely along the river.

Regardless of what the intentions of the killers were on the Keremeneno River so many years ago, the old woman's description of the confused and mistaken nature of the attack emphasized the closeness between Taremo's household and her own. Her story appeared to draw on an event of past violence in a way that reaffirmed her commitment to peaceful relations between former "enemy" groups. More specifically, her telling of the story speaks to the fact that Gaba has openly forgiven the killing of his father and that an enduring friendship has since developed between him and Minkaye's group. In this way, memories of violence, even those that establish the perpetrator's point of view, are part of a relational process in which Waorani people express a social and moral position in relation to the past.

While the story I heard told to Taremo emphasized the misunderstanding and mistaken nature of past violence, in other contexts people occasionally take pride in telling how their fathers and grandfathers have killed in the past. Even some of the same middle-aged adults who emphasize how their relatives became victims sometimes also describe violence from the killer's point of view. One of these was Awa, a man who described to me the feats of his deceased father in the days of intense violence between Waorani groups. As we sat alone in his home one day, he explained how his father (Niwa) was a fearless warrior, having taken the lives of many enemies in his day. Much of Niwa's notoriety comes from his tricking and killing Moipa, perhaps the most infamous of all Waorani warriors of his generation. Here I summarize this story as I recorded it in my field notes soon after I heard it from Awa:

> When I asked Awa about his parents, he told me a story about how his father killed Moipa. For years Moipa had been traveling angrily back and forth across the Waorani territory killing everyone he could and taking many women as his wives. He apparently had many wives and often killed women who refused to join his group after raids. When Moipa's group reached the house where Niwa's family lived, Niwa accepted them warmly and invited them to join him in a big feast, offering two of his own daughters as wives for Moipa himself. Moipa did not realize that Niwa and his group were plotting to trick him with the offering, having planned a surprise attack for the day of the feast. When Moipa's group arrived on the day agreed upon, they carried with them a massive bundle of spears. Niwa insisted that they put the spears to the side and drink from the large ceramic pots of manioc beer that had been placed out in the clearing in front of the house for their visitors (at this point Awa joked that the pots were actually nearly empty as his father's group attempted to trick Moipa into thinking they were full). Niwa and his followers had in fact hidden their own spears in the roof of their house in preparation for the surprise attack. When they finally pulled out the spears and attacked their unsuspecting visitors, Moipa was wounded in the side as he fled the scene. He was about to escape into the forest when he hit his head against a tree by accident and fell to the ground. Niwa then caught up and finished off Moipa with his spears.[2]

Awa then described how the survivors of Moipa's group fled deep into the forest and eventually joined the Tagaeri, one of the groups that refuses contact with all other Waorani people up to the present day and remains hostile to the incursions of kowori in their territory.[3]

Awa seemed to take pride in describing to me his father's achievement of killing Moipa and other enemies. This is partly due to Moipa's legendary status as one of the most feared and prolific killers of the generation that preceded missionary contact. Moipa is the subject of many victimhood narratives, including those told by Dayuma. Awa's description of his father as the killer of Moipa should also be understood in the context of

Awa's personal experiences with kowori people and generational changes within Waorani society. In contrast to elders (*pikenani*), who most often describe violence from the victim's point of view, Awa was closely involved in urban indigenous politics and relations with kowori people at the time of my fieldwork. This included participating regularly in political activities related to the official Waorani political organization, oil companies, and an internationally supported tourism project in his community. Probably in his late forties, Awa was also the elected "presidente" of his home community and spent a considerable amount of time outside the Waorani territory. At the time of my fieldwork, he was meeting regularly with representatives of an oil company that planned to expand its exploration and drilling on Waorani lands. Awa was in fact one of the most charismatic critics I knew on issues such as the behavior of oil companies and the presence of Quichua people and visiting missionaries in Waorani villages.[4]

While few Waorani are as vocal as Awa on these issues, the story he told about his father is characteristic of how younger generations of men today evoke past violence in their relations with outsiders. In telling me the story the way he did, Awa was not only recalling a notable part of his family history, he was also asserting his position in relation to the broader social and political circumstances in which he found himself. Waorani men like Awa are very much aware that their reputation for violence in some ways colors their relationships with other indigenous groups and kowori people in general. Their interactions with oil companies operating within the Waorani reserve are illustrative of this situation, as Waorani people know that spears and nudity inspire fear among oil workers and company representatives, in some cases allowing the Waorani a more immediate and advantageous position in their negotiations for gifts and services (Rival 1991). The emerging "ecotourism" industry in some villages promotes a similar scenario, rewarding Waorani people for exemplifying stereotypical features (such as nudity and warriorhood) that outsiders identify with indigenous Amazonian people and with the Waorani in particular.

This is not to say that Waorani people are so determined to acquire gifts and other benefits from outsiders that they simply narrate violence to impress visiting tourists, oil company representatives, and anthropologists. As we have seen, past violence is an important part of social memory within the intimate setting of Waorani households. However, we should not lose sight of the wider political and intercultural contexts in which social memory is (re)created in the present, as well as the divergent life experiences of the people who remember and perform violence. It is by examining shared and divergent perspectives on past violence in the "lived worlds" (Gow 2001) of different people that we can better understand the meanings, uses, and effects of social memory. By "lived worlds" I am not merely referring to the shared cultural understandings within which historical narratives are told, but equally to the ways in which people with diverse experiences and interests relate to society in different ways. The very different social contexts in which Awa, Gaba, and others find themselves in their own lived worlds are part of what motivated them to tell me their stories in the respective ways they did. They not only reproduce shared stories of how their family members and ancestors were killed, but they also draw on social memory in context-specific ways to define their relationship to Waorani society and beyond.

The *Aucas* of Colonial Imagination

Understanding the killer's point of view as a form of social memory requires recognition of the place of indigenous Amazonian people in colonial imagination and the history of regional interethnic relations. Even the earliest European explorers in Amazonia described the "wildness" of this unknown territory and the bellicosity of its native population. Whether soldiers, Christian missionaries, or fortune seekers in search of El Dorado, Europeans projected their own mythology of "Amazon warriors" onto the local populations of what is today called Amazonia. An image of violence and primitive wildness was thus ingrained in the very conception of the Amazon as a "place" in the colonial world. Today, nearly five centuries after the expedition of Spanish conquistador Francisco de Orellana and his crew became the first Europeans to traverse the Amazon River in 1542, colonial representations of Amazonia persist in popular imagination and in the experiences of indigenous people.

This imagery of violence and "wildness" can be seen in the social categories and processes of historical "ethnogenesis" (Whitten 1976b; Hill 1996) that emerged in the first centuries of colonialism. In Western Amazonia the term *auca* became a key social category in this process by distinguishing so-called *indios bravos* ("fierce Indians") from other people. While in Ecuador the term *auca* referred specifically to the Waorani during much of the twentieth century, the image of the auca "wild man" also holds an important symbolic place in many parts of South America. For centuries, images of wild yet powerful forest-dwelling people have been part of shamanic practices, ritual, and relations between highland and lowland people, particularly in the Andean countries (Salomon 1981; Taussig 1987; Whitten 1988; Taylor 1994). It is likely that even in pre-Columbian times the word *auca*, which is derived from the Quichua language, referred to social and geographical differences. The Incas appear to have used this term broadly in reference to a range of "enemy" Andean groups and other "warrior" peoples who remained outside the control of the Inca Empire (Platt 1987, 67). Colonial Europeans subsequently mapped onto this category a very specific and derogatory sense of untamed violence and "savagery" associated with the Amazon. Already by the late sixteenth century, Dominican Church personnel divided indigenous people into so-called "wild" and "tame" groups to establish themselves as a "civilizing evangelical force" in what is today Amazonian Ecuador (Whitten 2011a, 331).

Michael Taussig (1984) has described how, in the northwest Amazon, stories about the "savagery" of "wild" aucas became a powerful political force in conquest and the culture of terror wrought by the first rubber boom of 1880–1914. Colonial fantasies of the forest-dwelling "wild man" became a tool for political domination as Europeans projected onto indigenous people the forms of violence carried out by white people. It was a device used to justify ruthless forms of economic exploitation and terror suffered by indigenous people who were drawn, often by force, into collecting rubber. Taussig refers to how this colonial discourse became a "fictional reality" confirmed by the stories about aucas told by indigenous people themselves, as the imagined savagery of the mythical wild man "functioned to create, through magical realism, a culture of terror dominating both whites and Indians" (Taussig 1984, 492). The symbolic opposition between "wild" aucas and "civilized" white or mestizo people that emerged from colonial imagination continues to inform nationalist ideologies in Ecuador. Even after decades of indigenous political activism, these oppositions can be seen in discourses of "national pluralism" among both urban elites and indigenous peoples (Whitten 1981a; Whitten 1988, 304).

By the twentieth century, due to their reputation for isolation and conflicts with outsiders, the Waorani had become one of the archetypical "wild" auca groups in Ecuador, and as a result they are still commonly referred to by this name. Anne-Christine Taylor (2007) describes how the term *auca* was part of a wider system of social classification that emerged in the seventeenth and eighteenth centuries wherein people were defined as either *auca* ("wild Indian"), *manso* ("tame" or "domesticated Indian") or *blanco/ mestizo* ("white" or "mixed").[5] So-called "tame" groups consisted of multiethnic groups that formed at Jesuit missionary *reducciones* along major rivers during the colonial period (Taylor 1999, 234).[6] Those who survived the brutal epidemics at the missions adopted Quichua as a shared language along the Napo River in Ecuador and Peru (Muratorio 1991, 38; Taylor 1999, 225). This process of colonial "ethnogenesis" (Whitten 1976b) led to the various Quichua-speaking indigenous peoples becoming the largest ethnolinguistic grouping in Amazonian Ecuador.[7]

Taylor describes how certain Quichua-speaking people acquired the role of "brokers" in regional interethnic relations during the colonial period (Taylor 1999, 235). As "Christian Indians" living in relatively close proximity to whites and mestizos, their intercultural knowledge and access to manufactured goods gave them a unique position in relation to white people and so-called auca groups. In this process of historical ethnogenesis, in which some groups were (and continue to be) defined as "tame" and others as "wild," people are inscribed in colonial imagination not as who they say they are, but instead how they were "named, framed and written down" (Whitten 2011a, 327). Just as certain indigenous groups were seen by white people as "tame," their access to knowledge and material resources from urban areas also made them relatively powerful in relation to so-called auca peoples. In chapter 6 I explore how the pivotal role of Quichuas in intercultural relations contributed to their reputation as shamanic specialists in the region, a specialization that remains up to the present day (Gow 1996).

Although these colonial social categories appear to have persisted for centuries, Taylor describes a constant flow between so-called auca and manso groups as relatively isolated indigenous peoples were drawn into more permanent relations with their neighbors through trade, marriage, and mission settlement (Taylor 1999, 236–37). Rather than constituting the "acculturation" of indigenous people through conversion to Christianity (as envisioned by colonial authorities), this process reveals indigenous modes of social transformation and intercultural relations that can be seen still today (Whitten and Whitten 2011). Though construed in opposition to one another within the colonial order, Taylor suggests that the subsistence practices and other features of so-called "Christian" and "wild" indigenous peoples were in certain respects similar. In considering the mutual implication of these social categories, she argues that "rather than referring to fixed classes of beings, they designate positions, defined by cosmological, spatial, social, and economic correlates, within an integrated network of dependencies" (2007, 137). Taylor notes that, within the colonial order, so-called *auca* people could become *manso* by playing down salient features of being "wild" and emphasizing their transformation by adopting periodized forms of historicity—rather than having to learn a completely new order of cultural knowledge (Taylor 2007, 155).

The colonial categories described by Taylor should not be conflated with the actual experiences and identities of contemporary indigenous peoples. While the essentialist classifications of colonial imagination continue to inflect certain intercultural encounters in Amazonian Ecuador, it is important to avoid reifying or reproducing the imagined social boundaries that missionaries and other outsiders have strategically employed for centuries to control indigenous populations (Whitten 2011a). As Whitten warns, it is all too easy to allow colonial fantasies to inform contemporary concerns about whether one group or another is a more "authentic" representation of indigenous Amazonian culture. To accept the labeling of Waorani people, past or present, as "wild" aucas is as problematic as it would be to suggest that Quichuas are "tame" or "acculturated." Or, as Gow suggests, "The last thing we should do is decide in advance what such people are, and then interrogate them for their failure to live up to our own images of them" (1993, 341). The central question is instead what these categories mean to Amazonian peoples and how they draw on and move between them in their own ways. In Amazonia today, indigenous people also challenge the very categories of colonial imagination through diverse forms of political action, insisting on their own visions of ethnogenesis and social transformation that have little semblance to the notion of "wild" and "tame" people (Whitten 2011a). Both the relative historical isolation of Waorani people and the ethnogenesis of certain Quichua groups are related to intercultural processes in which "the cosmological scheme of a given people . . . articulates to the pragmatics of changing political economy" (Whitten 2011b, 179). In this context, the experiences of Amazonian people today should be understood in terms of historical transformations and indigenous practices that extend beyond the local.

Performing Warriorhood

While the very notion of aucas is steeped in colonial social imagination, ideas about fierce, forest-dwelling "wild Indians" continue to affect how Amazonian people experience intercultural relations today. The kinds of remembering and forgetting that emerge in contemporary contexts raise questions about the relationship between colonial history and indigenous forms of social memory. As Peter Gow asks, "If the colonial history of Western Amazonia has been articulated by images of 'wild Indians' and trackless forests, how is the product of that history lived as social reality by people in the region?" (1993, 328). My hosts in Toñampari remember and perform their symbolic role as aucas in a way that challenges the derogatory connotations of "wild" Amazonian people embraced by many Ecuadorians still today. Whether in public events organized by village schools or in larger multiethnic folklore festivals in Amazonian towns, young Waorani people present a view of Waorani history and ethnicity that appears to contradict the emphasis on victimhood and peaceful conviviality generally expressed in common across generations and genders.

Waorani people are aware of their symbolic status as aucas in the national society. They are also keenly aware that their legacy of spear-killing holds considerable meaning for other indigenous peoples, schoolteachers, politicians, tourists, anthropologists, and other kowori people. Although I have never heard a Waorani person accept being called an auca as anything less than an insult, in some situations they embrace the image of violence and "wildness" attributed to their ancestors and their ethnic group more generally. Young men often take an active interest in performing imagery of violence as an expression of temporal continuity with their ancestors and as a political statement of Waorani autonomy. Their public role as warriors is also sanctioned and encouraged by many of the same Waorani elders in Toñampari who insist on their own position as victims of violence in the stories they tell about how their relatives were killed in the past.

While relatively few Waorani live outside their territorial reserve, many young people, and especially young men, make regular visits to regional cities during school vacations. They are normally received by the families of Waorani political leaders who work at the indigenous political organization in the regional capital. Students also make occasional trips to cities organized by their local schools. These trips involve organized performances and competitions designed to give young people the opportunity to represent their "culture" in front of large Ecuadorian audiences. Village events are normally organized by schoolteachers and presented to local audiences and visitors from other Waorani communities. Major city events involve a greater degree of preparation by parents and students, including the production of body decorations and objects Waorani associate with acting "like the ancient ones" (*durani bai*). These public performances provide a stage for Waorani self-representation both within their own communities and to wider mestizo (non-indigenous) audiences. In both of these cases, young people are expected to represent Waorani "history" and "culture" by performing images of violence. Ideas about the past are fundamental to these performances, as they are judged explicitly in terms of their perceived degree of continuity with an imagined past of nakedness and warriorhood popularized in accounts of "wild aucas" in the region.

Young men typically have more experience with city life than do their parents and female siblings and are familiar with the often-blatant prejudices that mestizo Ecuadorians and foreign nationals have toward indigenous Amazonian people, particularly the Waorani. While racism in Ecuador and what Rahier (1998) calls the country's "racial-spatial order" has received considerable attention itself (Cervone and Rivera 1999; Whitten 2003, 2011), my interest here is in how Waorani people, and particularly young men, actively engage in and are rewarded for performing the symbol of Amazonian warriors in popular imagination. They engage in this form of social memory both as a generational role within Waorani society and as part of the wider intercultural dynamics of nationalism that symbolically links people across socially and geographically distinct regions of Ecuador (Whitten 1981a).

Local village schoolteachers have a key role in promoting representations of violence and other aspects of Waorani "culture" as they see appropriate. Historically, school education has discouraged much of what non-indigenous teachers associate with local customs (Rival 1992, 1996a). Today, however, teachers also have a role in promoting what they see as "typical" Waorani culture.[8] In Ecuador and especially in the Amazonian region, stereotyped images and practices associated with the past are often described as *típica*, a Spanish word best translated as "stereotypical" or an object or practice associated with one's "heritage." Waorani themselves have adopted this word and use it in similar contexts to the expression *durani bai* ("like the ancient ones") in their own language. In talking about their public performances, they often refer specifically to the practices of their ancestors.

Students perform "like the ancient ones" at a number of school-related events organized by schoolteachers in Waorani villages. One of these is the annual *juramento* (oath), when students line up and march in a single-file line before kneeling to kiss the Ecuadorian flag and pledging allegiance to their country. All over Ecuador this ceremony is meant to inspire sentiments of pride and bravery in defense of the republic. In the Amazonian provinces the ceremony carries added significance as a result of border disputes between Ecuador and Peru over their Amazonian border that have led to repeated armed military conflicts between the two countries since 1941. Male students march with spears and feathered crowns to communicate their

FIGURE 5. The annual juramento ceremony in Toñampari

readiness to defend the nation with the stereotyped weapons of Amazonian warriorhood. The spears are similar to those sold at tourist shops in regional cities, measuring about one-third the length of the two-meter spears used for hunting and very rarely in cases of warfare. However, the potent image of warriorhood is clear to viewers and participants. On these occasions female students are asked to wear feathered crowns and handmade palm-fiber bags (*digintai*) meant to represent the traditional Amazonian woman. Although these events are orchestrated by teachers, the parents of local students attend and take very seriously the *juramento* and other school activities involving images of warriorhood. As an essential part of completing an Ecuadorian education, the annual *juramento* explicitly rewards young people for representing imagery of violence and historical continuity.

The ways in which schoolteachers and other kowori encourage young Waorani people to perform this imagery can also be seen in the annual fiestas that commemorate the founding of the school in Toñampari. Here teachers choreograph dances and other performances, ranging from virtually naked young men with spears to female students dressed in American-style cheerleading outfits dancing to pop music. On these occasions students sometimes perform short theatrical plays, which mix comedy with stories of "uncontacted" Waorani people killing oil workers or other kowori. Although the teachers require that students participate, the students themselves choose the content of their performances, which often include semi-nudity and scenes of violence. As in the *juramento*, there is an expectation among teachers that young people should perform this kind of imagery.

The trope of "wild Indians" has a powerful presence in the ways kowori teachers talk about the Waorani. In my conversations with teachers, they frequently complained of the "wildness" and "primitiveness" of their students and attempted to exemplify their "civilizing" role as educators in public school-related events. They often encourage students to perform "traditional" images of violence and nudity alongside explicitly contemporary clothing styles, dance, and music in order to show how their efforts as educators have been successful in "taming" the assumed wildness of Waorani students. The students, much like their teachers, describe this imagery as típica or in some cases as *la cultura* ("culture"), which in local usage refers more to the past than to a sense of contemporary practice. They also joke about the fear and respect this violent imagery evokes among kowori outsiders. The notion of cultura embodied in these performances constitutes what Greg Urban (2001) describes as a "metacultural" discourse in which indigenous people express their own sense of cultural continuity. Students themselves explain that they are acting "like the ancient ones" in these events, drawing specifically on the past as an idealized image of warriorhood. In everyday life Waorani refer to various practices, such as hunting with blow-guns, climbing trees, long treks in the forest, and especially sharing abundant food with kin as being characteristically durani bai activities associated with their ancestors. It is the image of the Amazonian warrior, however, that takes center stage in Waorani public performances.

In contrast to official events organized at the school, ritual and dance at village feasts (*eëme*) organized by Waorani themselves do not usually involve spears or other stereotyped body décor. They initiate their own rituals, such as weddings, wearing the same street clothes used on their occasional visits to the city. In these contexts Waorani people are not so inclined to "dress up" as warriors for each other. This general lack of interest in performing past violence at village feasts and in everyday interactions is consistent with their critical views of past killings and the often expressed ideal of "living well."[9] For Waorani people, what they call *waponi kiwimonipa* ("living well") is characterized by peaceful conviviality and the collective consumption of abundant food, a process that leads to the creation of new people (Rival

FIGURE 6. Learning to be warriors: students march with spears at school

1998a; Overing and Passes 2000). In addition to the productive connotation of "living well," Waorani associate this ideal with the expansion of social relations beyond the village.

The Queen of Nationalities and the Warrior Princess

Choreographed performances of the historical Amazonian warrior have a significant role within Waorani communities beyond young people seeking approval from their schoolteachers. Parents take an active role in supporting youth performances at school and in urban folklore festivals outside the Waorani territory. The same elders who speak critically of past violence in their own oral histories carefully carve spears and craft body decorations so that their children and grandchildren can embody violent images of their ancestors. Many students enjoy dressing up this way for its entertainment value and, in the case of urban festivals, for the positive attention their performances receive from the wider Ecuadorian public. They take particular interest in events outside the villages, where they represent their "culture" in front of larger urban audiences. In contrast to the basic and sometimes humorous costumes used in school events, they wear beautiful palm-fiber necklaces, feathered headdresses, and other colorful regalia crafted by their families in anticipation of a big event in the city. For the most important events, such as a major protest in the capital against oil development or an urban folklore festival, they rehearse for weeks and arrive to dance and chant fully clad with their long spears, faces painted red with achiote dye, and necklaces full of peccary teeth.

One of these events was the 2003 Indigenous Nationalities Day festival of Pastaza Province, which included performances by a group of about twenty Waorani in the regional capital. Most were teenage students who came from Toñampari, where I watched them practice their dances and chants on several occasions in the weeks leading up to the event. Now they were competing on stage against several other indigenous Amazonian *nacionalidades* ("nationalities") to demonstrate what the festival presenters described as *cultura típica* ("typical culture"), such as cooking practices, hunting, the production of manioc beer, dancing, singing, and shamanic healing. Public festivals like these that promote the Waorani and other indigenous groups as distinct "nationalities" are part of an emerging political discourse of multiculturalism in Ecuador. Embraced by Ecuador's national indigenous movement, this idea of cultural pluralism challenges the hegemonic discourse of *mestizaje* ("blending" or "mixing") that has for centuries ranked Ecuadorians according to relative "whiteness" within a racial hierarchy rooted in colonialism (Whitten and Whitten 2011). Whereas colonial ideologies of mestizaje envisage hybrid racial types and "cultures" forged through the blending of "civilized" Europeans and "savage" people (de la Cadena 2000), the notion of indigenous nationalities asserts the sovereignty of indigenous peoples and recognizes their distinct languages and territories (Whitten and Whitten 2011, 104). In this process, the meanings of "culture" and "nation" are to some extent being redefined by indigenous people.

For Waorani people and other indigenous nationalities in Amazonian Ecuador, the 2003 festival presented an opportunity to engage creatively in this highly visible arena of interculturality. In some respects the Waorani troupe were the underdog in competition with much larger Quichua and Shuar groups. In other respects, however, the mixed audience of several hundred indigenous and mestizo Ecuadorians were impressed by the Waorani performances. While men from all participating nationalities appeared on stage wielding spears, it soon became clear that the Waorani were successful in winning the audience's gaze as "authentic" aucas through their semi-nudity, long spears, aggressive dancing and chanting, and lack of confidence in speaking Spanish.

FIGURE 7. Waorani youth sing before a festival judge in the city of Puyo

When the Waorani took the floor to present themselves in their introductory performance, the men and women entered in separate groups, both singing as they marched in a circle around the floor. The women walked calmly in front of the men in a horizontal line with their arms interlocked, chanting softly as the much larger group of men followed behind in a single-file line with their hands on each other's shoulders. This slow, repetitive dance continued until the entire group approached the judge's table to demonstrate a marriage ceremony for the judge and audience. The loudness of their repetitive chants and the aggressive posture of men wielding full-length spears captivated the audience, who watched with great curiosity from their seats.

The head presenter of the festival then introduced each candidate for the day's main event: the "Queen of Nationalities" competition. This consisted of a young woman from each indigenous nationality, accompanied by a spear-wielding man, who represented her group to the public. After the Achuar couple was introduced, two teenagers from Toñampari took the stage to represent the Waorani as an audio recording of chants in the Waorani language rang out over the loudspeakers. They appeared wearing short bark skirts and colorful feathered crowns, along with palm fiber bags slung around their shoulders and thin palm fiber cords crossed in an "x" around their otherwise bare upper bodies. While the young woman appeared uncomfortable as the only candidate in the competition whose breasts were exposed by her costume, the audience responded positively to the relative nudity and striking body decorations that distinguished the Waorani as "naked aucas."

The initial stage of the competition required each Queen of Nationalities candidate to respond to formal questions from the judges. Following the form of beauty pageants elsewhere in Ecuador, each woman was asked a question such as "What would you say to young people of your nationality about the importance of maintaining their culture?" or "How would you help promote intercultural relations between all the indigenous nationalities of Pastaza province?" The candidates' answers were somewhat formulaic, stating something to the effect that young people should not "forget their culture" and should work with provincial authorities to promote meetings with all of the indigenous nationalities to discuss their problems. After the Shuar and Quichua candidates gave confident responses in Spanish followed by translations in their indigenous languages, the Waorani student struggled with the speech in her own language and in Spanish.

In the next stage of the competition, each woman acted out various practices associated with her respective group, such as gardening, cooking, making manioc beer, and weaving hammocks and bags. Their male counterparts narrated the scenes to the audience, beginning each by saying "the Quichua woman . . ." or "the Wao woman . . ." in an attempt to demonstrate the archetypical practices of women of each indigenous group. The careful choreography of stereotyped practices and body imagery in the competition contributed to a sense of museum-like objectification in these explicitly metacultural performances. Although the Shuar appeared to have prepared best for this stage, the audience responded with even greater applause when the Wao candidate entered the stage holding a small boa snake. Just as Waorani spears are a powerful symbol of warriorhood in these intercultural encounters, bringing a live snake onto the stage appeared to similarly index the role of Waorani people as Amazonian warriors.

The final stage of the competition involved each candidate's singing in her native language. After the Quichua woman sang a well-rehearsed song accompanied by a full instrumental band, the Waorani woman performed, with much difficulty, a repetitive traditional chant without accompanying music. I had never before seen someone of her age sing in this way alone,

FIGURE 8. Performing on stage at the Día de Nacionalidades festival in Puyo

in part because public singing in Waorani communities is normally done harmonically in groups, with different individuals periodically interjecting new lines. Although unintelligible to most of the audience, her song was received enthusiastically, perhaps because of its clear contrast to popular Ecuadorian music.

Soon afterward the festival presenters invited all of the Queen of Nationalities candidates and their escorts back onto the stage to announce that the Quichua woman had been chosen as the winner. There were also prizes for the "princess of knowledge" and the "warrior princess," all of whom received gifts and were photographed by the public. It was little surprise when the Waorani candidate was named as the "warrior princess" and received a ribbon to confer her title. The prize confirmed the already unambiguous status of Waorani people as the competition's "warriors."

In events like these, the Waorani compete to represent their continuity with the past (*la cultura*) by performing historical imagery of the Amazonian warrior. For members of some other indigenous groups (especially Quichuas), this symbolism affirms their accounts of aucas killing their shamans and relatives with spears in the past. For mestizo audiences more generally it conveys the place of "wild aucas" in the dominant national memory—an idealized image through which they contrast themselves culturally and temporally as "civilized" Ecuadorians. What emerges in this context is a kind of symbolic interdependence in which oppositions like "wild" and "civilized" simultaneously create a heightened sense of national and ethnic identity (Whitten 1988, 306). Whether in a school *juramento* or the Indigenous Nationalities Day festival in the regional capital, Waorani people simultaneously present themselves as a distinct indigenous group and as Ecuadorian citizens when they perform as warriors. In this way, auca symbolism constitutes a dialogic relationship between national ideology and indigenous Amazonian understandings of alterity.

Waorani people are very much aware of the responses their performances provoke among kowori audiences. Urban festivals and other "performance spectacles" (Graham 2005) bring a sense of self-conscious irony to intercultural relations in Amazonia, as one group performs the role of wildness and violence in part as a response to the expectations of others. This process of perceiving oneself through the eyes of others results in multiple and changing self-images (Caiuby Novaes 1997, 45). These encounters and their place in the Ecuadorian national imagination reveal part of the complexity that characterizes the experiences of younger generations of indigenous people in contemporary Amazonia. As Ramos observes among indigenous leaders in Brazil: "Like actors on a gigantic stage, they strive to be acknowledged by the public in their roles as citizens of a double world—the Brazilian nation and their own societies" (1988, 233).

Embodied Memories

In festivals like the one I have described, bodily practices, ornamentation, and other material objects communicate powerfully the symbolic place of Waorani people in regional interethnic relations. In much of indigenous Amazonia, the body is a key point of reference in establishing social identity, perspective and difference.[10] Amazonian body painting, piercings, feather work, and other body imagery have attracted much attention from international audiences as a marker of "authentic" indigeneity (Conklin 1997). The relative nudity, hardwood spears, and aggressive movements in Waorani performances achieve a degree of perceived authenticity in the arena of folklore festivals. Spears are a particularly powerful symbol for participants and audiences alike due to their impressive length and the legacy of Waorani spear-killing in the region. When young Waorani perform on stage in the city, their body imagery and movements evoke a particular form of social memory, becoming what Stoller describes as "potent conveyors of meaning and memory" (1995, 30).[11] In Waorani performances, the body is also a key site upon which people contradict the narrative of victimhood that emerges in Waorani accounts of past violence and encounters with kowori people. In this way the performance of warrior imagery constitutes a distinct genre of Waorani memory—one that inverts the "victim" perspective often expressed in oral histories.

The image of warriorhood embodied in these events is closely linked to the intercultural relations that set the stage for auca performances. However, the young people who participate are involved in more than simply adopting popular stereotypes of Amazonian warriors. Even as they appear to contradict ideas about violence and sociality voiced in everyday life, they embrace a generational and gendered role that is to some extent sanctioned by elders and non-Waorani people alike. Performing "like the ancient ones" (durani bai) simultaneously articulates their designated position as "wild Indians" in the national imagination and conveys the autonomy and strength of their ethnic group—a claim supported by older generations of Waorani. Even as these performances draw in part on the oral narratives of elders, they invert the position of Waorani people from victims to killers in asserting Waorani autonomy and strength in the face of powerful outsiders. In protests against oil companies they block roads and appear with spears wearing little or no clothing to demand various gifts and services from oil workers. This engagement with the image of warriorhood has become part of Waorani self-representation in indigenous politics. The broader political significance of this symbolism became clear in 1992, when thousands of indigenous people marched from Amazonian Ecuador to the capital bearing spears and other objects associated with ancestral warriorhood in a successful campaign to secure land rights from the state (Whitten, Whitten, and Chango 2008).

The public spectacle of warrior performances also constitutes a form of self-reflexive social consciousness with implications beyond the pragmatic goals often associated with indigenous "identity politics." Anthropologists have described the practical political and economic gains of indigenous people who assert the distinctive value of their "culture" in response to the expectations of outsiders.[12] In Amazonia, Oakdale (2004) and Graham (2005) complicate this picture of the "politics of recognition" by suggesting that the meanings of indigenous discourses and public performances of cultural continuity should also be understood in reference to relations within indigenous societies. As Oakdale argues, : "The construction of a reified idea of culture and Indian identity is . . . not merely a two-sided affair, between indigenous and non-indigenous representatives. Rather, indigenous people actively refashion national-level identities that they know to have been attributed to them, as they put these identities to use for their own locally specific purposes" (2004, 61). Indigenous "cultural projects" and "performance spectacles" often have complex meanings and instrumental goals at the local level that are not always apparent to out-siders (Graham 2005, 625–26). While these performances appear to be a form of "cultural commodification" when choreographed specifically for interethnic audiences, indigenous people themselves do not necessarily view them as "inauthentic" self-representations (Oakdale 2005, 633). Like the theatrical cultural displays Graham describes among the Xavante, and the political discourses of Kayabi indigenous leaders described by Oakdale in Brazil, Waorani warrior performances are as much about generational experiences and relations within indigenous society as they are about the politics of indigenous identity. When Waorani students participate in cul-tural displays at school and in Ecuadorian cities, they embody imagery of violence as an expression of cultural continuity with what they see as their "uncivilized" ancestors. In contrast to elders, who generally associate past violence with suffering and personal loss, for young people performing as warriors provides a meaningful connection between the past and their present experiences. Like the dream performances described elsewhere in Amazonia, these practices engender "a subjective sense of continuity" in the context of changing circumstances, and "this sense of connection with the past empowers them as they move into the future" (Graham 1995, 6).

Whether in warrior performances or in talking about their ancestors, young Waorani people often refer to this sense of continuity as *cultura*. What distinguishes this reflexive "discourse of tradition" (Gewertz and Errington 1996) from the oral narratives of elders is not simply an inverted warrior/victim position in relation to past violence. Whereas stories about victimhood typically take the form of biographical narratives focused on the experiences of specific individuals, embodied memories of warriorhood in public performances refer to Waorani people (and their ancestors) as a generalized social whole. In conveying a sense of ethnic difference embraced widely by indigenous peoples in Ecuador, Waorani discourses of "national-ity" and "culture" illuminate the central importance of social memory in ongoing processes of ethnogenesis in contemporary Amazonia.

In Waorani communities, it is young people, and particularly young men, who engage most with urban indigenous politics and relations with kowori people more generally. From the point of view of elders, it is young people who should learn about kowori ways in school and on their trips to the city. As we shall see in the following chapter, Waorani understandings of masculine agency are closely linked to notions of exteriority and relations with people defined as "other"—whether kowori people, affines, or rival Waorani groups. Rather than simply conforming to external expectations of Amazonian "identity politics," warrior performances constitute a specific generational role within indigenous communities which, despite appearing to contradict the Waorani ideal of "living well," is embraced by young people and supported by older adults.

Remembering and Forgetting

Waorani "warrior" performances, and indigenous understandings of them, constitute a distinct way of relating to the past. Approached as an embodied form of social memory, they can be understood in relation to other practices in which Waorani people construct the past in the present. These urban spectacles are part of ongoing processes of ethnogenesis in contemporary Amazonia, which tends to be defined increasingly in terms of "interculturality" (Whitten and Whitten 2011). However, they also reveal the multiple and contrasting forms of historical consciousness that have defined social difference in Amazonia for centuries.

The ideas and images we encounter among young Waorani in urban contexts depart in significant ways from the oral narratives presented in the previous chapter. However, the killer's point of view expressed in their performances is also built out of the autobiographical narratives of victimhood told by Dayuma and other women and men of her generation. Young people are familiar with the life histories of people like Dayuma and come to know about their ancestors through similar accounts of how they were killed in the past. They tend to know the most famous of these stories even if they seldom tell them. In public "warrior" performances, however, the biographies of specific deceased kin are collapsed into a cultural narrative that celebrates spear-killing as an expression of what it means to be a Waorani person. Although this generational form of memory appears to invert the narratives of elders, young people are not confined to a single mode of historical consciousness. They too explain that Waorani have been and continue to be victims of powerful kowori, even if this perspective does not define the kind of remembering evoked within the increasingly intercultural environments in which they live.

The differences and interconnections between Waorani biographical narratives and urban performances point to how new forms of memory emerge in relations between indigenous people and national societies in Lowland South America. The emergence of contemporary ethnopolitics has coincided not only with the transformation of indigenous cosmology but also with a profound change in historical and political consciousness (Turner 1991, 1993). Turner describes how the Kayapó, who previously envisioned themselves to be a unique mythical creation, have come to see themselves as agents of their own history as a result of their entry into Brazilian national society as "indigenous people." This process resonates in many parts of Amazonia today, where intercultural relations and political mobilization have become an important part of contemporary social life for many indigenous peoples. These changes in historical and political consciousness also resonate with the contrasting forms of memory I have described across Waorani generations. Many young Waorani view themselves and their society in a radically different way than their grandparents, who distinguished themselves as the exclusive realm of real persons—in contrast to semi-human kowori cannibals. However, instead of accepting a trajectory in which a mythic register of alterity is replaced by a more "historical" consciousness, we should also be open to a reverse view of contemporary relations in Amazonia, one in which seemingly "mythical" cultural narratives are made out of the biographies of specific people.

In certain intercultural encounters young Waorani men embody a generalized killer's point of view that resonates with descriptions of other Amazonian societies in which the past is presented as a continuous series of adversarial relations, thus excluding non-indigenous people and marginalizing historical changes.[13] Earlier in this chapter I noted how colonial distinctions between so-called "wild" (auca) and "tame" (manso) Amazonian groups have more to do with contrasting regimes of historicity than they do questions of relative "acculturation" or "authenticity." This is to say that expressions of ethnic difference have as much do with how people understand the past as they do actual social and cultural differences in the present. Taylor, for example, draws a contrast between Amazonian groups who define themselves as a product of transformational processes of ethnogenesis and "civilization" (Whitten 1976a; Gow 1991; Muratorio 1991) and those for whom "individual memory is redistributed to build up a collective memory of adversarial relations" (Taylor 2007, 150). She points to the ways particular regimes of historicity are closely linked to indigenous concepts of personhood. Historically, in Amazonian Ecuador indigenous people have moved between colonial social categorizations such as auca ("wild") *and* manso ("tame"), not just by converting to Christianity but also by embracing a new kind of historical discourse that contrasts past times of "wildness" to a present state of "civilization" (Taylor 2007).

Waorani narratives of past violence to some extent fit Taylor's description of "auca" historicity in emphasizing a strict sense of alterity and adversarial relations. For many Waorani, however, these stories are also part of a wider narrative of "civilization" described in the previous chapter. In contrast to the image of Amazonian warriors that takes center stage in urban folklore festivals and political activism, narratives of civilization have a certain likeness to the "tame" forms of historicity Taylor attributes to Quichua-speaking groups. In their stories, "becoming civilized" refers precisely to processes of historical transformation involving conversion to Christianity and the increasing prominence of productive relations with kowori people. In Taylor's terms, we could describe these stories as evidence of Waorani people adopting a new form of historical consciousness as they enter into new kinds of relations within a regional system.

So are we then to view Waorani narratives of "civilization" as a recent example of an ongoing process of ethnogenesis rooted in colonial history, or do urban youth performances indicate a return to an "auca" regime of historicity? Rather than equating specific groups or social categories with a singular view of the past, I suggest that multiple and seemingly contradictory representations of the past coexist today as different aspects of social memory in Amazonia. Waorani autobiographies and embodied forms of memory constitute multiple modes of historical consciousness that contrast and build upon one another in the present. Being a Waorani person in some contexts means embracing a shared narrative of becoming victims and civilizados, while in others it expresses group autonomy and adversarial relations with kowori. These different forms of social memory reveal generational roles and experiences that emerge in the context of ongoing social transformations, rather than a generalized model of "traditional" versus "modern" forms of historical consciousness.

Taylor rightly points out the importance of memory as a key element in how indigenous Amazonian people experience continuity and change in culturally distinct ways. However, the complex and seemingly contradictory relationships that emerge within urban indigenous politics and Waorani performances require rethinking the place of memory in contemporary intercultural relations beyond a manso/auca typology rooted in colonial imagination. It would be difficult, if not misleading, to characterize these multiple forms of Waorani memory strictly in terms of a single regime of historicity focusing on continuity or change. What emerges most clearly in this context is that imagery of adversarial relations, autonomy, and continuity become most salient for Waorani people in urban intercultural relations. It is here that imagery of Amazonian warriorhood and discourses of cultura convey a strong sense of continuity and difference. It is in part the presence of kowori people, whether other indigenous groups or mestizos, that constitutes the social and political context of this kind of memory as a cultural expression.

As we have seen, in certain contexts narratives of victimhood and civilization incorporate non-indigenous people—namely kowori missionaries— into a Waorani social world. However, the image of warriorhood embraced by Waorani youth is oriented specifically toward relations of difference between Waorani people and kowori outsiders, even as this notion of difference departs significantly from elders' stories about kowori cannibals. Like the Jivaroan shamans described by Taylor and the generation of young "cultural brokers" described in much of Amazonia (Brown 1993), young Waorani men today also have an important position as "managers of alterity." They occupy this role of engaging in relations with other Ecuadorians not by dismissing the stories of victimhood with which they are so familiar but by building a new image of warriorhood out of the intersection of colonial imagination and the stories of elders.[14] In this way, autobiographical forms of memory become "history" in new social and political spheres, even where this history has many of the characteristics of "myth."

This multiplicity of Waorani memory reveals as much about what is "forgotten" in personal accounts and wider historical imagery as it does what is remembered. In Amazonia, cultural processes of forgetting are in some contexts vital for the production of new persons (Taylor 1993). Oakdale, for example, draws on Fogelson's (1989) concept of "nonevents" to describe how, among the Kayabi, mortuary songs "depersonalize and "de-eventualize" individual deaths by submerging them into a more all-encompassing process" (Oakdale 2001, 382). Waorani elders who tell stories about how their kin became victims of past violence tend to "forget" how these events were part of a wider series of revenge-killings in which their own families, and in some cases they themselves, were also involved as killers. When they describe spear-killings as *ononki* ("unprovoked"), they collapse these events into a broader narrative of victimhood that excludes other historical processes within which the events occurred. In the generational memories embraced by young people, past killings become "latent events" (Fogelson 1989) that are depersonalized in the construction of a "wild" Amazonian warrior image in urban interethnic relations. Here they "forget," albeit temporarily, the narrative of victimhood that has such an important place in the stories of their parents and grandparents.

While these seemingly conflicting narratives to some extent support Turner's (1988) claim that cultures not only have "multiple pasts" but also "multiple presents," I suggest that they also constitute different visions of the future. Narratives of victimhood and "civilization" embrace an idealized future in which new and productive relations are initiated across previous social boundaries. Such a future orientation suggests an "openness to the other" familiar to studies of indigenous Amazonian sociocosmologies (Lévi-Strauss 1995; Viveiros de Castro 1992; Ewart 2013). Young Waorani men, however, in contrast to their elders, manage these relations in certain contexts through embodied forms of memory that project a sense of closure and difference in the face of outsiders. The future they envision with their current political relations is one of strict differentiation, even as, or perhaps especially because, they become increasingly part of the wider politics of multiculturalism in Ecuador.

Conclusion

In this chapter I have brought into view the kinds of remembering that emerge at the interface of colonial history, indigenous understandings of the past, and urban intercultural relations in Amazonia. At first sight the public spectacle of warrior performances appears to contradict the emphasis on victimhood in Waorani narratives of violence. However, seen as an embodied form of memory, these performances conform to the enduring category of "wild" Amazonian people in the national imagination at the same time as they constitute a generational role in Waorani communities. As an expression of autonomy and continuity with past generations, they remind us that Waorani social memory is as much about changing intercultural relations as is it an indigenous model of alterity.

Rather than revealing specific groups or social categories with a singular view of the past, indigenous understandings of auca imagery illustrate the multiple and seemingly contradictory representations of the past that coexist today as different modes of remembering. In contrast to colonial social imagination, Waorani people do not appear to find a contradiction between their narratives of "civilization" and their assertions of being "like the ancient ones." What is at stake for Waorani when they perform as warriors is not simply a claim to authenticity according to Western criteria of indigeneity and "culture" but also their relationships with a growing range of kowori people with whom they interact on an increasingly regular basis. In this sense, the contrasting forms of social memory I have described should not be understood simply as "local" cultural phenomena. They illustrate specific generational experiences and strategies by which Waorani people engage with translocal processes in contemporary Amazonia.

CHAPTER 3

Like the Ancient Ones

The public performances of warriorhood described in the previous chapter and the generational changes of which they are part have an important gendered dimension. While both women and men take part in these performances at village schools and in the city, young men are more closely associated with the imagery of violence that defines Waorani people in these intercultural contexts. They also tend to have more experience with kowori people and Ecuadorian cities than do Waorani women and elders. This is partly the result of young men working for oil companies, their dominant presence in urban indigenous politics, and the increasing frequency of interethnic marriages between Waorani men and kowori women. In this chapter I consider how, despite a strongly egalitarian ethos in much of Waorani social life, women and men experience generational changes in different ways. This requires a closer look at indigenous understandings of gender, agency, and the body, and how these understandings relate to urban migration and the increasingly global images that have become part of everyday life in Waorani communities.

While these translocal encounters make new kinds of manhood imaginable, recent social and economic transformations have not led to the pronounced gender antagonisms between men and women familiar to many other parts of the world. Waorani people instead engage with these transformations in terms of indigenous understandings of gendered agency, in which women are associated with the production of "interiority" and men with relations of "exteriority." In a context where intergroup violence and missionary "pacification" are vivid in social memory, and where the local ideal of "living well" is expressed in terms of remaking past enmities into productive relations, certain practices associated with male elders are either unachievable or illegitimate within Waorani communities today. Whereas elders frequently contrast past warfare practices to what they call "civilization," imagery ranging from the rain-forest warrior in the national imagination to Bruce Lee and Rambo in popular film has become part of the way young men understand their own masculinity. This is not because indigenous Amazonian men (or men in general) have a universal need to express violence or antagonistic gender relations but because violence is a key facet of the cultural imagination produced at the intersection of Waorani and kowori worlds.

The ways specific generational forms of Waorani masculinity draw on global imagery of violence challenge the tendency to view indigenous peoples and cosmologies in isolation from broader political and economic relations in Amazonia. How, for example, might indigenous understandings of gender illuminate the ways Waorani youth interact with mestizos in urban areas? And how do Waorani men become "engendered" in the context of multiple and contradictory gender discourses? Understanding these processes requires viewing masculinity not as fixed in time but as constantly produced and remade in a dynamic process of historical transformation (Hodgson 1999). It is precisely in the context of translocal relations between Waorani and other people that these transformations come into view.

Gender and Agency in Amazonia

In recent years anthropologists working in Amazonia have prioritized the constitution of personhood, the body, and broader relations of alterity over those between men and women.[1] Descola, for example, argues that in Amazonia "the sexual division of labor is not based on a native discriminatory theory that would rank activities on a scale of prestige according to whether they are performed by men or women" (2001, 97). This view is consistent with a more general regional emphasis on egalitarianism and the collective production of consanguinity through living and eating together (Overing and Passes 2000). McCallum (2001) challenges the very notion that gendered relations in Amazonia can be characterized as a form of "hegemonic masculinity," instead framing Amazonian sociality in terms of non-dominant male and female agencies located in the body. She argues that since Amazonian cosmology posits a "unitary human identity" rather than "multiple gender identities inferred from a set of distinct subject positions" (165), sociality is not as much about producing women and men as it is about producing bodies and persons.

Even as being a victim can be seen as a generalized expression of Waorani personhood, there are also important gendered dimensions of indigenous cosmology and social life. Waorani men and women are not positioned in relation to violence in the same ways, even in a society in which people distinguish themselves as "prey" to predatory kowori. While Waorani men and women generally have equal social status, gendered differences emerge in the context of violence, as men are seen as susceptible to being overtaken by the non-human "predatory" desire to kill. Rival suggests that this is because men's "souls" are seen as less firmly attached to the body than are those of women, allowing the perspective of predatory spirits to control their minds and bodies (2005, 296). There is always the risk that a man who is overcome by anger (*pii*) after the death of a kinsman may himself become a predator, leading him to kill enemies or even members of his own household. While elders explain that men, women, and children died in past spear-killing raids, it was most often men who were targeted in these revenge killings.[2] Whether in oral histories or in commenting on contemporary marital relations, women are rarely singled out as specific targets of male violence.

Waorani understandings of gender can also be seen in the distinct roles that constitute married life. Adults describe marriage as a productive relationship between women and men that is closely linked to having children and collectively consuming abundant food through mutual support. This ideal is voiced at wedding ceremonies in which elders sing loudly to remind the bride and groom of their expected roles. It can also be seen in couvade practices in which men and women are expected to share dietary restrictions during and after pregnancy (Rival 1998a). While many marriages are arranged by elders, and a small number are polygynous, marital relations are generally stable and amicable.[3] Waorani marriage practices are characteristic of what anthropologists have called a "brideservice model," in which marriage does not involve a direct exchange or pooling of resources (Collier and Rosaldo 1981). Whereas the brideservice model suggests that conflicts and inequalities are generated by men's attempts to assert their rights over women (Collier 1988), such occurrences are rare in Waorani communities. The general absence of spousal abuse or a visible gender hierarchy, coupled with the flexibility and informality of most gendered activities, is part of a wider egalitarian ethos that pervades much of Waorani social and economic life. Whereas women typically reside in their natal homes after marriage and are associated with processes of regeneration and familiarization, a man ideally distances himself from his natal household, eventually to be incorporated into his wife's group.

Waorani understandings of male and female roles in violence and marriage practices illustrate what other ethnographers have described as a native distinction between masculine and feminine agencies in Amazonia. From this perspective, women are transformers of forest and garden products in the domestic sphere of consanguinity, while men are seen to have a predatory role in hunting, warfare, and affinal relations (Taylor 1983; Viveiros de Castro 2001).[4] The notion of gendered agency that I adopt, however, refers not just to the gender identities or actual roles of women and men, but also to an indigenous theory that attributes distinct capacities and symbolic values to male and female bodies. This formulation resonates with McCallum's argument that gender in Amazonia should be seen as "an epistemological condition for social action" embodied as male or female agency (McCallum 2001, 5).[5] In this context, emergent forms of Waorani masculinity reveal how specific embodied processes attributed to men and women enable particular capacities and relations, and how these processes change from one generation to the next.

Durani Bai: Hunting, Killing, and Masculinity

Understanding the place of violence and memory in contemporary Waorani gender dynamics requires closer attention to the meanings of the expression durani bai ("like the ancient ones") by which young people describe their public warrior performances. Statements about certain people, practices, and objects being durani bai have significance for Waorani people beyond the school events and folklore festivals described in the previous chapter. They constitute part of an everyday discourse through which young people comment on and identify themselves with practices they associate with previous generations. It is not uncommon to hear male teenagers using this term openly to admire elders and ancestors for their perceived autonomy, strength, and ability to kill. During my fieldwork they also praised as durani bai the few so-called "uncontacted" groups (*tagaeri taromenani*) who continue to refuse village settlement and peaceful relations with kowori outsiders, describing such groups as fearless and able to kill people by throwing spears from long distances.[6]

Members of my host family often used this expression to describe particular objects and actions associated with the past or in reference to previous generations. Blowguns, spears, gourd bowls, ceramic pots, and other locally produced objects are described as durani bai, as are traditional group dances and songs. Talk of this sort can often be heard at intervillage feasts, where people indulge in plentiful amounts of manioc beer and game meat, and dance and sing late into the night. In everyday life, durani bai is offered as an approving response to activities associated with past times of abundance. An elderly woman used this expression in describing to me a feast she attended in a distant village where the hosts provided enough food for guests to return home with extra monkey meat. For young men, it is a way of asserting one's own abilities and achievements in continuity with previous generations. [7]

One practice closely linked to the idea of durani bai yet seldom observed in Waorani households today is the whipping (*pangi*) of children with a forest vine after peccary hunts. When talking about their childhood, men and women recall how they suffered from the painful lashes they received from their fathers and grandfathers. On several occasions elders explained to me that this practice made children strong enough to hunt peccaries themselves one day. Beyond ascribing a role specifically to male elders, these explanations suggest that whipping is seen as a way of transmitting knowledge or ability from one person to another. In a parallel example described by a missionary in the late 1950s, one of the first Waorani men to be brought by missionaries to an Ecuadorian town commented that he wished to be beaten by a tractor driver so that he would acquire the ability to use the machinery in his home village (Wallis 1960, 256). Being subjected to physical beatings not only enables children to acquire the skills of adults but also reflects a more general Amazonian conceptualization of the "physical creation of social qualities through bodily states" (Fisher 2001, 122). Rather than being a form of punishment to correct misbehavior, the whipping of children reveals an understanding that bodily experiences constitute the acquisition of specific kinds of knowledge and agency. [8]

This notion of the body as a locus of acquired knowledge presents a contrast to what I described in the previous chapter as an embodied form of generational memory. Whereas performing on stage "like the ancient ones" involves remembering and performing a highly visible yet generic image of ancestral warriorhood that mediates intercultural relations, being whipped by an elder creates a kind of bodily memory that defines the subjective identity of an individual person in relation to ascending generations. As such, it is a kind of social memory that, instead of uniting them in a generalized image of "Waorani people," differentiates people based on their individual experiences. In his famous characterization of the body as a "social skin" (1980), Turner describes how Amazonian people alter the external form of the body in order to "mark and help bring about transformations in the social identity and subjective perspective of persons" (2009, 33). While visible body ornamentation such as spears, feathers, and body paint establish a certain kind of "social identity" for Waorani youth in folklore festivals, it is the experience of being whipped by elders that is seen to bring about the transformations by which they become strong and able to carry out the tasks exemplified by elders.

Although Waorani elders in Toñampari say that they stopped whipping children during the missionary period, this practice continues to have a presence in how Waorani people envision gendered and generational relations today. Parents lament that the current generation of boys and girls is weaker than previous ones, who they describe as stronger and better able to withstand long treks in the forest. Elders explain that this deficiency is a consequence of children today not having been whipped like they themselves were in past times. While the resulting lack of embodied knowledge is said to have affected boys and girls alike, the absence of this practice appears to have had a disproportionate effect on the skills and abilities of young men, who are said to be unable to hunt peccaries with spears because they were not whipped as children. Given the importance Waorani place on peccary hunting and its association with masculinity, it was difficult for me to see why most people abandoned the practice of whipping children. When I asked the senior man in my host family why he does not whip his children, he responded that young people today cannot withstand the lashes because they eat too much "foreign food" (*kowori kengi*), referring to the rice, noodles, oatmeal, and other features of the lunches supplied by local schools. He explained that, as a result, their arms and legs are too weak and would break from the whipping.[9]

This idea that people, and particularly men, are becoming physically and culturally deficient as a result of changing ritual practices resonates with Conklin's work in Brazil with the Wari, who say that previous generations of men grew larger, stronger, and more capable than men today who have never experienced specific enemy-killing rites after warfare. What becomes clear in both of these cases is that men are seen as unable to "actualize their masculine potential" (Conklin 2001, 155) as a result of not experiencing specific bodily transformations. In contexts like these, the perceived problem is not just that men today are failing to fulfill their expected gender roles but also that they lack specific capacities attributed to previous generations of men. Whereas younger Waorani generations are seen as being less "hard" or "strong" (*teëmo*) than elders, the few remaining "uncontacted" groups are said to have remarkable physical abilities due to their strict diet of "Waorani" foods and because, in contrast to "civilized" Waorani who became Christian and today live in villages, they continue to whip their children. This understanding of how knowledge and agency depend on specific bodily practices has important consequences for the ways young men today envision their own masculinity. The following brief sketches of men from different generations point to how the experiences of Waorani men have changed dramatically in recent decades:

Pego is one of the oldest men in Toñampari, having grown up in the decades prior to the arrival of the first missionaries. He was born in the eastern part of the Waorani territory, where his father was killed in a series of revenge killings with other Waorani groups. Pego, who is known for his humor and exciting hunting stories, describes how he was brutally whipped as a child by his senior kin and as a result became an expert hunter of monkeys, birds, and peccaries at an early age. When he was a young man, he married a woman his kinsmen abducted in a raid against an enemy group. In the late 1960s Pego and his wife joined the missionary settlement at Tiweno, where they lived for several years and had four children. In the late 1970s they joined several other families to establish the village of Toñampari, where they have remained intermittently ever since. Pego has voiced to me his frustrations about the noisiness of village life and often goes on hunting trips alone for days or weeks at a time. He has built a hunting lodge about a day's walk away from the village along the bank of a small river, where he receives visits from his children and many grandchildren during school holidays. He also makes extended visits to his ancestral territory far to the east, where he says he enjoys better hunting, visits with relatives, and food gifts from oil companies operating in the area. An old and gregarious man, Pego complains that young men spend too much time in the cities, where their laziness and diet causes them to become "like outsiders" (*kowori bai*). Yet he also asks his grown children to bring him manufactured goods and medicines when they visit urban areas, and he is known to block oil roads on Waorani lands with felled trees, demanding that oil workers provide him food and other gifts. When in the village, Pego and his wife live in the home of his oldest son, Wareka.

Pego's relationship with Wareka is generally relaxed, friendly, and informal. Although Pego is a major provider of game meat to Wareka's large household, he says he prefers to live away from the village and often decides to leave without consulting his son's family. Wareka, who is in his late thirties, grew up on the mission and later attended a missionary school in the city for about a year. As a boy he enjoyed hunting birds and monkeys but has never killed peccaries or other large game. As a teenager he married a Quichua woman with whom he today has seven children. While his parents' generation consists primarily of monolingual speakers of the Waorani language, Wareka speaks Waorani, Quichua, and Spanish. After working intermittently for several oil companies, he was among a group of young men who established the official Waorani political organization in the early 1990s. As a result, he spends several months at a time working and living in the regional capital. In his home village he has been elected to various community offices and is active in local school events. Wareka speaks of his father and other senior kin with admiration, as people who live durani bai ("like the ancient ones"). He praises his father's ability to live on his own in the forest, never failing to return home with meat. On occasions when Wareka is able to provide large amounts of fish, game meat, or goods procured in the city, he often compares these acts to his father's providing monkeys and other meat for his family and neighbors. He explains that he is able to work hard because, as a child, his father whipped him after peccary hunts. Wareka regularly takes his children to visit his parents' distant hunting lodge, where his father joins the young men on fishing trips and enjoys entertaining the children with his storytelling in the evenings.

Dabo, who is twenty-two years old and unmarried, grew up in the largest Waorani village and is the third oldest of nine siblings. His father grew up on the mission in the 1960s and is today one of the few remaining Waorani active in the local evangelical church. Dabo was among the first Waorani to graduate from the new village high school, speaks Spanish fairly well, and often goes by the name Juan. He is a skilled fisherman and also enjoys dancing to Ecuadorian pop music. Since graduating, Dabo has worked on temporary contracts to clear roads for oil companies. He says that the work, in addition to providing wages, allows him to visit friends in other parts of the Waorani reserve. Dabo also makes frequent visits to the regional capital where he sees relatives, shops for clothes, and occasionally joins friends at local bars and dance clubs. Despite his experience in the city, he says he is uninterested in becoming involved in the Waorani political organization and instead aspires to study business or tourism at a university in the capital. When in his home village he stays with his parents and younger siblings, though he is frequently away for extended periods. Dabo often described his father to me as a skilled hunter who, like his ancestors, is able to kill monkeys, peccaries, and other large game. He seldom accompanies his father on hunting trips but occasionally joins him on group peccary hunts near the village, despite never having killed large game himself. At times Dabo insists that he will someday establish his own longhouse deep in the forest, where he and his older brother will live and hunt "like the ancient ones." At other times he speaks of his desire to become an oil company truck driver and to travel abroad.

The contrasting life experiences of these three men hint at how the roles and expectations of Waorani men have changed considerably from one generation to the next. While each grew up in radically different historical contexts, they emphasize a common ideal of autonomy and providing game meat associated with being "durani bai." It is striking that peccary hunting is a particularly important expression of manhood for men of all three age groups. Waorani people make strong symbolic associations between hunting peccaries and killing people in warfare (Rival 1996b), a link that has been described in much of Amazonia and is even represented in the urban Andean "Yumbada" festival in Quito (Salomon 1981; Whitten and Whitten 2011). In previous times peccaries were among the only animals hunted with the same type of spears used for killing people, and there remains a link between killing peccaries and the admired strength and bravery of men who have killed people. Some of the most impressive and long-winded household stories are about the fortunes and misfortunes of men hunting peccaries. In recalling past hunts, they describe the act of killing large animals and collectively eating and sharing the meat as durani bai and *waponi* (pleasing) activities. Peccary hunting is today emblematic of a masculinity idealized by young men, despite the fact that few have themselves speared peccaries. They show great interest in these hunts and tend to know who has killed a peccary and who has not, much like they know who has killed a human enemy. When older men return to the village with a dead peccary, an adult woman may whip its body with her hands or the dull edge of a machete. Treating the dead animal in this way is said to bring about successful hunts in the future and prevent other peccaries from invading manioc gardens.

The fact that both peccaries and (in previous times) children were whipped after the hunt suggests a degree of perceived continuity between

FIGURE 9. *Durani bai*: a man returns from the hunt with a peccary

people and peccaries familiar to studies of animist and perspectival cosmologies in Amazonia (Descola 1994; Århem 1996; Viveiros de Castro 1998a). In everyday life Waorani jokingly compare human behavior to that of peccaries, such as leaving behind a muddy path in the forest when large groups travel together. It is these perceived parallels between killing people and peccaries that make peccary hunting a key index of Waorani masculinity for young men today. Whereas most living male elders and ancestors are known to have killed people in warfare, and many of the men who grew up at the mission settlement in the 1960s have speared peccaries (and not people), few young men today have killed animals or people with spears. For teenage and young adult men whose parents converted to Christianity and all but ended the revenge-killing vendettas of preceding generations, peccary hunting has come to be seen as a quintessentially durani bai practice through which they claim a certain connection with "the ancient ones."

The ways the current generation of young men embrace peccary hunting as an expression of masculinity can be seen in the exaggerated or completely embellished stories they tell about killing peccaries. On one occasion a young man named Nenki approached my house carrying a massive, white-lipped peccary over his back. That morning, about a dozen men had raced down the river in canoes after a local man spotted a large herd crossing the river upstream from the village. After dropping the animal on the ground in front of the house, Nenki explained how he and the other men tracked the peccaries to a swamp where several animals were trapped in the mud. As is typical of hunting stories, he showed the movements of the flailing animals with body gestures and mimicked the noises made by the peccaries. The account culminated with Nenki's killing two large animals and subsequently giving one of them to his relatives. I later heard from two older men who participated in the hunt that Nenki's story had been almost completely contrived; he had little to do with killing the peccaries, having trailed behind the lead group of armed men and arrived only after the animals were killed. Apparently, Nenki received the animal he carried to our house from another hunter who killed two peccaries and had more meat than he needed. I later discovered from Nenki's close relatives that Nenki has in fact never killed a peccary himself.

Another young man explained to me that in order to marry his Quichua wife, he had to hunt enough game meat to fill several large baskets for her family. After hearing his stories about tirelessly hunting peccaries, tapir, and other animals, I later discovered that his senior male kin actually did the hunting because the young man was unable to kill peccaries himself. Just as young adult men attempt to position themselves as durani bai in embellishing stories about peccary hunting, male teenagers claim that their experiences of being whipped as children have made them stronger than younger siblings who they say were not whipped.[10] In this way young men associate themselves with the assumed strength, endurance, and knowledge of older men, even if they admit to not having carried out a number of durani bai practices themselves.

Violent Imagery and Masculine Fantasy

Of course, peccary hunting and warfare are not the only measure of Waorani manhood. To understand the seemingly contradictory ways Waorani masculinities are produced today requires consideration not only of Amazonian cosmology and generational changes but also the experiences of young men in broader political, economic, and intercultural contexts. This is because young Waorani people, especially men, spend an increasing amount of time in Ecuador's frontier cities and because mass-media sources are becoming more readily available within Waorani communities. All of this contributes to new masculine fantasies in which Waorani men draw on both popular film imagery and notions of ancestral continuity.

The characters young people see in popular Hollywood films are among the diverse images and practices they describe as *durani bai*. Films have become more accessible in the past decade with the arrival of televisions and video players in Waorani communities. Violent action-adventure movies are especially popular and attract large audiences to the few homes equipped with electric generators. As a result, many young Waorani are as likely as North Americans to be familiar with actors such as Jean-Claude Van Damme, Sylvester Stallone, and Jackie Chan.[11] At the time of my primary fieldwork between 2002 and 2004, *Rambo II* was the most popular movie among young Waorani men, who appeared to be fascinated by imagery of violence in film. After viewing scenes of Rambo killing people in the forests of Southeast Asia, they compared his ability to trick and kill enemies from hidden positions to their own ancestors, describing him as *durani bai*.[12] While watching a Rambo film, a male teenager explained to me that, upon finishing his studies at the village school, he planned to move to a remote part of the Waorani territory where, like his ancestors and Rambo, he would live "free" in the forest. Statements like these often emphasized an ideal of autonomy and independence from larger settlements and *kowori* people, as well as a desire to live in traditional longhouses (*durani onko*) and hunt game with spears and blowguns used by elders.

Bruce Lee and the martial arts are another popular image, particularly for the male teenage students who stay at the school boarding house in Toñampari.[13] At the time of my fieldwork, they would hang Bruce Lee posters and painted Chinese calligraphy copied from the packages of videos onto the inner walls of the building.[14] Martial arts fighting became so popular among young men that the students' residence was transformed into a martial arts clubhouse. In the household where I lived, a teenager decorated the wall with posters of Bruce Lee, which he placed next to a small wooden spear and a feathered crown. When asked about the images and objects displayed on his wall, he described them as "durani bai" and explained that his ancestors refused to become "civilized" and live in villages like the Waorani today. He said that, like Bruce Lee, they defended themselves fearlessly against many enemies. Other young men involved in the martial arts club evoked similar comparisons in describing their fighting abilities as "durani bai." Without assuming that young men see in Rambo or Bruce Lee practices that they envision carrying out themselves in the future, the imagery in these films resonates with capacities that young people ascribe to previous generations of men. Much like their parents killing peccaries and their ancestors killing enemies, they represent a form of manhood characterized by autonomy, strength, and endurance in the face of physical danger.

The enthusiastic reception of violent imagery associated with characters like Rambo is not uncommon around the world, especially among young men with historical or first-hand experiences of war (Kulick and Wilson 1994; Richards 1996; Wood 2006). Whereas male youth elsewhere have been described as seeing these images as "tools for the active construction of their own modernity" to be emulated in actual warfare (Richards 1996, 105), young Waorani men emphasize the continuities between Rambo and an idealized form of masculinity associated with their ancestors. Despite this emphasis on generational continuity, such an ideal is itself a product of historical transformation. In various contexts colonialism, the presence of missionaries, and tourism campaigns have all had a role in the historical production of masculinities that emphasize "warriorhood" (Hodgson 1999). Young Waorani men, who interact with mestizo Ecuadorians on a regular basis, draw in part on popular imagery of "Amazonian warriors" when they compare themselves to Rambo. I suggest that violence in film is attractive to these men because it constitutes what gender theorists have described as a "fantasy" of masculine power. The notion of fantasy is useful here in referring to the sense of what kind of person an individual aspires to be and how he or she wants to be seen by others (Moore 1994, 66). While voicing plans to engage in specific acts of physical violence is very rare in Waorani communities, Bruce Lee and Rambo embody a fantasy of masculine power and generational continuity that young men both idealize and fail to demonstrate in everyday life. In this context of shifting male roles, masculinity is produced out of multiple, coexistent discourses and images that speak to the widening gap between how gender is constructed culturally and how it is lived in the present. This tension has considerable bearing on the experiences of young Waorani men who migrate to urban areas.

Not all Waorani place the same values on practices they describe as durani bai. Just as the imagery of violence that attracts young men differs from the emphasis on suffering and victimhood in narratives told by older generations, men and women place themselves differently in relation to the past. While for young men, masculinity is associated with the perceived strength, violence, and autonomy of their ancestors, women associate themselves more closely with the creation of interiority out of differences. Women at times also make comparisons between violent movie characters and their ancestors but are less inclined to praise imagery of Rambo and Bruce Lee. This is not because older generations or the past in general is associated exclusively with male practices. While killing people and peccaries is an unambiguous expression of masculine agency, other practices described as durani bai, such as the collective consumption of plentiful food and generously hosting visitors, are associated with both men and women.

The ability to provide for visitors in the home and at village-wide feasts (*eëme*), though less exclusively gendered than warfare and hunting, is more closely linked to female agency. For example, the production of manioc beer (*tepe*)—a key component of the Waorani diet and an expected feature of visits between households—is clearly demarcated as the realm of women. They brew this drink by masticating boiled manioc roots (*kene*) to make a thick pulp (*keë*), which is later mixed with water to be served.[15] The transformational power of manioc beer is evident in the Waorani notion that its repeated consumption over time leads to household members sharing a single, distinctive body. Since the making and serving of manioc beer is one of the few exclusively female activities, women have a special part in the creation of internal consanguinity, just as masculinity is more closely associated with relations of exteriority wherein men become detached from the social body, such as warfare and uxorilocal marriages (Rival 2005). Despite the contrasting capacities associated with women and men, Waorani adults often emphasize the necessity of both male and female activities for tranquil marital relations, the production of children, and "living well."

Alongside accounts of past violence, the oral histories of Waorani men and women also reach back nostalgically to an idyllic past when related households invited one another to drink massive amounts of manioc beer together. These events continue today in festivals sponsored by schools or entire villages. In addition to making and serving manioc beer at these events, women sing songs that emphasize closeness and solidarity between different Waorani communities. These songs often welcome visitors and emphasize alliance and friendship between the hosts and visiting groups. Whether through providing manioc beer and songs for outsiders or familiarizing in-marrying husbands into their natal households, women's agency is characterized by the ability to incorporate and transform exteriority into interiority and thus constitute the household group. These understandings of gender and agency support the broader assertion from masculinity studies that manhood should be considered in terms of relations between women and men (Brandes 1980; Gutmann 1997). However, rather than asserting masculinity and femininity as gendered oppositions, Waorani men express their gendered agency in relation to previous generations and kowori people and images. It is perhaps for this reason that emerging masculinities are not predicated on gendered antagonisms and seldom lead to male violence against women.

Urban Masculinity: Gender in Crisis?

As in many other parts of the world, the gendered experiences of men and women in Amazonia have changed dramatically as indigenous people become increasingly involved in wage labor and the market economy (Seymour-Smith 1991). In these contexts emerging idioms of "modernity" and aspirations to acquire commodities often contribute significantly to gender antagonism and inequality. In much of Amazonian and Melanesia, as men earn cash and prestige through wage labor and urban political leadership, women's roles in agriculture and domestic life are devalued in relation to the cash income of men (Knauft 1997). These changes reveal that femininities and masculinities are never fixed but instead are "formed and reformed through interactions with broader historical processes and events" (Hodgson 1999, 125). Given the shifting nature of gendered experiences, masculinity should be understood not only as historical but also as multiple and contradictory.

The experiences of Waorani men have changed considerably in the past few decades, even beyond the general transition from warfare to relative peace. The majority of young men older than about age eighteen have at some point left their communities to work for oil companies or at the Waorani political office in the regional capital. As their expected roles outside the home have transformed from that of killers and hunters to students, oil workers, and politicians within just a couple of generations, it appears that the lives of men have changed to a greater degree than those of women.

FIGURE 10. A young man hunts birds along the Keremeneno River

The emphasis many Waorani place today on being "civilized" and living in a "community" conveys a stark contrast to stories about young men in the past being trained in the methods of spear-killing.

Although women's lives have also changed considerably in the past fifty years, there are few, if any, gendered practices associated with previous generations that Waorani women are today unable to carry out. The establishment of larger villages with schools and the decrease in intergroup violence have probably expanded the possibilities for feminine agency as a broader

FIGURE 11. Feeding a household pet

range of outsiders, including former "enemies," are incorporated more readily into kinship relations and household visits. While older women lament
the difficulty of producing manioc and other garden foods in past times
when revenge-killings demanded constant relocation, younger adult women
often proudly describe how they serve plentiful amounts of manioc beer to
their guests. Even if men's involvement in the wider national economy and
indigenous politics has increased women's domestic labor burden, it can
equally be said that Waorani men are less successful than women in terms
of fulfilling their expected gender roles.

With the growing expectation that boys should attend school, learn Spanish, and eventually work for wages, oil development and indigenous political
activism have become part of a new masculine ideal for young men. In contrast to previous generations in which elders arranged marriages between
cross-cousins in their early teenage years, parents have explained to me that
their male children should work for oil companies to earn money before
marriage.[16] Young men tend to agree and often attempt to avoid marrying
until reaching their twenties. In this context, masculinity is seldom stated
against a notion of "tradition" but is instead cast much in the same light

as older adults providing abundance for their household. Whether as oil company employees or urban politicians, young men are expected to bring large amounts of goods from the city back to their family and community. This expectation is particularly strong for men who are elected to positions in the Waorani organization.

While some young men achieve a degree of prestige through wage labor and politics, their roles have changed in ways that reveal their diminishing ability to achieve particular forms of masculinity associated with previous generations. Insofar as women's agency is associated with the creation, re-generation, and expansion of the group, women have become increasingly successful in their expected gendered roles in the decades since mission settlement—a period marked by wider intergroup alliances and rapid popu-lation growth.[17] Men, however, even when successful in urban politics and wage labor, are compared in various ways to past generations of killers and successful hunters. Waorani political leaders, who are almost exclusively young men, face criticism from their kin when they fail to satisfy the expec-tation that they generously provide large amounts of goods obtained from external (kowori) sources. When they fail to provide generously enough, they are contrasted to elders and ancestors who are said to have shared plentiful game meat for their household and neighbors. These men come to be seen by their male and female peers as becoming more like "outsid-ers" and are described as *kowori bai* ("like non-Waorani people")

Young men respond to this situation in a number of ways. For the ini-tial generation of Waorani political leaders based in the regional capital, one strategy has been to negotiate contracts with oil companies. Enkeri, a man in his late twenties who has worked at the Waorani political office for several years, explained to me the difficulties of reconciling urban life with the expectations he faces in his home village. He complained that, in contrast to his home community, where his kin provide food for each other without payment, one needs money to live among kowori people in the city. Enkeri lamented that his low wages make it impossible for him to provide the wealth of manufactured goods that his kin have come to expect from him. Despite having participated in a number of protests against oil development on indigenous lands, this same man proudly explained to me his role in signing an agreement with an oil company that he hopes will provide school and health supplies to his home community.

These contexts reveal how, through wage labor, men come to be mea-sured increasingly in terms of the cash and commodity goods they provide for their families. This process has not led, however, to the gender polarity and antagonism anticipated by theorists who envision an emerging global hegemonic masculinity based on male domination. Spousal abuse remains extremely rare and is a much-criticized practice that Waorani associate with kowori Ecuadorians. Women are not expected to be subordinate to their husbands, nor has female sexuality become commodified or noticeably more restricted. Even as it is generally young men who are elected to leadership positions within the official Waorani political office, women continue to have an active role in voicing their opinions and influencing decisions in local political debates. Conflicts in Waorani communities are very rarely voiced in terms of gender oppositions. Like men, women complain that indigenous leaders are selfish—not because they are men but because they fail to demonstrate the generosity expected of both men and women.

Urban indigenous politics are in part an extension of the Waorani logic that, just as female agency is associated with creating, expanding, and regenerating sociality within Waorani communities, relations with kowori "outsiders" involves a specifically masculine form of agency.[18] Rather than having mutually antagonistic gendered roles in their engagement with broader political and economic processes, men and women demonstrate distinct capacities within indigenous Amazonian notions of gendered agency. In the context of recent social transformations, crisis and antagonism are instead expressed primarily in terms of generational differences and interethnic relations that put the masculinity of young men in question. This is not to say that Waorani gender relations are entirely equal, harmonious, or unchanging. As we have seen, the roles of men have changed considerably in recent decades, and it remains to be seen whether the forms of manhood produced in ever-expanding Waorani villages and in urban interethnic contexts will lead to a more pronounced gender hierarchy in the future.

Young Waorani men inhabit a world of multiple, contradictory, and constantly shifting masculinities (Cornwall and Lindisfarne 1994). They increasingly find themselves in urban contexts where, in the eyes of other Ecuadorians, they embody a specific image of warriorhood. As we have seen, although they are unable to demonstrate many local durani bai practices, in the city these men sometimes embrace their allocated position as "wild Amazonian warriors" in popular Ecuadorian imagination. Just as they celebrate stories about peccary hunting, images of Rambo, and the idea of superhuman "uncontacted" relatives living "free" in the forest, performing as warriors in front of mestizo Ecuadorians and tourists confers a form of masculinity that is elusive in the villages where young men grow up. In these urban settings, the Amazonian warrior becomes yet another element

FIGURE 12. *Kowori onko*: the Amazonian frontier city of Puyo

of masculine fantasy for young men who themselves describe their dress and performances as being "like the ancient ones."

Indigenous Amazonian notions of gendered agency are today only part of the lived experiences of Waorani people, especially for men who stay in the regional capital for months or years at a time. Some of them befriend mestizo Ecuadorians and join them in drinking sessions and the male sexual banter familiar to studies of masculinity elsewhere in Latin America (Brandes 2002; Gutmann 1996; Wade 1994). Young Waorani men say that drinking at bars is an important part of being "amigos" (friends) with mestizos and other Waorani men in the city. In these urban environments, what Knauft describes as "a new collective life of male fraternity" can be seen in relations between Waorani and mestizo men (1997, 241). These friendships, coupled with popular stereotypes about Waorani violence, have placed young men at the crossroads of contradictory forms of masculinity. Even as leaving one's household was part of becoming a man in previous generations, young Waorani men now find themselves in a position where they must negotiate the demands of their home communities and the expectations of urban Ecuadorian society.

While male bonding in urban areas has not led to the devaluation of women or strict gendered oppositions, recent social transformations reveal the tensions and contradictions between indigenous and popular Ecuadorian measures of masculinity.[19] Whereas manhood in Waorani communities is measured in terms of a man's ability to demonstrate autonomy, provide abundantly for his family, and engage in productive relations with kowori people, the expectations of urban mestizo masculinity tend to emphasize sexuality, gender hierarchy, and solidarity between men through the collective consumption of alcohol.[20] Without attempting to draw an all-encompassing contrast between "egalitarian" Waorani and "patriarchal" mestizos, it is clear that young Waorani men are measured differently in urban areas than in their home communities. Increasingly, Waorani men fail to satisfy specific expectations of manhood both locally and in the city. While they lack the "hard" bodies that make older generations of men able to hunt with spears, they are also seen as deficient in key aspects of mestizo masculinity. Waorani political leaders, who come from villages where alcohol has only recently become available, are said to be unable to handle social drinking, often ending up belligerently drunk on the streets at night. Even as Waorani public folklore performances are consistent with mestizo Ecuadorian ideas about "wild Amazonian warriors," these men often fail to fulfill the expectations of masculinity on the streets of the regional capital, where they are as likely to be accused by mestizos of "losing their culture" when they drink as they are of being anti-social if they don't.

Conclusion

Anthropological studies of masculinity often evoke the challenges and contradictions men face when their identities and practices are "out of synch with those regarded as 'traditional'" (Viveros Vigoya 2004, 28). In contrast to questions of identity and sexual antagonism that have preoccupied much writing about gender, the young Waorani men whom I have described in this chapter are involved in a struggle to reconcile urban intercultural relations with idealized forms of manhood associated with previous generations of Waorani men. In specific contexts, such as the village martial arts club and urban "warrior" performances, they are able to emulate the practices they attribute to elders and "the ancient ones." And yet the expectations of peaceful conviviality in contemporary Waorani communities and new forms of interethnic male fraternity have transformed the ways masculine agency is produced and performed. Rather than approaching these changes only through the lens of indigenous Amazonian cosmology, I have attempted to explain how contemporary Waorani manhood is also made and remade through increasingly global media imagery and intercultural relations. In situations like these, masculine fantasies of power draw simultaneously on multiple gender discourses rooted in indigenous Amazonian understandings of gendered agency, local oral histories of violence, global media, and colonial imagination.

Even as would-be warriors and peccary hunters are today becoming oil workers and urban political leaders, these changes have not led to widespread violence and gender antagonism between men and women. Without implying that Waorani sociality is fixed in time or entirely egalitarian, the experiences of young men reflect Amazonian understandings of gender and agency that associate women more closely with interiority and men with exteriority. While previous studies of "men as men" demonstrate that masculinity is often constructed and performed in opposition to women (Bourdieu 2001), what is striking about Waorani forms of masculinity is how they are seldom constructed explicitly against or even in reference to femininity. This is not to ignore the important differences Waorani and other Amazonian people envision between women and men. Since masculinities are always a product of historical transformations, it remains to be seen whether urban migration and intercultural relations will lead to more hierarchical gender relations in the future. For young Waorani men today memories of ancestral warriorhood, mestizo Ecuadorians, and Bruce Lee are all part of the generational and intercultural relations through which they express their own ways of being men.

Lost People and Distant Kin

The Taromenani Massacre of 2003

In May 2003, after having spent most of the previous year in Toñampari and other Waorani villages along the Curaray River, I was visiting the frontier city of Puyo when a group of young men from the Waorani political office approached me at an open-air restaurant frequented by local indigenous leaders. They told me the latest news: a group of Waorani men had attacked the longhouse of an "uncontacted" group living in voluntary isolation within the Waorani reserve. Visibly concerned, they explained to me that a large but unknown number of people were killed in the raid, which was carried out by men from Waorani villages to the east of Toñampari. At this point they did not appear to know many details about the attack, but shared with me a letter from the organization's president to the local military authorities estimating that as many as twenty-five people described as "Taromenani" had lost their lives in the massacre.

In the days that followed, news of the killings spread across Amazonian Ecuador, before long becoming a headline story in the national media. I soon found myself sitting in the homes of Waorani officials in Puyo, listening to their accounts of the killings between news reports on the television about "tribal violence" in the Amazon with chronological lists of past Waorani spear-killings. It was during one of these visits that a Waorani friend showed me a necklace that had been taken from one of the bodies at the scene of the killings. It was made of a dozen or so palm fiber strings tied together to form a single, thick necklace. Around the moist and pungent-smelling strings were many small pieces of colorful plastic, rubber, and aluminum strung up as beads. Some of the beads were made from chopping up plastic tubing into small pieces, which were placed in alternating colors alongside bottle caps and peccary teeth. For me, this chilling object conveyed powerfully its owner's social isolation from and material coexistence with the oil camps that surround many of the most remote parts of the Waorani reserve.

Sometime later, amid growing gossip and speculation about the attack, another Waorani man in Puyo invited me to his home to show me a video he recorded at the site of the massacre a few days after it occurred. He had joined a group of Waorani men from ONHAE and Ecuadorian soldiers on a trip in a military helicopter to investigate the scene. I sat with him, his wife, and their two small children as we watched the footage of ONHAE representatives looking through the contents of a burned longhouse that was ignited by the attackers during the struggle. It looked very much like a *durani onko* (traditional Waorani house) in size and shape, and the blowgun and spears recovered from the scene appeared similar to those used by Waorani. Keenly interested in these objects, my host pulled down from his wall a blowgun he found at the scene, comparing its likeness and specific differences to a blowgun made by his uncle.[1]

The video then focused on the bodies of several victims, which were riddled with spears. My host explained to me that the men at the scene were fearful, knowing that survivors could be hiding nearby, waiting to take revenge. He and his wife then spelled out to me the further danger that any contact with blood spilled in killings can cause sickness, as touching the blood of a person who is killed causes wounds to form on the surface of the skin. The man was concerned that his trip to the site of the attack might affect his infant son and other members of his household. In order to prevent becoming sick from contact with the blood, he said, he would need to be whipped with a vine by an elder—and preferably someone who has killed in the past.

The man who recorded the video was one of many Waorani who expressed deep concern about the killings and curiosity about the victims. Both in Puyo and upon my return to Toñampari I heard varied accounts of the attack from Waorani people. In the months that followed, much of the gossip, conversation, and reflection on the past that I heard around the cooking hearth in the evenings turned specifically to this event. Some reported that nine men from Tiguino and other Waorani villages to the east carried out the attack, shooting scores of victims with rifles supplied by illegal Colombian loggers operating along the Tiguino River.[2] Others explained the attack as an act of revenge for killings carried out by "uncontacted" people decades earlier. Some described how the killers decapitated their victims after spearing them, placing their heads on the ends of spears left protruding from the ground.

Now, a decade later, the series of events that preceded the attack has become somewhat clearer, as have some of the motives of the killers. The 2003 massacre and more recent killings have become a telling example of how so-called uncontacted groups are caught between processes of aggressive economic development, the indigenous rights movement, and frontier policies in present-day Amazonia.[3] Establishing an accurate picture of what happened is important for addressing the current situation of these marginal groups and defending their human rights in the face of increasing threats to their very existence and way of life (Cabodevilla 2004a). Useful as this knowledge may be for preventing violent encounters between "uncontacted" people and their neighbors in the future, it is equally important to understand what these groups living in voluntary isolation mean to Waorani people with whom they share a territorial reserve and certain aspects of social organization and material culture.

Up to this point I have focused on how Waorani people remember violent encounters from the relatively distant past and how colonial imagery of Amazonian people has itself become part of indigenous social imagination. The point of this book, however, is not to attempt to reconstruct a more accurate picture of the past but to explore violence and memory in terms of how Waorani people experience contemporary social life. Since the initial period of mission settlement half a century ago, missionaries and anthropologists alike have noted a remarkable transition from intergroup revenge killings to relative peace among the Waorani (Yost 1981; Robarchek and Robarchek 1996; Boster, Yost and Peeke 2004). These transformational processes, and indigenous understandings of them, emerge as an important part of social memory in Waorani villages today (High 2009a). However, we should be careful not to adopt uncritically an Evangelical narrative of change from "pre-contact" violence to "post-contact" peace that ignores the forms of violence that Waorani people experience today, both as victims and as perpetrators. Violence is a key concern in Waorani villages today beyond the oral narratives and "warrior" performances described in the previous chapters. Whether in describing revenge killings or speculating about the existence of distant kin among "uncontacted" groups, Waorani perspectives on recent events point to the role of memory in indigenous understandings of sociality and alterity.

The killings that occurred during my fieldwork reveal how Waorani understandings of violence are interconnected with ongoing political and economic transformations in Amazonia. The presence of multinational oil development and illegal logging on indigenous lands are among the eco-logically destructive and socially disruptive forces that Waorani and other indigenous Amazonian people face today. These and other kowori-driven processes contribute to violent conflicts within and between indigenous communities in unpredictable ways. Rather than viewing Waorani people simply as victims of powerful outsiders, here I focus on how these processes are also embedded in Waorani understandings of sociality, alterity, and revenge. How, for example, are loggers, oil workers, and other kowori incorporated into conflicts between indigenous groups, and how do Waorani people characterize the victims and perpetrators in these events?

In a recent ethnography of Papua New Guinea, Stasch (2009) observes that his Korowai hosts "know relations by events, and . . . search for relational meanings in events" (17). For Waorani people violence appears to set off a particular kind of search for relational meanings. While my hosts and neighbors in Toñampari were generally critical of the killings that occurred during my fieldwork, these events appeared to create new kinds of relations in a society where victimhood is a key marker of social proximity. This becomes particularly clear in Waorani speculations about groups living in what has been described as "voluntary isolation" within the Waorani reserve (Cabodevilla and Berraondo 2005). Typical Western understandings of "uncontacted" or "isolated" people conjure an image of "wild" and "primitive" populations untouched by the corrupting influences of history and civilization. In contrast to this enduring image, Waorani people understand their "uncontacted" neighbors to be both fierce warriors reminiscent of their ancestors and kinsmen who became disconnected from other Waorani in past times. These enigmatic "lost people" have become both a valued source of potential relations in the aftermath of violence and a potent image of indigenous strength and autonomy.

Waorani, Tagaeri, Taromenani

In Toñampari, one of the major concerns after the 2003 killings was the question of who the victims actually were. Waorani generally describe "uncontacted" people within their territory as Tagaeri—referring to the legendary group of Tagae, who fled into isolation many years ago when most Waorani came to live at the missionary settlements. They became famous in the region for their nomadism and hostile resistance to contact with Waorani villages, missionaries, oil workers, and other outsiders.[4] Although "Tagaeri" is a general term for people described locally as "uncivilized" or durani bai ("like the ancient ones"), most Waorani are familiar with the specific story of Tagae and, in some cases, their kin relation to him or members of his following. While the Tagaeri have a prominent place in social memory, most Waorani say that Tagae himself was killed years ago and that few, if any, members of his original group survive today. Despite their reputation for hostility toward kowori and Waorani villages, my hosts identify the Tagaeri and their descendants unambiguously as Waorani people.

In the aftermath of the 2003 killings, many Waorani referred to the victims as Taromenani, a group they described as distinct but similar to the Tagaeri. They live in the central and eastern part of the Waorani reserve in an area that was designated by Ecuadorian law in 1999 as the Tagaeri Untouchable Zone.[5] Extending north from the middle course of the Curaray River, the Untouchable Zone was intended to offer a degree of protection to the Tagaeri and other uncontacted groups whose lands have been encroached upon by oil development and illegal logging in recent years. While Toñampari and other Waorani villages near the headwaters of the Curaray River are located several days' walk to the west of the Untouchable Zone, many Waorani to the north and east live much closer to this reserve within a reserve. The village of Tiguino, for example, is connected to the city of Coca by an old oil road (the "Via Auca") that has become a major conduit for the colonization of Waorani lands by mestizos and the trade in hardwoods extracted illegally from the reserve. It was from this frontier village that the men involved in the 2003 massacre began their journey downriver to attack the Taromenani.

While ecological factors were a consideration in creating the Untouchable Zone, the reserve was established for the benefit of people in "voluntary isolation" who may in fact not be aware of its precise existence. Despite the official reserve, "uncontacted" indigenous groups continue to live in the path of extractive industries with few state controls. As in previous decades with the Tagaeri, who were repeatedly involved in violent clashes with kowori and Waorani people, there were concerns before 2003 about the Taromenani and their violent encounters with loggers, oil camps, and

MAP 3. The Yasuní National Park, and the Tagaeri-Taromenani Untouchable Zone, and Waorani Territory

Waorani. In the year prior to the 2003 attack, my hosts described other encounters in which loggers and uncontacted people were killed.

But who, exactly, are these Taromenani people? In the weeks following the attack I heard dozens of explanations, many from Waorani who disagreed about whether or not the Taromenani victims were indeed "Waorani" people. Although some suggested that the Taromenani are survivors of the original Tagaeri group, their actual identity appeared to be somewhat a mystery to most people in Toñampari. Some insisted that they speak the Waorani language (*Wao-terero*), while others claimed that they do not and are from a completely different indigenous group. Several people insisted that they are tall, have whitish skin "like gringos," and come from far away in Peru to the east. Despite the disagreements and uncertainties, everyone attributed great strength and speed to these forest-dwelling people, much as they do to the Tagaeri and their ancestors.[6]

A Political Economy of Revenge

Both in the national media and in indigenous communities there was much controversy and intrigue about what caused the unprecedented scale of violence in 2003. It has become increasingly clear, however, that indigenous cosmology and the changing face of economic development in Amazonia had their part in the killings. The area around the village of Tiguino, where the killers assembled before the attack, has long since been a zone of frontier violence and tension between Waorani, oil companies, and colonists (Cabodevilla 2004a, 27). In the early years of the twenty-first century, these tensions were exacerbated by an influx of illegal loggers who used the old oil road between Tiguino and the frontier city of Coca to extract timber from Waorani lands. This is the same oil road built in the 1960s to open the area up to oil development, which ultimately resulted in the loss of a significant part of Waorani ancestral lands to colonization, deforestation, and industrial pollution.[7] By 2003 one of the men who led the raid was a local gatekeeper between the loggers and the village of Tiguino, receiving payment for allowing timber extraction downriver in the direction of the Untouchable Zone and the Yasuní National Park (Cabodevilla 2004b, 19–21).[8] According to many Waorani, the loggers, who sought to eliminate the famously hostile uncontacted groups in an area they routinely exploited for timber, provided rifles, ammunition, and payment to the killers in compensation for carrying out the attack. While it is difficult to establish whether or not logging interests were directly involved in supporting the 2003 massacre, it is clear that past and present extractive economies have contributed in a major way to the tensions that persist in the area.

According to the accounts of my Waorani hosts after the attack, the external influences of money, guns, and frontier development in Amazonia were only part of the story behind the 2003 massacre. Even as many Waorani lamented the killings, their accounts also address the logic that motivated the killers. They explained that it was carried out according to indigenous understandings of revenge, whereby the death of a kinsman should be avenged even decades after the initial killing. Lingering memories of absent kin can evoke grief, anger, and in some cases retaliation against not only specific people but also against a killer's entire household. Several Waorani explained that the 2003 killings were intended to avenge the death of Carlos Omene, a Waorani man who was killed by Tagaeri in 1993. Omene was speared on an incursion into the Untouchable Zone, where he and other men from Tiguino intended to return a young Tagaeri woman previously captured by Waorani.[9] The fact that several of the men who carried out the 2003 killings were close kin of Omene indicates that the violence in 2003 was part of a series of confrontations that extends decades into the past. Cabodevilla reports, for example, that prior to the attack, Omene's widow tearfully recounted her husband's death at the hands of the Tagaeri, reminding the men in Tiguino that his death ten years before still had not been avenged (2004b, 23).

Much debate remains about several details of the actual attack, especially as this event has rapidly become part of both Waorani oral history and media intrigue in Ecuador. What we do know is that none of the killers were arrested or prosecuted by the Ecuadorian authorities. One question raised by Waorani and kowori commentators alike is the extent to which guns were used in the attack. In their interviews soon after the massacre some of the killers insisted that they fired their guns initially only to frighten the Taromenani upon entering the dark longhouse, which they set ablaze before chasing and spearing their victims outside.[10] While it is difficult to confirm or deny many of the details reported by the killers and other Waorani, it appears that guns, spears, and machetes were used extensively. Regardless of these details, the dramatic economic changes of recent decades are only part of the story of how and why the Taromenani massacre occurred.

Kin as Victims

Given the enthusiastic use of radio communication between even the most remote Waorani villages, news of the Taromenani killings quickly became a heated topic of conversation and speculation. From the beginning there was much debate surrounding both the motives of the killers and the actual identity of the victim group. After hearing people in Toñampari lament and criticize past killings in their oral histories, I was not completely surprised to hear them denounce the May 2003 attack. What did surprise me was how upset they were about the fate of a reportedly hostile group living far away and in isolation from their own homes and lives. Their critical accounts illustrate how, for many Waorani, the killings led to a sense of shared experience with the victim group. Instead of attempting to elucidate a complete or objectively true account of what happened, I am concerned here with the particular discourses that emerged in the aftermath of the attack and what they reveal about Waorani perspectives on intergroup violence.

Although nobody in the villages where I carried out long-term fieldwork participated in the killings, this event and the fate of the victims loomed large in Toñampari in the following months. People frequently offered their interpretations and explanations of what happened without my asking, using as much narrative detail and bodily mimicry as they did when telling stories about spear-killing raids in the distant past.[11] Some were concerned that the surviving Taromenani would soon take revenge on Waorani villages. The most pressing concern for many people in Toñampari, however, was the possibility that some of the victims may in fact have been distant kin. Despite the still unresolved debate about who the victims were, some Waorani speculated about cousins and other relatives who may have been living among the Taromenani. They explained that, although the Tagaeri fled into voluntary isolation many years ago, some members of Tagae's original following could still be alive, having been incorporated into the mysterious Taromenani after years of intergroup violence. Some even spoke of local elders weeping over the massacre of specific Tagaeri relatives. They described the Taromenani as people who, despite their reputation for hostility and isolation, were actually hoping to settle among Waorani neighbors like themselves. Much like the stories Waorani tell about their ancestors being killed, they positioned the Taromenani unambiguously as victims of unjustified violence.

People in Toñampari generally described the killings in morally charged terms, referring to them as *ononki* (unjustified, mistaken) and the killers themselves as *wene* (bad, evil). They lamented that most of the victims were women and children, which for local people added to the deplorable nature of the violence.[12] Many adults objected to the 2003 massacre in much the same way they talk about killings that occurred in the distant past. Despite the different versions and details of the attack that were circulating at the time, most people could list most or all of the men who participated.[13] Alongside accounts of how loggers supported the attack and descriptions of the specific methods used, some told of the dialogue between the killers and their victims and about stories of children being abducted from the scene. Nearly all of the accounts I collected in the months following the attack, however, deeply sympathized with the plight of the Taromenani.

I heard one of these accounts from Wakewe, a man who described the attack to me a few days after it happened. He explained how his uncle, a well-known elder, was one of the men who led the raid. According to Wakewe, after a journey by canoe downriver followed by a long trek through the forest, his uncle was the one who began the shooting upon entering the dark interior of the Taromenani longhouse. While some of the unsuspecting victims managed to escape from the house, others pleaded with the attackers not to kill them, insisting that they wanted to live together with Waorani people in Tiguino. Since other people had told me that the Taromenani did not speak the Waorani language, I asked Wakewe about how the victims communicated with their killers. He assured me that at least some of the Taromenani do speak Wao-terero, albeit in a different way, and that during the attack these individuals communicated a desire to end their isolation.

This desire for closer relations with Waorani neighbors appeared to be the very basis of Wakewe's frustration with his uncle and his collaborators. He explained, in much the same way that Waorani elders describe their own history of missionary settlement, that the Taromenani wanted to become "civilized." He also described how one of the men who participated in the attack tried unsuccessfully to prevent the others' firing their guns on the Taromenani. Wakewe, who has many relatives who live near the Tagaeri Untouchable Zone, predicted that the survivors would go into hiding before eventually seeking revenge by attacking Waorani villages.

Wakewe was not alone in seeing the attack as a missed opportunity to bring the Taromenani into peaceful contact with Waorani villages. Kowe, a Toñampari elder, expressed a similar concern about possible revenge killings. In lamenting the attack, he referred to his own specific kinship links with the Tagaeri at the point when Tagae and his followers became isolated from other Waorani decades ago. Kowe explained that Tagae himself was his cousin and listed the names of several other people in Toñampari who may have living relatives among the Taromenani. Despite the dangers associated with these "uncontacted" people, Kowe spoke of them with respect and admiration. He described them as physically superior to what he called "civilized" Waorani, emphasizing their strength, speed, and stamina in moving through the forest, and their ability to throw spears at amazing lengths. What stood out most prominently in my discussions with Kowe after the attack was his keen interest in establishing social ties with the isolated group. He even spoke of his desire to travel personally to the Untouchable Zone with other elders to attempt to bring them into the realm of "civilization."

Both of these men not only denounced the attack, but they also raised the possibility of (re)establishing social ties with the uncontacted group. For Wakewe, the basis of this was the actual desire of the Taromenani to live among "civilized" people like himself. Kowe too expressed a desire to incorporate the Taromenani into his own social world and even asserted his kinship links to members of the Tagaeri who may or may not still be alive. Whereas the men who participated in the attack apparently intended to eliminate as many Taromenani as possible, most of my Waorani hosts were more interested in them as a source of past or future relations.

This emphasis on expanding the possibilities for intergroup sociality and engaging in relations with dangerous or unknown outsiders is a common theme of discussion in Waorani communities that often emerges in accounts of missionary settlement in the 1960s. Despite the central place of violence that persists in social memory across genders and generations, many Waorani envision themselves today living in a period of growth and expansion in terms of territory, population, and the making of social ties beyond local households and villages. Recognizing the 2003 attack as a potential threat to this period of relative peace, they denounced what they saw as the dangerous consequences of the massacre. Above all, they remembered their social links with the Tagaeri to a much greater extent after the attack than they had before.

These responses to the Taromenani attack point to how violence creates new ways of conceptualizing Waorani kinship and sociality. Such an indigenous emphasis on social closeness to victims and their kin is also extended to kowori people who were killed in the past. In chapter 1 I described how the two principle North American missionaries who established the evangelical mission settlement at Tiweno in the 1960s were the widow and sister of a missionary killed by Waorani in 1956. It appears likely that Waorani people accepted the missionaries in part because they understood them to be, like themselves, the close kin of victims previously killed by Waorani (High 2008, 2009b). Even as any interpretation of this historical encounter is necessarily conjectural, elders today remember the early missionaries in much the same way that they define themselves: as kin of victims.

Waorani people describe in a similar light some of the Catholic missionaries who have worked in the eastern part of the Waorani territory since around 1965. In 1987 the Spanish priest Alejandro Labaka and a nun (Ines Arango) who accompanied him were killed in an attempt to make contact with a Tagaeri group. They were speared soon after being dropped by helicopter near an isolated longhouse in what is today the Untouchable Zone. At the time Labaka was hoping to negotiate a truce between "uncontacted" groups and oil companies after the expansion of oil exploration on Waorani lands had already led to several violent confrontations between Tagaeri and oil workers. Labaka's death has become an important part of Waorani lore, in which the priest is presented as an archetypical victim of violence. Fondly remembered by many Waorani today, Labaka is described in much the same way as kinsmen killed by enemies in past spear-killing raids.

While Labaka, like other missionaries, preached against violence, it appears that some Waorani were intent on avenging his death at the hands of an uncontacted group more than fifteen years after he was killed. His status as kin to many Waorani appears to have had at least some bearing on the 2003 killings. One of the killers who arrived at the Catholic mission in the town of Coca soon after the attack announced that he and his group had avenged the death of both Carlos Omene and Father Labaka (Cabodevilla 2004a, 62). Without exaggerating the influence Labaka's death had in motivating the Taromenani massacre, examples like these illustrate how relations with missionaries and other intimate kowori are interwoven with Waorani revenge killings as much as they are kinship. They suggest that it is not only the external political and economic forces of oil development and illegal logging that effect local forms of violence, but also that intercultural relations that have become part of the most intimate aspects of Waorani memory and experience.

Lost People and Proximate Others

There is no denying that anthropologists working in Amazonia and elsewhere have at times been seduced by an image of indigenous people living in isolation from other societies, the reach of nation-states, or the effects of "Western" culture. Napoleon Chagnon's (1988) claim that his study of Yanomami warfare in the 1960s revealed a state of human nature uncorrupted by Western contact is a famous example of this tendency—one that has been widely refuted by other anthropologists (Albert 1989; Ferguson 1995, 1999). While anthropologists and historians have done much to counter this image, the idea that certain "lost tribes" live in a state of "primitive" isolation from outside influences remains a powerful popular media representation of indigenous people. Rarely does a year pass without a major news story about aerial sightings of an "uncontacted" Amazonian tribe or a dangerous encounter with people assumed to be living as if in the "stone age."

While the myth of "lost tribes" presents indigenous populations as living in a "natural" state of isolation, the situation of specific uncontacted groups is invariably at least in part a result of political and economic processes that extend well beyond the local (Kirsch 1997, 64). In many cases, as with the groups living in voluntary isolation within the Untouchable Zone, this isolation appears to be, above all, an active refusal to engage in unequal or undesirable relations with powerful outsiders. In this way they are indicative of a much wider historical process of intercultural relations in Amazonia. As Kirsch suggests, "The lost tribes of the Amazon are the product of centuries of colonial relations. Their discovery is made possible by virtue of their long history of retreat and resistance; their isolation is a social creation rather than a natural condition" (62). Even if much about "uncontacted" people living in or near the Waorani reserve remains a mystery, it is clear that the changing social, political, and economic landscape of Amazonian Ecuador contributed to their relative isolation, whether in the form of missionization, oil development, or the more general condition of frontier violence and displacement that indigenous Amazonian people have suffered for centuries. By ignoring the historical power relations from which "uncontacted" groups continue to emerge, the myth of lost tribes implicitly absolves Western society from responsibility for the often precarious situation of these groups (Lutz and Collins 1993, 214–15; Kirsch 1997, 59). Rather than reproducing the myth that "uncontacted" or "lost" tribes constitute a state of pristine nature, we should recognize how these transformative processes effect and become part of indigenous formulations of violence, alterity, and kinship.

In the contemporary world, the image of naturally isolated "tribes" is not merely an object of media fascination, it is also an aspect of legal discussions of culture and rights on a global stage. In what Bessire (2012) describes as the contemporary politics of isolation, indigenous people living in voluntary isolation have come to be valued as the most "pure" form of multiculturalism. The politico-legal category of isolation, Bessire observes, "presumes that social relation itself is a line of exclusion cutting through the category of culture. It thus parses indigenous kinds of life into opposing regimes of authenticity based on a degree of associative relations, which are then set against one another and vertically ranked by politics" (470). Isolation, construed as a natural state rather than a product of social relations, has become an important feature of indigenous rights campaigns. Whether in the adoption of new national laws in Ecuador or in the United Nations Human Rights Council's *Draft Guidelines on the Protection of Indigenous Peoples in Voluntary Isolation and in Initial Contact* (2009), "non-relational life" has come to be seen as the ultimate expression of indigenous peoples' right to self-determination (Bessire 2012, 477). The paradox of this notion of isolation-as-right, Bessire notes, is that it "presupposes a legal subject that must remain outside the law itself" whereby "segregation is the only possible form of solidarity with isolated subjects" (477–80).

While this politics of isolation has deep roots in Western imaginings of indigenous peoples in places like Amazonia, Waorani understandings of "uncontacted" people suggest an alternative to our own insistence on social and ontological boundaries defined ultimately by segregation and unified collectivities. Rather than focusing on the processes by which indigenous Amazonian people have become an object of Western fascination, or the contemporary politics of indigenous identity in Amazonia, my interest is in how Waorani themselves imagine and engage in relations with their own others. The act of defining a certain person or group as other to oneself is not simply a statement about difference but also a boundary through which people posit and engage in relations of unity and closeness (Stasch 2009). Rather than assuming people in other places engage in these processes in ways that parallel the contemporary politics of isolation, we should be open to alternate ways of conceptualizing and organizing relations of alterity.[14]

While anthropologists have challenged popular stereotypes about "lost" or "uncontacted" people, rarely do we stop to consider seriously what indigenous people like the Waorani have to say about their neighbors who live in voluntary isolation. This may be the result of our general reluctance to engage at all with the idea of uncontacted peoples after the self-conscious purging of the concept of isolated, primitive societies from anthropology.[15] While anthropologists were surely right to shed this image, approaching the position of seemingly enigmatic groups like the Taromenani in terms of Amazonian notions of alterity and kinship can open up new ways of thinking about how and why indigenous Amazonian people respond to key contemporary events in the ways they do.

The 2003 attack and its aftermath reveal the multiple ways that Waorani people conceptualize, cultivate, and in some contexts violently demand relations with their uncontacted neighbors. For many Waorani, the Taromenani are an object of social othering at the same time as they present, at least for some, an ideal source of potential relations. As Stasch observes in Melanesia, the very qualities of alterity are in some contexts a focus of social connection, such that social bonds are a synthesis of otherness and intimacy that "exist[s] through concrete channels of communicative contact and separateness" (16). In Waorani accounts of "uncontacted" people, this process of living separately and cultivating or imagining closeness involves very little in the way of communication. Whether in describing the Taromenani as long-lost kin or taking revenge on them for previous killings, the kind of alterity that Waorani people find in the Taromenani is one that diverges significantly from the paradigm of nonrelational life promoted in indigenous rights advocacy.

As my hosts lamented the deaths of people they described as their potential kin, it became clear that the 2003 killings contributed to a growing sense of closeness to the Taromenani. In a cultural context where people define themselves collectively as "prey" to violence (Rival 1998b), the attacks were a catalyst for Waorani to imagine what they share in common with their uncontacted neighbors. For Waorani people, being a victim of violence presents a contrast to the aggression associated with rival groups and kowori people. Rival describes how, for Waorani people, killing creates "otherness," both in terms of the killer's anger transforming him from kin (*guirinani*) to non-kin (*warani*) and in precipitating future revenge killings (Rival 2002, 64). After the Taromenani attack, however, my hosts were more concerned with asserting their identification with the survivors based on a shared position as kin of victims rather than mounting a raid against the men they denounced for the killings.[16]

Waorani descriptions of Taromenani people after the attack allow for rethinking some of the key features of Amazonian kinship and sociality. Ethnographies of this part of the world evoke examples of how kinship is conceived as an effect of shared experience, where everyday conviviality forms bodies and makes transpersonal unities.[17] In certain ways Amazonian concepts of consanguinity and affinity present a radical alternative to notions of biological relatedness in Western kinship ideologies and the focus on procreation that guided classical anthropological studies of kinship (Schneider 1984). As consanguinity in Amazonia is often understood to be the result of human action or intention—rather than procreation—kinship is constituted more by memory than it is by genealogical descent, that is, "as a set of relations between living people which are actively produced in time" (Gow 1991, 288).[18] Waorani understandings of marriage, procreation, and the effects of living together evoke a sense of relatedness that is "made" through shared experience. Rival notes that Waorani who live in the same longhouse become "of the same flesh": "The physical reality of living together, that is, of continually feeding each other, eating the same food and sleeping together, develops into a common physicality, which is far more real than genealogical ties" (1998a, 621). Whether it is through consuming the same things collectively or avoiding them, the notion that "the repeated and undifferentiated *action* of sharing . . . turns co-residents into a single, indistinct substance" (Rival 1998a, 621) has come to define the kinds of mutuality and well-being associated with the "moral economy of intimacy" in Amazonia (Viveiros de Castro 1996, 189).

Waorani concepts of consanguinity and affinity not only challenge Western assumptions about the biological basis of kinship, they also illustrate the need to sidestep the traditional dichotomy between the "biological" and "social" (Carsten 2013, 249). My hosts' descriptions of "uncontacted" people as their kin after the 2003 killings resonate with Sahlins's approach to kinship as "a manifold of intersubjective participations, founded on mutualities of being" (2011a, 12). Drawing on Aristotle's *Nicomachean Ethics* and a range of other theorists, Sahlins views kinship in terms of the "larger meanings of mutual belonging" by which people come to sense "the same entity in discrete subjects" (10). Challenging the traditional focus on pro-creation in anthropological discussions of kinship, he notes that mutuality of being "encompasses and goes beyond the notions of common substance, however such consubstantiality is locally defined and established" (14).

The comments I heard from Waorani people in response to the 2003 kill-ings insisted on a certain mutuality of being that has little or no reference to shared substance or the conviviality often emphasized in studies of kinship and sociality in Amazonia. Rather than positing kinship only in terms of local commensality and physical closeness, they expressed a sense of social proximity and mutuality at a spatial distance. For many Waorani, the Taro-menani are their kin not because they live together or even know each other in person, but because, to use Sahlins's phrasing, they envision themselves as people who "live each other's lives and die each other's deaths" (14). It was precisely the 2003 attack and the status of the Taromenani as victims of violence that contributed to this expression of mutuality between themselves and their "uncontacted" neighbors. While Sahlins describes mutuality as a fundamentally human sentiment of belonging shared between people who are "co-present in each other" (11), after the attack many Waorani expressed a similar sentiment in contemplating unknown people as their kin.

Cultivating Contact

My hosts' frequent reiteration of the Taromenani as a source of past or po-tential kinship, whether in remembering kin in the past or desiring relations with them in the future, presents a contrast to Western ideas about "lost" or "uncontacted" people. Just as many Waorani insist on the social closeness they see in uncontacted people, outsiders tend to define and value these groups essentially in terms of segregation and the assumed cultural purity that their isolation confers in Western imagination. And yet Waorani claims to mutuality with the Taromenani do not necessarily entail a sense of shared substance or even physical presence. As Sahlins notes in his proposal for a sociocentric perspective on kinship:

> "[B]eing" in a kinship sense denies the necessary independence of the entities so related, as well as the necessary substantiality and physical-ity of the relationship. . . . If kinsmen are members of one another, then in the manner and to the extent that they are so, experience is diffused

among them. Not in the sense of direct sensation . . . but at the level of meaning. . . . More or less solidary in their being, kinsmen accordingly know each other's doings and sufferings as their own. (2011b, 227–31)

I do not know if the Taromenani share this sense of kinship with their Waorani neighbors in the way some of my hosts claim, but this is beside the point. It is clear, however, that many Waorani embraced a certain sense of mutuality with "uncontacted" people as they came to see their "doings and sufferings as their own." Despite the physical distance that separates them, many Waorani came to see the Taromenani as victims of violence or, more specifically, people who died their own deaths and today live their own lives as kin of victims. Both in this vision of mutual victimhood and in the killers' logic of revenge, death can be seen to rearrange relations among the living in important ways (Lambek 2011). This rearrangement is intense and potentially far reaching in cases of violent death, which has been described in Amazonia to both produce and dissolve relations.[19]

While Waorani ideas about "uncontacted" people appear to sit well with Sahlins's project of decoupling kinship from questions of biology, substance and procreation, they also reveal something of the temporal dimensions of mutuality. Carsten, noting the tendency in anthropology to prioritize the positive qualities of kinship over its negative and coercive qualities, describes how mutual belonging also "accumulates or dissolves over time" (2013, 247). This temporality refers not just to how people and relations are part of a remembered past but also, as we see with Waorani comments on the Taromenani, how they imagine potential kinship futures that "remain unknowable" (Carsten 2013, 248). While it remains to be seen whether my hosts will someday actualize the kinship they see in "uncontacted" people, their status as victims of violence appears to present an opening to a potential future.[20]

Even as Waorani have come to understand the Taromenani in terms of their own concepts of kinship, alterity, and revenge, the politics of isolation described by Bessire (2012), like the politics of indigeneity more generally, has important implications for Amazonian peoples regardless of their degree of integration within national societies. Like Waorani youth who wield spears at frontier folklore festivals and Kayapó elders who draw international media attention from their lip-plugs and colorful body decoration at protests in Brazil, isolation is a potent marker of cultural authenticity in the modern world. In some cases, indigenous people draw effectively on this trope in their engagements with non-indigenous people. Those who fail to live up to these expectations of autonomy and authenticity risk being accused of "losing their culture" and, as a result, having their rights claims ignored in national and global political arenas (Conklin 1997).

At the same time, indigenous Amazonian perspectives on "uncontacted" people tend to be more complex than the Western fantasy of "lost tribes." Whereas most outsiders view "contact" with isolated groups as necessarily degrading a "pure" or "natural" state of being, many Waorani view the isolation of the Taromenani as a tragic and dangerous situation that should be overcome. Their stories about past spear-killings describe a time when Waorani groups lived in relative isolation in distant parts of the forest, a time when confusion and fear made visits and marriage alliances between families extremely difficult. In these stories, it is not the past in general that elders lament but more specifically the sense of fear, loss, and social isolation associated with past revenge killings. While a strongly egalitarian ethos leaves considerable scope for individual and household autonomy, there is also a sense that being alone for too long can be dangerous and should generally be avoided. The association between isolation and potential violence can be seen in how Waorani people express, on the one hand, the importance of living in villages, while on the other hand they insist on their ability to abandon villages in times of conflict. In a similar way, they embrace the Taromenani as exemplars of Waorani autonomy and strength while at the same time recognizing their isolation as a dangerous condition.

It was this concern about the dangers of isolation that people in Toñampari appeared to be voicing after the 2003 attack when they identified the Taromenani as potential kin and called for their "civilization" and incorporation into Waorani communities. For Waorani who live much closer to the Untouchable Zone, this at least partial identification with the Taromenani can be seen as both an act of self-protection and of cultivating contact. Since the attack in 2003, some Waorani have built traditional longhouses (*durani onko*) for the first time in decades so that Taromenani in the area might recognize them as Waorani and not outsiders. The majority of Waorani houses today are similar to those throughout much of rural Amazonian Ecuador, consisting of a basic square construction of machined hardwood planks raised above the ground, with a thatch or corrugated sheet-metal roof. A traditional longhouse, in contrast, can be distinguished clearly by its long, bending roofline that extends unbroken from the ground up to the apex of an A-frame structure, which is almost entirely covered with interwoven palm leaves on all sides. These longhouses, which were the mainstay of large extended families prior to the mission, are in fact very similar in

FIGURE 13. A typical house in a Woarani village along the Curaray River

FIGURE 14. *Durani onko*: living like the ancient ones

appearance to those of the Taromenani discovered at the site of the 2003 massacre and aerial photographs of groups living in the Untouchable Zone.

While uncontacted people are widely thought to be hostile to contact with outsiders, including Waorani, some of my hosts describe how the Taromenani are able to distinguish between Waorani houses and those of non-indigenous people. One young man explained that his relatives replaced their previous kowori-style house with a traditional longhouse to deter potential attacks by Taromenani. In his view, the widespread use of Western construction materials and clothing risk making Waorani indistinguishable in appearance from kowori, leading Taromenani to think he and his neighbors are in fact kowori. A similar concern about misrecognition emerged in discussions of hunting, whereby some men began hunting without clothes so that the Taromenani who see them in the forest would not mistake them for kowori colonists or loggers. In recent years Waorani have reported fleeting encounters with uncontacted people while hunting or traveling through remote parts of the reserve. Some of them describe Taromenani visiting Waorani gardens to gather food or even seeking shelter in abandoned houses near a village. They also describe peaceful encounters prior to the 2003 attack, in which Taromenani approached Waorani elders in remote areas and explained their tentative desire to live among the Waorani. Regardless of what actually happened in these encounters, many Waorani emphasize the need to prevent revenge attacks and to make peaceful contact with the Taromenani possible.[21]

Since the 2003 killings, the Taromenani have become an object not only of fear but also of respect and fascination for many Waorani, particularly young people. One young man described to me how he wished to marry a Taromenani woman and join her group to live, as he described, "like the ancestors" (durani bai). While in certain intercultural contexts Waorani reproduce colonial fantasies about "wild" Amazonian warriors, their response to the 2003 killings and their comments on the Taromenani also challenge popular ideas of what it means to be "uncontacted." For many Waorani these are not "naturally" isolated people but are instead long-lost relatives, potential spouses, and a powerful symbol of ancestral power, autonomy, and violence in the face of colonization.

In Amazonia and elsewhere, anthropologists have described how and why indigenous people have sought contact with white people and other outsiders at specific historical moments. In some cases, such as that of the Wari described by Vilaça (2010) in Brazil, these encounters presented opportunities to make or renew relations within indigenous societies. Despite the proliferation of writing on alterity among anthropologists, few consider indigenous perspectives on encounters with so-called uncontacted people.[22] One exception is Myers's (1988) description of how, in the context of a headline story about the discovery of a "lost tribe" in Australia in 1984, his aboriginal Pintupi interlocutors insisted that their newly contacted neighbors in the Western Desert were in fact "relatives" who were tragically "left behind" in previous times (614). Like my Waorani friends today, the Pintupi fundamentally challenged the nonrelational status often attributed to so-called uncontacted people. But more important, in both of these cases indigenous people can be seen to draw on such encounters to insist on their own cultural autonomy. For the Pintupi, the ability to define the event of "contact" on their own terms constituted a political stance against the intervention of white people and the government. At the same time, a global politics of isolation that presumes segregation to be the will of "isolated subjects" can render indigenous leaders "inaudible in the name of self-determination" when they seek interventions that would challenge segregation (Bessire 2012, 480–81).

After the 2003 killings Waorani political leaders drew on a combination of this politics of isolation and popular media representations of "tribal violence" to deter state intervention. As the massacre came to be defined as an "indigenous issue," the national media wasted little time in presenting it as the latest outbreak of Waorani violence, reminding the wider public of missionaries and oil workers killed by Waorani since the 1940s. Stories that circulated about the attackers using traditional spears, rather than guns, and images of a severed head taken from a victim only reaffirmed the "primitive" nature of the attack. So excited were journalists about the prospect of documenting apparently genuine tribal violence that some of the killers were offered trips to the Ecuadorian coast for interviewing and sightseeing (Cabodevilla 2004c, 62). Rather than being prosecuted for acts of murder, which some of the killers openly admitted to, they became an emblem of indigenous autonomy and exotic savagery, the "wild" Amazonian warriors of colonial imagination (Salomon 1981; Taussig 1987; Whitten 1988). What appeared to be ignored in this articulation of the politics of isolation were the external causes of violence and isolation in Amazonia. Instead, the taking of a Taromenani head and the killers' insistence that they used only spears asserted indigenous autonomy and appealed to popular imagery of Waorani violence.

Conclusion

Whether we consider the logic of revenge that appears to have motivated the killers or Waorani concerns about losing potential kin, the Taromenani massacre illustrates how violence at once creates and transcends boundaries between kinship and enmity. Anthropologists have described how relations of enmity and revenge are an integral part of Amazonian symbolic economies, where personhood and the reproduction of society are often closely tied to ideas about killing and predation.[23] Yet Waorani reactions to the recent killings also reveal how indigenous understandings of violence are closely related to wider political and economic processes that extend beyond relations within and between indigenous societies. However, rather than explaining violence as simply an effect of externally driven power relations, whether the force of colonial history or contemporary development agendas in Amazonia, in this chapter I have focused on how Waorani people make sense of these translocal relations according to their own concepts of how relations are constituted.

Their interpretations of the 2003 Taromenani attack point to how the revitalization of so-called "tribal" violence in Amazonia cannot be simply explained as the result of either external forces or a preexisting "traditional" cosmological order. Rather than affirming, as a Western politics of isolation would have it, an artificial analytical divide between "traditional" forms of violence and "modern" processes, I suggest that these two seemingly distinct levels of analysis cannot in fact be separated. As Stasch (2009) argues, one of the key tasks of anthropology is not simply to examine how "people's social lives are structured by non-local institutions and cultural influences" but to study otherness "as an internal feature of local social relations and local social practices" (9). In this way, missionaries, oil companies, loggers, and anthropologists all emerge as part of a Waorani lived world, whether as dangerous enemies or as kin. After the transformations of recent decades it should not be completely surprising that missionaries and Taromenani have become part of indigenous conceptualizations of this changing social world. For many Waorani certain kowori appear, like the Taromenani, not just dangerous but also familiar and close to themselves.

One of the major obstacles missionaries faced in attempting to make peaceful contact in the 1950s was that the Waorani feared kowori outsiders to be cannibals bent on killing and devouring them. As most Waorani today are confident that this is not the case, the notion that real or potential kin are victims of violence has been extended to include those kowori with whom they appear to share this position. Both the mysterious Taromenani and particular missionaries have come to be seen as socially proximate to Waorani people, as people with whom they share a certain sense of mutuality. In many Amazonian societies the act of killing an enemy, perhaps the ultimate act of crossing socio-cosmological boundaries, produces new kinds of people and new relations. For Waorani people, however, it is the status of being kin of victims that distinguishes internal sociality in contrast to the violence of outsiders, even if people as close as kin are always at risk of becoming something else through their grief and anger. While the notion of being a common community of victims is central to how relations are conceptually transformed between Waorani groups and in relation to the Taromenani, the following two chapters examine how people attempt to create the conditions for peaceful conviviality in the village of Toñampari.

CHAPTER 5

Intimate Others

Whether distinguishing victims from perpetrators and Waorani from kowori people or envisioning kinship relations with "uncontacted" groups, the kinds of remembering I have described are as much about mutual experiences as they are social differences. In Toñampari, where my hosts interact with and evaluate the practices of their Waorani and kowori neighbors in their everyday lives, Quichua people are a key point of reference in Waorani discussions of violence, translocal relations, and everyday interactions. For decades they have been the archetypical kowori—a category that I translate at different points in this book as "outsiders," "enemies," or simply "non-Waorani people." Since the period of mission settlement, Quichua-speaking people have been the kowori with whom Waorani people are most familiar and, in many ways, most concerned.

This chapter and the next focus on what Waorani people say about their Quichua neighbors and how they interact with them. Quichuas have a seemingly enigmatic position in Toñampari, where they are described as morally deficient in Waorani discourse at the same time as they are highly desired spouses. While Waorani distinguish the consumption of alcohol as a key feature of kowori behavior, they also associate Quichuas more specifically with envy, the use of money, and witchcraft. Despite these moral evaluations, a growing number of Quichua people are coming to live alongside the Waorani through interethnic marriages.[1] The perspectives of people involved in these marriages and those of young men aspiring to marry Quichua women illuminate the indigenous logic by which by which "enemies" are incorporated into Waorani communities. Young men prefer Quichua brides not only for the translocal links and exchange relations they bring but also for the kinds of autonomy these marriages allow them in the villages where they live. Wao-Quichua marriages are part of both a dynamic history of intercultural relations and indigenous understandings of kinship and marriage. In placing the present ethnography in the context of wider debates about alterity in Amazonia, I hope to make sense of why, for Waorani people in Toñampari and elsewhere, "enemies" make such good affines.

Placing Quichuas

The violence and isolation for which the Waorani have come to be known often obscures the complex history of intercultural relations of which they are part. At first sight, the increasing presence of Quichua people in Toñampari and other Waorani villages sits strangely alongside elders' stories about aggressive kowori whom they until recently assumed to be cannibals. Today many Waorani are choosing to marry these former "enemies," bringing Quichua and other kowori spouses to live with them and raise families in their own homes and villages. Although they have changed significantly in form, scale, and importance over the past century, Wao-Quichua marriages are not a completely new phenomenon and are part of a wider historical context of social transformation in Amazonian Ecuador.

Located on the left bank of the Curaray River, the village of Toñampari is in an area that only relatively recently came to be inhabited by Waorani people. The Curaray was once home to the Zapara, an indigenous population that all but disappeared as a result of warfare and disease in the nineteenth and early twentieth centuries. Quichua families from surrounding areas subsequently moved to the Curaray, where they intermarried with the surviving Zapara and remained until they abandoned the Curaray in the 1930s as a result of a yellow fever epidemic (Reeve 1988, 1993a, 2002). It was at this time that Waorani from the east moved to the Curaray, a place many Waorani acknowledge as having previously been inhabited by Quichuas. The original Quichua/Zapara population returned to the Curaray later in the 1930s, as did Napo Quichuas from the north and Achuar from the south (Reeve and High 2012, 145). This process of repopulation along the Curaray coincided with violent conflicts between Waorani and Quichuas during much of the twentieth century, with Waorani people defending their lands from what they saw as kowori intruders and Quichuas seeking access to key resources on lands they once inhabited.

Historical evidence suggests that Wao-Quichua relations were not exclusively violent prior to mission settlement. As in much of Amazonia (Lévi-Strauss [1943] 1976), interethnic relations between Waorani and Quichua people have oscillated between, on the one hand, fear and violence, and on the other, tentative friendship, exchange, and alliance (Reeve and High 2012). In many cases, colonial history, missionaries, and new forms of economic development have had an important role in these shifts. In the 1940s, Royal Dutch Shell began oil exploration in Amazonian Ecuador, exacerbating the violence between Waorani groups and conflicts with Quichuas. At this time, several oil company employees were killed as they encroached on Waorani lands, while a number of Waorani died at the hands of kowori shotguns. As Waorani carried out spear-killing raids against kowori and each other in some cases to acquire steel tools (Blomberg 1956; Cipolletti 2002), Wao-Quichua relations became increasingly characterized by avoidance and violence. Stories about Waorani people killing Quichuas at this time contributed to popular Ecuadorian representations of the Waorani as "wild" aucas.

Even as Waorani feared kowori intruders, in some contexts they accommodated their presence and reportedly engaged in sporadic forms of exchange with Quichuas who worked as oil company employees. According to the account of one missionary, Quichuas were allowed access to fishing along certain rivers in the Waorani territory (Elliot 1957). Even from the scant historical documentation prior to the 1960s, it appears that Waorani were intent on incorporating Quichuas into their households. This can be seen in the accounts of Quichua women who were abducted by Waorani in the first half of the twentieth century. One of these women was Joaquina Grefa, who was abducted in 1944 and later told the story of her abduction to English missionary Wilfred Tidmarsh (Tidmarsh and Grefa 1945). Grefa, whose account includes a list of Waorani words and the names of people with whom she lived for one year, explained how she was accepted and incorporated as a wife by her captors until she escaped and returned to her Quichua relatives.[2] Later accounts describe other Quichua women who were abducted and incorporated into Waorani households as wives, one of whom was later returned to her Quichua family upon the request of missionaries (Wallis 1973).[3]

Wao-Quichua relations changed dramatically in the 1960s, when many Waorani joined the Evangelical mission in Tiweno near the headwaters of the Curaray. In addition to bringing rival "upriver" and "downriver" Waorani groups together to live in a single village, the missionaries facilitated interethnic marriages between Waorani and Quichuas. For the missionaries, these marriages were part of a strategy to overcome decades of violence and distrust between rival Waorani groups and between Waorani and Quichuas. They envisioned interethnic marriages as part of a "civilizing" process they hoped would replace the traditional Waorani practices of polygyny and cross-cousin marriage. Although the missionaries had a clear agenda in this process, many Waorani were attracted to the mission precisely because of the intercultural opportunities it offered. Interethnic marriages presented an alternative to marriages between Waorani groups with a long history of violence and mutual distrust. Elders today explain how, at the time preceding the mission, the possibilities for arranging marriages were restricted as a result of revenge killings between Waorani groups. In the context of killing vendettas and violent encounters with kowori that had depleted and isolated Waorani groups, they found in the mission a valued source of manufactured goods and potential marriage alliances (Yost 1981).

According to missionary writings (Wallis 1973) and the accounts of Toñampari residents today, Rachel Saint and Dayuma had a key role in promoting interethnic marriages at the mission. Yost (1981) describes how Dayuma and the other recent Christian converts became "cultural brokers" who benefited from arranging Wao-Quichua marriages. As Waorani men joined oil company crews in the late 1970s, they forged formal friendships with Quichuas from Napo and Curaray that led to several interethnic marriages. While relations between Waorani and Quichua people have generally remained apprehensive in recent decades, including occasional killings, specific extended family ties dating back to the mission continue to be the basis of interethnic marriages in Toñampari and other Waorani villages along the Curaray River (Reeve and High 2012). The pattern of interethnic marriage that began at Tiweno has continued and increased since the official departure of SIL missionaries more than thirty years ago. Today Quichuas have become the preferred spouses in many Waorani villages, and some communities like Toñampari are attracting ever-larger numbers of Quichua residents.

Waorani describe a diverse range of Quichua-speaking indigenous people under the label of "Quichuas." Many Quichuas, who call themselves *Runa*, are descendants of indigenous people who intermarried across different territories and languages of the Upper Amazon in part as a survival strategy in the wake of colonialism (Whitten and Whitten 2008, 52). Historically, the dispersal and aggregation of distinct indigenous groups, often at mission settlements, has been an important aspect of ongoing processes of ethnogenesis in the region (Whitten 1976b). Many Quichuas who live along the Curaray today are descendants of other ethnic groups, and as a result are bilingual in Quichua and Achuar or Shuar (Reeve and High, 144). Rather than "acculturated" or degraded remnants of "authentic" indigenous societies, the contemporary practices and cosmologies of these groups constitute an indigenous Amazonian cultural form that has transformed and adapted to historical processes of ethnogenesis (Whitten and Whitten 2011).[4] For many Quichua and other indigenous peoples in Ecuador, multilingualism and intercultural relations are not new phenomena but enduring aspects of ethnic identity and historical consciousness.

Quichua-speaking communities constitute the largest indigenous ethnicity in Amazonian Ecuador, likely numbering more than one hundred thousand people.[5] Quichua villages can be found in some of the most remote jungles of eastern Ecuador and in the outskirts of sprawling regional cities, such as Puyo, Tena, and Coca. Some of these communities have grown into local hubs of commerce and transport where mestizos and members of different indigenous groups are attracted to the marketplace. In recent decades they have demonstrated formidable political solidarity as an ethnic bloc in regional and national indigenous movements (Sawyer 2004; Whitten 1997; Whitten and Whitten 2011). Quichua people also embrace more specific local identities in reference to prominent rivers, communities, and provinces. Some of these distinct groups include the Napo Runa (or Napo Quichua) (Macdonald 1999; Uzendoski 2005); Curaray Quichua (Reeve 2002); and Canelos Quichua (Whitten 1976a). Being native speakers of the Quichua language is one of the key features that unites these indigenous people across several areas of Amazonian Ecuador.

Quichuas generally have more sustained interactions with urban centers and popular Ecuadorian culture than Waorani people and therefore tend to speak more Spanish. They have adopted diverse subsistence strategies, ranging from agriculture and cattle ranching (Macdonald 1981) to a variety of urban business enterprises, including shops, restaurants, and ecotourism projects. Rival (2002) contrasts the Waorani as mobile forest trekkers to Quichuas and other indigenous groups who have a much longer history of contact with colonial influences and the cash economy. For Rival, even manioc cultivation and other gardening practices are peripheral to the hunting and trekking culture of the Waorani. This is contrasted to other indigenous Amazonian people like Quichuas, who have a tradition of intensive sedentary gardening. While autonomy, mobility, and hunting are certainly important to Waorani people, popular stereotypes tend to exaggerate the actual cultural differences between supposedly "wild" Waorani and "civilized" Quichuas. Regardless of the similarities and differences between these groups, Waorani and Quichua people tend to emphasize strong social differences in reference to each other. In the following section I explore how Waorani people assign moral values to these perceived differences.

Moral Others

As I sat around the warm hearth early one evening, Gaba was entertaining his family with stories about the day's hunt. He had returned with two *yawe* (toucans), which he had shot along a river some three hours' walk to the north, and a spider monkey he had encountered on the edge of a manioc garden outside the village. His wife seemed pleased as she cut up the monkey meat and her daughters carefully plucked the birds' feathers. Soon Gaba launched into a story about how he and his friend Iteka had encountered a large *ore* (white lipped peccary) that narrowly escaped a close-range shot from Iteka's shotgun. Mimicking the animal's movements after the shot was fired, he explained how the peccary stood strangely still as the hunters initially approached it. Despite the peccary's narrow escape, Gaba and his small audience appeared pleased with the daily hunting report as they laughed and ate their meat along with boiled manioc, the staple accompaniment to meat.

Perhaps because of the good food and entertaining stories, on this evening we stayed up later than usual. Before long we heard the sound of Ecuadorian pop music bursting from a stereo system powered by a gas generator near the village airstrip, about one kilometer away. In recent weeks a couple of families had been hosting parties attended by teenagers from the school and their teachers. Along with the loud music, which persists until the host's supply of petrol runs dry, these "fiestas" consist primarily of Ecuadorian-style dancing and drinking alcohol. I attended several of these parties in Toñampari during my fieldwork, both in people's homes and at official events organized at the *ñene onko* (communal house).

Two of the teenagers in my host family had already left for the party when I asked Gaba about the parties and the people who attend them. Gaba described the music we could hear in the distance as a kowori phenomenon, which he contrasted sharply to Waorani behavior. In particular, Gaba rejects the consumption of *tiname* (hard cane liquor) as a kowori practice. For many of his generation, part of being a Waorani person is drinking unfermented variations of *tepe* (manioc beer), *peneme* (a sweet mashed plantain drink), and seasonal drinks such as *dagengkai*, made from the delicious cooked chonta fruit between December and April. None of these drinks have a significant alcohol content and are often consumed in massive quantities that swell the belly to a tight roundness. Gaba and other Waorani are aware that they are the only indigenous group in the region that does not let their manioc beer sit to ferment for days or weeks. Most families are more inclined to throw out the manioc pulp if any remains after a few days than to drink it. They associate "strong" manioc beer (Spanish: *chicha fuerte*) with Quichua people, who they say have a long tradition of making alcoholic drinks and purchasing tiname (Spanish: *puro*) produced in frontier areas of Amazonian Ecuador.

As Gaba spoke about the party, he attributed what he sees as objectionable kowori behavior to the presence of Quichua people in Toñampari. He explained that it is Quichuas who bring tiname into the community, produce strong manioc beer, and host drinking and dancing into the late hours of the night. For Gaba and many other adults alcohol is part of how they distinguish Quichuas as people who are morally different to themselves. Gaba frequently pointed out that Quichua men beat their wives and children when they drink and become too lazy to hunt. This was not the first time I heard Gaba criticize drinking or his Quichua neighbors. During my fieldwork I saw him warn his neighbors and peers of the dangers of this behavior at community meetings. Despite the generally amicable relations in Toñampari, I encountered a number of situations where my Waorani hosts contrasted Quichua practices to their own. These caricatures became a lens through which I was to interpret what living alongside kowori neighbors means to them.

While many young Waorani men now take part in the binge drinking found throughout much of Amazonian Ecuador, the consumption of alcohol is still considered by most to be a particularly kowori activity. Waorani are aware that much, though not all, alcohol consumed in villages like Toñampari is of Quichua origin. Since "strong" manioc beer is made from ingredients readily available in the area, Quichua women in Toñampari often produce this alcoholic beverage and serve it in their homes and at village meetings, school celebrations, and household parties. In recent years fermented manioc beer (mixed with mature plantain for higher potency) has become a typical feature of these events. Quichua men in Toñampari also bring large drums of cheap cane liquor back from their trips to the city. While the locally produced brew causes occasional drunkenness, the potency of commercial liquor sometimes leads to severe inebriation, especially among Waorani who have relatively little experience with distilled spirits.[6] In 2003 there were occasional fights between young Waorani men after drinking parties, an occurrence that was unknown in Toñampari during my first fieldwork in the late 1990s. The presence of alcohol has caught the attention of Waorani elders who speak out against young people for behaving *kowori bai* ("like *kowori* people"). One of the oldest women in Toñampari went as far as sending a letter to the pilots who fly into the village, imploring them not to allow alcohol to be transported on their flights.

When asked about the differences between Waorani and Quichua people, many Waorani say that Quichuas drink strong manioc beer and *trago* (liquor), whereas they themselves drink manioc beer fresh with relatively little alcohol. Some of these same Waorani adults drink heavily at community events in the village alongside their Quichua neighbors. Despite associating alcohol consumption specifically with Quichuas and other kowori, sharing in these practices does not appear to erode the sense that drinking alcohol is a particularly Quichua activity. Commentaries about drinking are just one of many ways that Waorani people contrast Quichua practices to their own. Given the history and social geography of eastern Ecuador, it is no coincidence that Waorani people draw a sharp distinction between themselves and the indigenous group with the largest presence in and around their territory. They are well aware that Quichuas constitute a larger group and have more experience in urban areas of Ecuador. Although Waorani criticize behavior they associate with non-Waorani people generally, Quichuas are the paradigmatic kowori in local discourse.

At the time of my main fieldwork, Waorani also associated Quichuas specifically with money and commerce. In Toñampari some Quichua women had established a form of local micro-enterprise through contacts in the city who sent basic foodstuffs and manufactured goods to them for resale in the village. One such woman, for example, had a small stock of rice, oatmeal, cooking oil, soap, cookies, cigarettes, and bottled cane liquor in her home. At any one time she was unlikely to have all of these items on hand, but occasionally she had a limited number of additional manufactured goods, such as tins of meat or candles. Although Quichua men and the Waorani spouses of Quichua women sometimes support this form of business by bringing goods back from their trips to the city, the commerce in Toñampari is handled almost exclusively by Quichua women. In contrast to houses, which are normally known by the name of the father or senior male resident, shops are associated with the women who run them. According to local residents, this small-scale commerce and the consumption of alcohol in Toñampari originated with the arrival of Quichua and mestizo school-teachers, who used shops as a way of supplementing their low salaries.[7]

Waorani people are aware that, more often than not, they must pay for kowori goods or *cosas de afuera* ("things from outside") when visiting towns and cities. However, they often cite payment for goods as a distinguishing feature of Quichua relations. They explicitly contrast monetary transactions to the sharing economy of their own households, where guests are to be served food or drink without compensation or expectation of repayment. Indeed, I have never seen a Waorani person ask for money in exchange for food. Although in practice they accept the commercial practices of Quichuas and occasionally buy items from them with money received from distant oil work or school scholarships, they reject this form of exchange in their own homes. On several occasions my hosts proudly explained to me that, unlike Quichuas, who demand payment, Waorani people always share their food and manioc beer with visitors.[8] Without simply accepting this claim, commerce appears to be a key marker of social difference between Waorani and Quichua people in Toñampari.

In practice, rather than rejecting commerce altogether, Waorani people generally keep the commercial practices of Quichuas separate from the sharing economy within Waorani household clusters. These efforts can be seen in the following description of two of the households I know best in Toñampari.

Maria is a Quichua woman who runs a shop in her home in Toñampari. At the time of my fieldwork, she lived with her Wao husband and children not far from Gaba's house. Since her husband is the younger sibling of Gaba's wife, the two families were part of the same group of households who regularly visit, work in the gardens together, and share food. Since Gaba is a skilled hunter, Maria and her husband often received excess meat from his household. Although her family seldom had sufficient game meat to share with others, to my knowledge they never incorporated the wares of her shop into this network of sharing. The sale of kowori goods was controlled exclusively by Maria and was kept separate from the circulation of food between households. I never saw a member of Gaba's household make a purchase from her, nor did her husband sell the goods. When asked about Maria's shop, Gaba commented that *kowori kengi* ("outsider food") is expensive and tastes bad, insisting that he can hunt better food in the forest without having to pay anything. This criticism of city food did not stop my hosts from happily accepting the bags of rice, beans, and other foodstuffs I occasionally brought with me to the village or the handouts of bread or candy made by visiting politicians and missionaries. Gifts of kowori goods are in fact highly coveted and even demanded in the context of relations with oil companies (Rival 2000). It is not so much the taste or quality of the food that Waorani people reject in this context but rather the kind of relation that purchasing food from a neighbor presents for them. They often contrasted Maria's shop to their own generosity as hosts and the Waorani logic that food is abundant and can be exploited freely by anyone willing to do so.

For many Waorani who criticize the practices of Quichuas, the moral connotations of alcohol and commerce are closely linked, as local shops are at times a source of hard liquor. The ways many Waorani youth embrace drinking and the availability of "outside" goods in Toñampari is part of an increasing gap between generations. However, many of the same Waorani teenagers who embrace drinking tiname and eating rice contrast themselves to Quichua people in much the same way as their parents do. Although they are less likely to draw on these distinctions in the presence of Quichuas at drinking parties or when buying items at shops, they voice this sense of difference in the presence of their parents and elders.

Practices associated with Quichuas are not always seen in purely negative terms. On a number of occasions my Waorani hosts demonstrated enthusiastically to me their knowledge of Quichua practices. Maria's Wao husband once proudly taught me to prepare smoked fish (*maito*) by wrapping it in leaves with salt and manioc "like Quichua people do." This same man, who often praised the novelty of Quichua foods, money, and other things he associates with his wife's background, on other occasions insisted on the superiority of Waorani practices, such as providing food for guests and boiling meat in a pot without spices. This ambiguity also emerged in his attitude toward alcohol, which he both consumes regularly and has denounced publicly as a kowori or Quichua practice. In this way Quichua people are a key reference point in indigenous understandings of social difference at the same time as their presence in Toñampari has become increasingly acceptable and desirable.

Living Together

One feature that distinguishes Toñampari from other Waorani villages is the proportion of Quichua people who live there. Most Quichua adults in Toñampari have married a Waorani spouse. At the time of my main fieldwork in 2004, approximately half the twenty-eight households in the village included one Quichua spouse. While the number of Quichua women is significantly higher than that of men, there are also several Quichua men in Toñampari who are married to Waorani women. These men are often close relatives (siblings or first cousins) of Quichua women who previously married into Waorani families. Some of the most recent Quichua brides to arrive in Toñampari have explained to me that having close relatives already in the village makes life more pleasant for them, especially in their initial months living in a foreign community. In addition to the convenience of having at least a few neighbors from one's home community who speak the same native language, this tendency for Quichua spouses to follow the lines of previous interethnic marriages to Waorani villages reflects enduring alliances between specific extended families (Reeve and High 2012). Some Quichua men in Toñampari have links to the Waorani that extend back to their childhood and the mission settlement. Two were adopted by Waorani families in Tiweno in the 1960s, and one explained to me that he was abducted by Waorani during a raid prior to the missionary period in which his parents were killed. After the death of his Waorani wife, the man now lives in Toñampari with his Quichua wife.

There are also Quichua students in Toñampari who, with the invitation of their kin already living in the village, come from areas around the cities of Puyo and Tena to study at the village school. They typically describe life in Toñampari as an opportunity to study without the costs of living "afuera" ("on the outside"). Despite the negative stereotypes of the Waorani in much of Amazonian Ecuador, Quichuas see advantages in living in the vast and seemingly inexhaustible Waorani territory. Quichua people I encountered in frontier towns often described to me the rich forestlands and wealth of animals that the Waorani enjoy on their reserve. There are frequent conflicts between Quichua communities located on the borders of the reserve and Waorani who resent their hunting, fishing, and logging on Waorani lands. These clashes have led to the killing of a number of Quichuas in recent years, and serious tensions remain in some areas. While Waorani often describe these conflicts as a "Quichua problem," the enduring alliances between specific Waorani and Quichua extended family groups established through past marriages persist despite these tensions (Reeve and High 2012).

When I asked Quichua men why they came to live in the Waorani territory, they sometimes mentioned the relative economic independence of living far from roads and cities. Quichua women seldom describe coming to live with the Waorani as their own choice but rather the result of a decision made by their fathers. My Waorani hosts often explained to me the desire of Quichuas to inhabit their lands, citing their perceived envy as an explanation for witchcraft (see chapter 6). Waorani motives for marrying Quichuas appear to be slightly different from the economic factors that reportedly attract Quichua families to interethnic marriages. Young Waorani men often told me that they hoped to eventually marry a Quichua woman. When I asked why, they generally had little to say about their reasoning: some simply replied "I don't know" (*iñinamai*) or that Quichua women are "beautiful" (*waimo*). Their short and inconsistent explanations left me confused after hearing their critical views of Quichua people and their practices. When I asked women and elders why young men seek Quichua brides, they often said something to the effect that marrying a Quichua would bring more access to kowori goods, relationships, and lifestyle. I found this explanation insufficient because, although some people who marry Quichuas are involved in broader social networks outside their territory, they appear to gain few material advantages through interethnic marriages and almost invariably continue to live in their own community.

I began to understand more of the Waorani logic in these interethnic marriages only by listening to the reflections of men and women already involved in them and the plans of young men hoping to marry a Quichua. Wareka, a Waorani man who has raised six children with his Quichua wife over the past twenty years, told me the following story in response to my question about why he sought a Quichua wife:

> I went with two friends to Arajuno, where the Quichuas live . . . where my father-in-law lives. We went to his house. All three of us were looking for Quichuas to marry, so we asked him if we could marry his daughters. He only had one daughter to marry. He was a good man. He said I could marry his daughter if I brought ten large baskets of meat for him (showing me the size with his hands). There were no women for my friends, so they couldn't marry. I went back to Toñampari and went hunting in the forest. I hunted for weeks, and killed a big tapir, howler monkeys, and white-lipped peccaries. There was so much meat! It was a lot of work, but we filled ten baskets with meat for my father-in-law. We took it to him and I got my wife. That is how the Quichuas marry.

According to Wareka, he had not met his wife before arriving in Arajuno to make his request. Like other men of his generation, he went because he wanted to marry a Quichua woman rather than to court a particular woman he had met previously. Soon after delivering the meat to his father-in-law,

Wareka and his wife left for Toñampari to live with his parents. They later had children, built their own house, and became part of a cluster of three sharing households that included Wareka's parents and his older sister and her husband's family. While Wareka reflected on his own experience of interethnic marriage with a sense of humor and exotic adventure, his wife Luisa's account of their marriage had a different tone:

> When he (Wareka) came to our house, I didn't know him. I was scared. My father told me Wareka wanted to marry me, and I was scared. I didn't want to marry him, but my father said I had to. I cried a lot and wondered what would happen to me. I didn't know the Waorani or speak their language. I only heard that they killed people with spears and lived in the forest. I was scared that they would kill me and did not want to leave my father. But my father made me go with him. . . .
>
> I came here [Toñampari] to his family. I thought they were going to kill me. Everything was different, and I didn't understand anything because I didn't speak Wao. We lived here with Wareka's mother and father. They kept talking to me but I didn't understand anything. I was scared and I cried a lot. In Arajuno we live differently. . . .

Like most Quichua women and men who marry Waorani in Toñampari, Luisa eventually learned to speak Wao-terero and has adapted to life in what she sees as a radically different social environment. Wao-terero is normally the primary language in these households, though many Waorani men with Quichua spouses, and to some extent their children, speak at least basic Quichua. As a result, despite the dominance of Waorani language in much of everyday life, a considerable amount of code-switching between Wao-terero and Quichua occurs in households like Wareka and Luisa's, especially when Quichua neighbors come to visit. While Luisa came from Arajuno, a large Quichua settlement two days' walk from Toñampari, other Quichua residents in Toñampari come from several other areas, including the communities along the road to Tena and the village of Curaray to the east. There are also a small number of marriages between Waorani and Shuar, most of whom come from the southern part of Amazonian Ecuador.

Many of the young men who said little about why they wanted to marry a Quichua woman did explain *how* they intended to marry. Their plans were in many ways similar to Wareka's dealings with Luisa's father. Two young men complained to me about the difficulty of acquiring a Quichua wife due to the expense of compensating her family and starting one's own household. They described these marriages as "expensive," contrasting this

FIGURE 15. Waorani on an oil company truck in the Yasuní National Park

practice of brideprice to Waorani marriages in which no payment is made. The answer to this problem for Wareka twenty years ago was to embark on a massive hunting expedition with the help of kin and to live with his parents upon marrying his new bride. Today many young men see employment with oil companies as an opportunity to accumulate the money necessary to marry a Quichua wife. One young man explained to me in detail his plan to work a few months for an oil company in the far eastern region of the Waorani reserve to earn enough money to buy a cooking stove and other manufactured items to deliver to a Quichua family with an eligible daughter. I heard similar plans from men who said their parents insisted that they establish themselves through oil work before marriage. Although nobody mentioned having made prior arrangements with a particular Quichua family, the specifics of their plans suggested to me that some men had perhaps already made formal arrangements to marry.

It is commonplace for young Waorani men to be employed by oil companies in the eastern part of the Waorani reserve, where they tend to work short contracts for two or three months before returning to live in their home villages. The work is well paid relative to other jobs in Ecuador. In

2003 men were paid around $400 per month for clearing vegetation along oil roads and other labor-intensive jobs. A few Waorani men have been trained as truck drivers, and others are employed in *relaciones comunitarias* ("community relations") to negotiate conflicts between oil companies and Waorani who live in the path of oil development. The contracts of these briefly well-paid negotiators are normally terminated once an agreement is reached with the community in question. In addition to the income that short-term employment provides, working for the oil companies brings Waorani men into contact with more kowori people, including oil company representatives and Quichuas. In the early years of the twenty-first century, it was at least partially through the income and personal contacts of oil work that Quichua spouses become more attainable for young Waorani men. Opportunities to visit distant villages, familiarize themselves with other ecological areas, and meet kowori people are all factors that draw them to work in the oil areas.

Like young men, young Waorani women in Toñampari to some extent appear also to prefer Quichua spouses. However, they were even less willing than their male counterparts to discuss the topic with me during my fieldwork.[9] My questions about why women marry Quichuas were often met with nervous laughter or silence. Women I knew well sometimes responded that they would not marry a kowori man. Occasionally, however, the teenage daughters of "mixed" marriages stated that they preferred not to marry a Wao man but rather a Quichua, without any subsequent explanation of why. It is unclear whether the current pattern of Waorani women marrying Quichua men is a response to the lack of eligible men not already married to Quichuas or if it reflects a more specific preference for Quichua men.

From Enemies to Affines

The Christian mission had an important role in facilitating interethnic marriages in the 1960s and 1970s. However, the large number of these marriages in Waorani villages today is also part of an indigenous logic of kinship and marriage. Marrying Quichuas has become a desirable alternative for people and households who seek to maintain a degree of autonomy in the context of recent social transformations. This becomes particularly clear in the context of changing postmarital residence that interethnic marriages bring to Waorani villages.

In part as a result of the traditional practice of cross-cousin marriage that is still prevalent today, previous ethnographers have described the Wa-

FIGURE 16. A man collects fish with his son-in-law

orani in terms of a Dravidian kinship terminology (Rival 2002; Robarchek and Robarchek 1998). Upon marriage a man is normally expected to move into the house of his bride's family, where he contributes to the household economy through hunting, fishing, and clearing gardens with his affines. This period of matrilocal residence continues until the couple has children and establishes a new household of their own. Although there is nothing in the way of "brideprice," marriage does involve, for the man, a certain level of obligation to his in-laws, especially during his co-residence with them.

The dramatic transition that marriage marks in a person's life can be seen in how Waorani couples are married and what this relationship entails. Marriage implies different things for men and women in terms of residential movement, but for both it involves a transition from the freedom of adolescence to the roles and expectations of a productive adult life. Having children is a central part of this productive capacity (Rival 1996), as is the expectation that women establish their own larger gardens, and that men hunt and fish more regularly to support the household. While people are capable in these tasks from an early age, upon marriage men and women are expected to become the key productive members of the woman's natal household and eventually their own. Aware that marriage in many ways involves more definite demands on everyday life, young people of both sexes tend to avoid marriage as long as possible.

This avoidance of marriage has important implications in relatively large villages like Toñampari. Young people take great care not to make premarital sexual relations known, especially to older adults. As public recognition of these relations (epitomized by a woman becoming pregnant) may lead elders to arrange for the couple's marriage, teenagers tend to keep cross-sex intimacy more hidden than same-sex intimacy. It is not uncommon to see young men sitting on one another's lap or holding hands at an eëme festival or girls walking arm in arm along the village airstrip or in the forest. In contrast, one rarely sees intimacy between young people of the opposite sex in Waorani villages, and the Ecuadorian practice of having a "boyfriend" or "girlfriend" was all but completely absent during my fieldwork. Making a heterosexual relationship public in this way would place the couple at risk of being married against their will. It was not long after beginning fieldwork that I realized how young people seldom even refer to people of the opposite sex (especially of their same generation) as "friends," as the Spanish word *amiga* or *amigo* implies that the person might be a lover.[10] As a result, my descriptions of women as "friends" and the visit of my then girlfriend in Toñampari were met with much laughter.

It is precisely this danger of sexual relations slipping into the expectations of productive married adult life that is the subject of much sexual banter between Waorani men. Male teenagers often tease one another with accusations that someone or another has made a woman pregnant. They jokingly refer to such a man as a *geremempo* ("baby-father"), a status in which a man is expected to observe the same dietary taboos as women associated with the couvade.[11] A geremempo, like a pregnant woman, can also expect to suffer a number of calamities, such as the inability to hunt or fish and general fatigue. Unsuccessful collective fishing trips are attributed to either a pregnant woman (*geremara*) or a geremempo being in the water at the time of fishing, causing the fish poison to lose its potency. Men who appear lazy or tired as they sit in their hammocks risk being called a *geremempo* by their male friends. My hosts described to me how animals approach a geremempo in the forest to tease him before invariably escaping his clumsy hunting efforts. This banter draws on a very real anxiety among young men regarding sexuality and marriage. In the case of an actual pregnancy, these joking accusations may become real as the man is recognized as the actual geremempo and is pressured into marriage and the productive expectations of adulthood.

FIGURE 17. A young couple at their cooking hearth

Attempts at maintaining the relative independence of unmarried life are ultimately futile, as the decision to marry is often not made by the couple themselves. In contrast to other aspects of social life in which individual autonomy is respected and authority spurious, a marriage can be forced upon a couple if it is agreed between elders. Marriages are normally arranged at an ëeme feast in which one household or village hosts visitors. Marriage ceremonies are dramatic rituals wherein a group of adults spontaneously gathers around an often-unsuspecting couple, physically forces them together, and performs loud and repetitive chants emphasizing the expected roles of married life. Since young people generally prefer to avoid the obligations associated with marriage, these ceremonies can be dramatic events in which fearful couples attempt to escape. In the end, however, most young couples reluctantly accept their new role as productive members of society.

Rival (1992) writes that approximately half of the marriages during her fieldwork in the late 1980s involved Waorani couples who decided to live together against the will of their parents (97). She describes how marriage rituals were often enacted only jokingly, as Waorani couples "eloped" and registered their marriages away in towns. While these elopements still occurred in the early part of the twenty-first century, the apparent revitalization of "traditional" marriage rituals at the time of my fieldwork suggests that marriage practices continue to transform as young Waorani people are increasingly attracted to marrying kowori. There also appears to be a decreasing emphasis on the long-term obligations between Waorani men and their Quichua affines described by Rival (1992, 144). In contrast to middle-aged Wao-Quichua couples like Wareka and Luisa, who host Luisa's brothers and parents in Toñampari for long periods and make regular visits to her home village, young men today often emphasize interethnic marriage as a virtual one-off transaction.

There are certain structural continuities between traditional cross-cousin marriages and interethnic marriages, as "pre-contact" marriages also required making dangerous alliances beyond the local group with untrusted "enemy" Waorani (Rival 1992, 147). However, the frequency of marriages between Waorani men and Quichua women has also led to significant changes in postmarital residence patterns. In contrast to the traditional practice of matrilocality between Waorani spouses, whereby a husband resides with his wife's family upon marriage, Quichua men and women almost always relocate to Waorani villages after marrying a Waorani person. Since the most common form of interethnic marriage is between Quichua women and Waorani men, this has marked a general transition from matrilocality to patrilocality in villages like Toñampari. As we can see in Luisa's story earlier in this chapter, the move from a Quichua community to a house full of affines in a foreign place is not always easy or desirable, especially in the beginning. This is not to say that marrying a Waorani man does not have certain advantages for Quichua women themselves. Some Quichua women say that, unlike Quichua men, Waorani men seldom beat their wives (see also Rival 1992). When considered from the perspective of young Waorani men, however, there are a number of potential advantages in these marriages.

Some Waorani explain the preference for Quichua wives in terms of the translocal ties these marriages bring. With the exception of Waorani politicians who live and work in the city, Waorani men married to Quichuas generally have more contacts and friends outside their territory who may assist them financially or in other ways when they travel to the city. This can be advantageous for men who would otherwise have few sources of support in urban areas. However, men who marry Quichuas are less likely to be elected to offices in the Waorani political organization. All of the married men who held political offices during my fieldwork, including the Waorani *presidentes,* were married to Waorani women.[12] Some men voiced the view that these positions should be available exclusively to Waorani people with

Waorani spouses. This despite the fact that the majority of Waorani political leaders come from the areas where interethnic marriages are most common, such as Toñampari. As the political organization continues to be one of the primary sources of employment and assistance for Waorani people outside their territory, marrying a Quichua does not appear to be an obvious strategy to gain access to kowori goods, money, or political power.

While interethnic marriages create new links with people outside Toñampari, there are other local factors that motivate young men to seek kowori wives.[13] Bringing a Quichua woman to live with his natal household allows a man to forgo leaving his family to live with affines. This is particularly important in a context where interhousehold relations are apprehensive after decades of revenge killings. Given Waorani ideas about Quichuas as moral others, interethnic marriages do little to solidify the already uncertain relations between Waorani households. According to many of my male friends, marrying a Quichua woman is akin to a one-off transaction that carries few interfamilial obligations beyond the initial payment of meat, goods, or cash. These marriages preserve the independence of young men who would otherwise be expected to observe the obligations of a local cross-cousin marriage. Perhaps most important, for young men, marrying a Quichua is a choice they make. This is a clear contrast to Waorani couples being forced into marriage at village feasts. Although men are equally expected to fulfill their productive adult roles after marrying Quichuas, their ability to choose and free themselves from obligations to potential Waorani affines preserves the all-important Waorani ideal of individual autonomy.

At first sight it appears that interethnic marriages undermine one of the few contexts in which young adults are subject to the authority of elders.[14] Despite their misgivings about Quichua practices, many elders in fact endorse and encourage these marriages. When men bring Quichua wives to live with their parents, they increase the size and productive capacity of the local group. As we have seen, for many Waorani today the growth and expansion of households and villages is part of a more general ideal of "civilization" they express in contrast to the isolation and depletion associated with past violence. This helps to explain why, in Toñampari, marriages between Waorani men and Quichua women are more common than those between Waorani women and Quichua men. As the traditional practice of matrilocal marriage residence already brings the groom to the house of his new wife, it is Waorani men marrying Quichua women that allows households to retain young men and to incorporate new members through interethnic marriage.

Incorporating Others

An important consequence of married life is the incorporation of new individuals into a household. This involves more than taking up residence with one's affines or giving birth to children. Waorani understand kinship to be constituted as much through living and eating together as it is by descent from a common ancestor. In this way, a person's residential movement involves a process of being incorporated into the local household over time.[15] While village membership has become more important in recent years, households remain the central focus of Waorani social life. Waorani say that people who eat, drink, and work together in the same household eventually come to share a common physical substance (Rival 1998a). This notion of creating a shared body through conviviality and collective consumption, rather than through descent, appears to be a widely distributed feature of kinship in Amazonia (Overing and Passes 2000). It has led Viveiros de Castro (2001) to suggest that in Amazonian societies consanguinity is "constructed," while an encompassing notion of affinity is "given" or "naturalized."

In describing Quichuas as kowori people who are morally different from themselves, Waorani construe them in terms of an absence of relations, an absence that defines all non-Waorani groups. However, Quichuas are also people who come to live in villages like Toñampari and are incorporated into Waorani kinship and sociality through marriage. In this way kinship—or more specifically consanguinity—is made out of an encompassing background of potential affines (Viveiros de Castro 2001). In Viveiros de Castro's terms, "potential affinity" refers to how, in Amazonia, affinity is a dominant principle by which generic relations with unknown people are marked as a kind of "virtual sociality," such that "the Other is first and foremost an affine" (2001, 23–24).[16] The distinction between affinity (as virtuality) and kinship (as actualization) can be seen in how Waorani men address their male kowori co-workers in oil camps by the term *menki* ("brother-in-law" or "cross-cousin"), while in actual marriages a Waorani man is understood to be an outsider who gradually comes to share the same substance as his affines by living with them and sharing dietary restrictions with his wife before and after the birth of their child (see Rival 1992, 1998a).

In Toñampari some Wao-Quichua couples have in fact lived together for decades and have households that are just as large and prosperous as others. Quichua men enjoy hunting much like other men, even if they tend to prefer different animals and eat more foods from the city. Quichua women are apt in learning local customs and maintain many of their native practices that differ from the Waorani, such as specific cooking and craft techniques, planting a wider variety of crops in their gardens, and speaking the Quichua language. They are also praised for their hard work and ability to prepare food and manioc beer according to Waorani conventions.

While in many ways kinship in Amazonia is made processually out of others (Vilaça 2002), there remain essences of difference that are not transcended simply by living together (Lepri 2005). Waorani appear to emphasize differences between themselves and Quichuas at the same time as they transcend them. Despite their status as kowori, Quichuas to some extent come to share the common body of their household group after a period of conviviality. In the Wao-Quichua households I came to know well in Toñampari, Quichua spouses were subject to dietary taboos during pregnancy associated with the couvade. However, ideas and practices surrounding bodily substance and sharing are described differently in these "mixed" households. The parents of one such family explained to me how the entire household observed the taboo on eating meat and manioc beer when their daughter suffered a snakebite. However, they explained that, in contrast to Waorani households, these taboos are observed only for a person who is of the "same blood." That is, a Wao-Quichua couple would not have to avoid meat and manioc beer for each other in a case of snakebite, whereas both would observe these restrictions for their children. This suggests that although Wao-Quichua households subscribe to even the most intimate aspects of Waorani sociality, the emphasis on shared substance as the basis of relatedness is more pronounced in households with two Waorani parents.

After decades of interethnic marriages, many children and young people in Toñampari have one Wao and one Quichua parent.[17] The changing composition of the village can be seen in the local school, where Waorani, Quichua, and ethnically "mixed" students study together. When asked whether they see themselves as Waorani or Quichua, students from mixed households normally answer unambiguously that they are Waorani. When asked specifically about their parents' backgrounds, some of the same students explained to me that they are both Waorani and Quichua and in a few cases referred to themselves as *mestizo* ("mixed"). This identity as "mixed," however, is rarely emphasized in daily interactions between students. During my fieldwork some "mixed" students were in fact selected by the community to participate as representatives of the Waorani nationality at the *Dia de Nacionalidades Indígenas* (Indigenous Nationalities Day) festival in the capital. I have also seen Quichua students perform in "traditional" Waorani costumes alongside their Waorani classmates at events in Toñampari.

Young people born of interethnic marriages are in some contexts defined more by their perceived behavior than a unitary ethnic identity. According to Waorani parents with a Quichua spouse, their children are first and foremost Waorani. Elders and other adults without a Quichua spouse are more ambiguous in their descriptions of "mixed" children. In response to certain situations, such as a drinking party or theft in the village, they attribute transgressive behavior to these children being Quichuas. During my fieldwork this often emerged in moral evaluations of youth conduct. When the children of two Waorani parents were criticized for drinking alcohol or not sharing with kin, they were accused of acting "like kowori people." That is, while being Waorani is expressed in contrast to being kowori, the children of interethnic marriages are classified contextually based on what they do.[18] This ambiguity between perceived essences and practices is nothing new to anthropology, as Astuti has demonstrated in the context of gender and ethnic identities (1995, 1998). Waorani understandings of relatedness reflect the widely held notion in Amazonia that a common group identity is made through commensality and conviviality. However, the incorporation of Quichua spouses and "mixed" children also illustrates the limits of transcending difference in Waorani households and villages.

Alterity Transformed

The preference for Quichua spouses in Toñampari raises questions about indigenous formulations of difference that have long been familiar to the anthropology of Amazonia. Lévi-Strauss ([1943] 1976) was among the first to note that, in Central Brazil, the same "enemy" groups that people feared and raided were also those with whom they intermarried and exchanged highly valued gifts. For Lévi-Strauss, these relations, characterized by both fear and necessity, are the source through which kinship ties are built. In analyzing this dialectic between hostility and reciprocity, and the classificatory nature of Amazonian kinship that splits each generation into halves (siblings and affines), he highlighted affinity as the principle that orders relations between groups. He observed that a special "brother-in-law" relationship is characteristic of relations formed between allied groups, usually involving the same term used between actual affines within the group. As marriage alliances between previously hostile groups replicate the process of exchange in cross-cousin marriages within the group, indigenous understandings of kinship and affinity constitute the link to wider social relations. In describing how difference, rather than identity, is the "principle of relationality" in Amazonia, Viveiros de Castro notes, "The common word for the relation, in Amazonian worlds, is the term translated by 'brother-in-law' or 'cross-cousin.' This is the term we call people we do not know how to call, those with whom we wish to establish a generic relation. In sum, 'cousin/brother-in-law' is the term that creates a relation where none existed. It is the form through which the unknown is made known" (2004, 18).

Following Lévi-Strauss, Viveiros de Castro (2001) and others have noted the symbolic importance of "enemies" and exchange across sociopolitical boundaries in Amazonia where notions of predation, "other-becoming," and exchange are often expressed in terms of affinal relations.[19] As the process of mixing with or incorporating people from beyond the local group is central to indigenous understandings of social reproduction, it becomes increasingly difficult to view Amazonian societies in isolation from one another, even as indigenous people tend to emphasize what they see as key moral differences between themselves and other groups. This helps to explain why relations of affinity and friendship between specific Waorani and Quichua extended families have endured for decades despite ongoing revenge killings and disputes over land that indigenous people often present as ethnic conflicts between Waorani and kowori people (Reeve and High 2012).

Links between affinity and exchange can be seen in the "brother-in-law" relationship that Waorani men establish with Quichuas and other kowori. They often address their male kowori friends by the term *menki* (brother-in-law), a term that denotes mutual support and potential affinity. In the early 1990s Waorani men addressed their kowori co-workers in oil camps as menki and typically requested money and goods from them (Rival 1992). This relationship, characterized by joking and friendship, acquired sexual connotations when Waorani men visited their menki accompanied by their sisters who sought lovers in the camps. Just as it does between unrelated warani groups within Waorani society, the term *menki* expressed social distance and sharing between Waorani and kowori oil-workers (Rival 1992). While Rival emphasizes the semantic shift of the term *menki* from referring to relations between Waorani groups to those between indigenous and non-indigenous people, the actual form of this reciprocal relationship appears much the same.

While marginal in much of Waorani social life, exchange is not alien or inimical to a society in the process of establishing enduring relations with outsiders that were not possible only a few decades ago. Marriages between "enemy" groups, and the violence that resumes when relations of affinity break down, are a common feature of intergroup relations in much of Amazonia (Fausto 2012). This process of transforming relations of enmity to affinity also emerges alongside what Waorani people envision as the current period's relative peace that allows new opportunities for alliance and social expansion. Despite the violence and generalized distrust that remains between the two groups, Quichuas are people with whom Waorani see the possibility of new alliances. They welcome interethnic marriages as an opportunity to incorporate wider networks of people into their own households and communities. It is only if we assume that particular societies live in "natural" isolation from one another that marriages between Waorani and Quichua people appear alien or problematic.

Conclusion

As Lévi-Strauss (1995) argued, the relationship between self and other, the basis of human sociality, is in constant transformation. For Waorani people, Quichuas have gone from being "cannibal" enemies to ideal spouses in the past few decades. Rather than evidence of social breakdown or "acculturation," this process reflects indigenous understandings of kinship and sociality in a context where Waorani people emphasize "living well" and repopulating their vast territory in the aftermath of intense violence. Isolation and violence should not be the only measure of Waorani culture or society, even if revenge killings are a recurring theme in social memory today. Although we know relatively little about Waorani history prior to the 1950s, relations between Waorani and kowori people, as well as those between different Waorani groups, have oscillated between violence, friendship, and alliance for many years.

Waorani people criticize Quichuas as morally different from themselves at the same time as they welcome them into their homes to live and raise children together. Despite ongoing conflicts that sometimes erupt into interethnic violence, relations with Quichuas and other kowori have an important value for Waorani men and women. More than simply bringing greater access to manufactured goods and urban centers, marrying Quichuas allows Waorani men to escape some of the obligations that marrying a

Waorani woman entails. Even if Wao-Quichua marriages to some extent involve exchange relations, they also preserve the Waorani ideal of autonomy. The transition from enmity to affinity that I have described coincides with the formation of larger Waorani villages and is part of a wider emphasis people in Toñampari place on living in a "community." In the next chapter I consider some of the challenges and dangers that living among so many potential and actual affines present for them.

CHAPTER 6

Shamans and Enemies

Even as a growing number of kowori have come to live in Waorani villages, Quichua people continue to have a prominent place in local discussions of enmity and violence. This sense of alterity can be seen in Waorani ideas about shamanism, a practice that is associated closely with Quichuas. Building on my analysis in the previous chapter of the dual status of Quichuas as people who are both distinguished by Waorani as morally different and desired as spouses, in this chapter I consider how Quichuas have become the primary source of both shamanic curing and witchcraft accusations. This seemingly paradoxical situation reflects indigenous understandings of shamanism and Waorani efforts to "live well" in contemporary villages in the aftermath of violence. Waorani people in Toñampari object to shamanism not because of a lack of belief in its efficacy but because shamanic power presents a threat to the idealized conditions of living in what they call a *comunidad*.

From Household to Comunidad

One of the key changes in Waorani social life in recent decades has been the establishment of multihousehold villages along major rivers. The origins of many of these villages, like Toñampari, can be traced to elders who joined the Tiweno mission in the 1960s and later founded new communities along the Curaray River and surrounding areas. Today some of these villages have local schools and incorporate twenty or more households in the same area. This process has coincided with the emergence of a certain degree of Waorani solidarity as an ethnic group alongside regional and national indigenous movements in Ecuador. After the intensity of revenge killings that preceded mission settlement, village life was initially characterized by fear and suspicion between rival groups who, for the first time, found themselves living in close proximity to each other (Yost 1981). Still today, many daily activities are carried out within specific household groups that maintain a strong degree of social and economic independence. With the exception of community fiestas and the school, people tend to interact primarily with members of their own household or within a group of mutually supporting households (*waomoni*). This is not to ignore school activities or the occasional visits people make between houses outside their local group and to other villages, but to emphasize the spatial and social independence by which households tend to carry out much of their everyday lives.

Before the missionaries arrived, the Waorani lived in longhouses that were often large enough to house multiple nuclear families, each with its own cooking hearth (Rival 1996a). While members of a particular *nanicabo* generally had regular contact with a small number of neighbors in the vicinity, households maintained a remarkable degree of independence, as intergroup relations were often fraught with violence and distrust. Since the process of living, eating, and drinking together is seen to have a formative role in creating relatedness within the group, the relative autonomy of households has important implications in Waorani understandings of kinship and sociality. The ways household identity is established through shared experience can be seen in the practices by which Waorani people incorporate newborn children and men marrying into the household group. By taking part in the same dietary taboos as their wives during pregnancy associated with the couvade, a man begins to share the same body as his wife and her natal household. Similarly, a newborn baby is initially a guest to be incorporated into the group only after consuming the same food and drink as other household members (Rival 1998a, 626).

The incorporation of new people into the nanicabo exemplifies a more general Waorani emphasis on the effects of sharing and living together. In some contexts a person's physical well-being depends on his or her kin collectively eating or avoiding certain foods. When a household member falls ill, such as in cases of snakebite, co-residents are expected to conform to taboos on eating most game meat. Waorani explain that failing to observe these restrictions collectively results in the wound growing more severe, bleeding profusely, or rotting (High 2006, 161). Fish and certain bird species are the only game that should be eaten, and everyone in the household drinks a special type of unmasticated manioc mash (*mine*) in a collective effort to restore the ill person's health. Ordinary manioc beer (*tepe*) and *peneme* (mature plantain drink) are avoided at these times since, like most game meat, they are associated with rotting. At one point during my fieldwork, a teenager studying in Toñampari was said to be observing this special diet after hearing on the radio that a member of his home household in another village was bitten by a snake. Similarly, when a teenage girl was hospitalized after a snakebite, her household avoided eating meat for more than a month, despite the fact that during much of this time she was away in the city.

While anthropologists and ethnobotanists have pointed to the remarkable variety of plant species used in indigenous health practices in Amazonia,[1] there is much less attention given to how sickness and health are related to indigenous understandings of consanguinity that result from people living together. Evan as Waorani generally value individual autonomy, in certain contexts the well-being of each person is understood to be inseparable from that of the group, such that the collective actions of the household have direct effects on particular individuals. Waorani people show great concern when a member of their household falls ill, insisting that the person will quickly recover. The death of one person may be a sign that the nanicabo is becoming vulnerable and is seen as a threat to the entire group. The couvade and ethnomedical practices illustrate how processes of living, eating, and drinking together are at the heart of everyday sociality and household identity. Whether it is through consuming the same things collectively or avoiding them, the notion that "the repeated and undifferentiated *action* of sharing . . . turns co-residents into a single, indistinct substance" (Rival 1998a, 621) has come to define the kinds of mutuality and well-being associated with the "moral economy of intimacy" in Amazonia.

Even in the largest villages, the social composition and spatial positioning of Waorani houses to some extent replicates traditional longhouses. Today, nuclear family households tend to form a close spatial cluster based on the same relations of kinship and affinity that previously constituted a single longhouse. Instead of moving directly into the home of his parents-in-law upon marriage, a young man today may build a separate house directly next to that of his in-laws and perform much the same social role expected in a single longhouse. The houses of adult opposite-sex siblings, which before would normally have been located at a distance, may be only fifty meters away and in plain view of one another. In Toñampari this spatial organization of houses is intentional, as groups of close kin and affines tend to occupy specific sections of the village that in most contexts maintain relative independence from other family clusters. I began to realize just how separate the everyday lives of these groups were from one another when I spoke with people at the school or in other parts of the village. They often knew little of what was going on in the cluster of households where I lived, such as the building of a new house or of changes in the social composition of a particular household. In contrast to the popular image of a tightly knit community where everyone knows everything about everybody else and shares the same social experience (Stasch 2009), these household clusters maintain and respect a social distance from one another in most aspects of daily life.

One of the central concerns in Toñampari and other villages is what Waorani people refer to in Spanish as *comunidad*. The idea of living in a community is part of a wider moral and sociopolitical discourse in Ecuador promoted by schoolteachers, state institutions, and NGOs. Stasch (2009) describes how the idea of community as a kind of social unity or "mutual identification" has had an important place in the history of anthropology and European thought more generally. Whether in Henry Maine's writing about permanent collectivities in *Ancient Law* (1871), Ferdinand Tönnies's influential concept of *Gemeinschaft* (community) as a "perfect unity of wills" ([1887] 1957, 37), or Durkheim's concept of mechanical solidarity, modern social science has contributed to "the stereotype of 'tribal' and 'family' sociality as [an] undifferentiated, space-based unity of consciousness" (Stasch 2009, 8–9). In Ecuador, the idea that indigenous people, as opposed to whites or mestizos, are members of an undifferentiated community with a single conscience is part of an enduring colonial legacy that continues to inform popular imagination and relations between the state and indigenous peoples.

While notions of community can be traced in various directions in popular Ecuadorian culture, international development agendas, and Western thought more generally, my specific interest here is what living in a comunidad means to Waorani people in the context of recent social transformations. Rival (2002) has described how Waorani villages exist primarily due to the presence of schools, often despite the economic hardships of living in depleted hunting areas. While Waorani people embrace living in a comunidad as a key social value, their understandings of what this means departs significantly from popular Western notions of community as integration or a "communitarian oneness" that subsumes personal differences (Stasch 2009, 8). They instead envision comunidad as a delicate combination of living in a village alongside various Waorani and kowori people while at the same time maintaining a strong sense of household and personal autonomy.[2] For many Waorani, the idea of comunidad refers to participation in a limited number of collective social practices and a commitment to preventing and resolving conflicts between households. This vision has certain parallels with the way elders contrast present conditions to the violence of past times in their memories of "civilization."

Avoidance and Confrontation

In Toñampari, the idea of living in a comunidad is closely linked to the village school. Kowori schoolteachers are centrally involved in organizing village events, such as meetings, *mingas* (collective work parties),[3] and fiestas to commemorate national holidays. They see this as an integral aspect of their job, that of "civilizing" and "integrating" the Waorani so that young people might graduate from the local school and subsequently find work in the city or enroll at an Ecuadorian university. For many Waorani adults, living in a comunidad means supporting the formal education of their children, participating in school events, and avoiding potential conflicts between individuals and households. While young people participate enthusiastically in soccer tournaments and other activities organized by the school, meetings at the *ñene onko* (community house) have become a key arena in which parents, teachers, and elders voice their concerns about the village. In village meetings and in other contexts, Waorani people address conflicts without directly confronting the specific individuals implicated in them.

At the time of my fieldwork, meetings in Toñampari were formally organized by schoolteachers and the village president.[4] While they were generally dominated by speeches in which teachers complained about poor student performance and implored parents to prioritize education, Waorani men and women also raised their own concerns about the community and even the conduct of teachers. Rival (1992, 2002) describes the support and respect given to teachers despite the economic demands they make on local households and their general hostility toward the practices of Waorani elders.[5] During my fieldwork, however, Waorani people publicly challenged the behavior of kowori teachers in village meetings. While they generally avoid confronting individuals with whom a conflict arises directly, these meetings are a unique space for voicing concerns about threats to the co-munidad without confronting specific people.

This space for criticism in community meetings became clear in 2002, when several Quichua schoolteachers who had recently arrived in the village brought cane liquor (*puro*) with them and regularly appeared drunk. Before long, parents were complaining that the teachers were missing classes as a result of their drunkenness. Teachers were also seen drinking with teenage students in the boarding house built for students who come from other villages to study in Toñampari. These same teachers began visiting the homes of Quichua residents to drink late into the night. As I described in the previous chapter, drinking alcohol is a practice by which Waorani adults often distinguish kowori people from themselves. Although parents explained to me their concerns about the teachers' missing classes and en-couraging students to drink "like kowori people," to my knowledge they never directly confronted the teachers about the problem. Waorani adults appeared unwilling to interfere with or attempt to stop the drinking that was becoming a regular feature of village parties.

Despite their reluctance to confront the teachers individually, about two months after the drinking began several parents and elders denounced the teachers collectively for their behavior at a community meeting. They in-sisted that the drinking was causing serious problems in the comunidad, leading to conflicts between households and undermining education at the school. In their complaints that drinking was threatening the local ideal of "living well" in a comunidad, parents voiced their own understanding of the relationship between knowledge and experience. Waorani people view the transmission of knowledge from one generation to the next as a process wherein young people learn by replicating the actions of people with experi-ence rather than observing a strict power relationship between parent and child or teacher and student. Parents were concerned not only about the contradiction between drunkenness and the kinds of social relations they envision as a comunidad but also that teachers drinking with students was causing young people to become "like kowori people." Since parents place a strong emphasis on their children's formal education, they also complained that the teachers were failing to fulfill their commitments at the school. At the meeting parents demanded that the teachers stop drinking with students and that they drink only on weekends. Rather than singling out particular teachers for their behavior, the parents at the meeting addressed them as a group, even as the teachers involved clearly knew they were the targets of criticism.

Parents later submitted a letter to the Waorani political organization and educational directive in the regional capital about the drinking problem, which eventually led to the removal of two teachers from the village. By this point in my fieldwork I had mistakenly concluded that Waorani parents would sooner allow the drinking to continue than confront the teachers. Despite their legacy of violence and criticisms of kowori ways, I never saw a Waorani person confront someone else in the form of an argument, threat, or physical assault. The general reluctance to directly challenge the actions or statements of other individuals reflects the importance Waorani people generally place on individual autonomy (Rival 2002; High 2007). I found this lack of confrontation remarkable after hearing my hosts' stories about how other villagers had wronged them in various ways. These criticisms are a context in which people frequently evoke the imagery of victimhood that is central to Waorani understandings of personhood. Residents often complained to me that someone stole their clothes or other items from their home while they were away fishing, gardening, or visiting another village. However, I never saw or heard of someone confronting the suspected thieves, even when they were seen wearing or using the stolen items.

For my Waorani hosts comunidad connotes a form of sociality in which people avoid the violence that has such a strong presence in social memory.[6] The emphasis on nonconfrontation appears to have become more prevalent in recent decades since the intervention of missionaries and state institutions. Yost (1981) describes how, at the mission settlement in the 1970s, Waorani openly challenged one another in verbal confrontations. Without suggesting that Waorani people have become passive in response to perceived problems in their villages, it appears that an emphasis on avoiding potential conflicts has gained greater resonance in the context of living in a comunidad. When I asked one man why he did not confront a group of young people who reportedly stole his clothes, he explained that, although the thieves had "done badly" (*wiwa keranitapa*), he did not want a "problem." Waorani often use the Spanish word *problema* in drawing a contrast to the notion of comunidad, referring to situations and practices that they fear may lead to violent conflicts. The same man who had his clothes stolen proudly contrasted his large comunidad to the problems of previous generations and other villages. Even as Waorani people criticize the behavior of their neighbors, living in proximity to various other people has become part of the everyday experience of living in a comunidad.

The kinds of sociality associated with comunidad can also be seen in relations between households. While Waorani people seldom attempt to

FIGURE 18. Toñampari and the village school

interfere with the affairs of other households, they are often concerned about conflicts in the village that pose a threat to the ideal of "living well." This became clear after a rare incidence of domestic violence in which Pego, a middle-aged Waorani man, reportedly hit his Quichua wife in the head with a machete during a drunken tirade, causing minor injury. As suggested previously, domestic violence between spouses is extremely rare and generally unacceptable to Waorani, and Pego's behavior caused much concern among his neighbors.[7]

The morning after the incident Pego retreated to his home, claiming to be sick with malaria and refusing to leave even to go hunting or fishing. Several neighbors explained that Pego was simply too embarrassed to appear in public after his outlandish behavior. When he failed to attend a minga to clear foliage from the village airstrip, his neighbors became concerned about Pego's withdrawal from the community.[8] At the minga they voiced concerns about the lack of meat for Pego's family and his lack of participation in the comunidad. To my knowledge nobody went to Pego's house to reprimand him or encourage him to resume his daily activities. As in most aspects of everyday life in Toñampari, Pego's autonomy was respected even as his behavior was widely criticized as *wiwa* ("bad" or "ugly"). Although it is common for households to have little regular interaction with one another, Pego's neighbors were concerned about the continuing problems his inactivity was creating for his family. It was only after Pego finally emerged from his house a few days later that they were convinced that he was still committed to taking part in peaceful relations in the community.

Shamanic Agency

If village life reveals certain continuities in social organization and indigenous understandings of autonomy, the notion of comunidad also presents a Waorani vision of social transformation. For many people in Toñampari and other villages, living in a comunidad involves rejecting certain practices associated with the past. Just as local narratives of "civilization" emphasize village settlement and the cessation of revenge-killings, many Waorani today see shamanism as a practice that is difficult to reconcile with the notion of "living well." The rejection of shamanism reflects local concerns about preventing violent conflicts and achieving an idealized mode of sociality associated with a comunidad. In this context, shamanism illuminates the dual status of Quichua people as a source of both witchcraft and curing.

One of the odd things in writing about Waorani shamanism is that there are remarkably few Waorani shamans. As elsewhere in Amazonia, evangelical missionaries who lived among the Waorani in the 1960s and 1970s sought to combat shamanic beliefs and practices through their Christian teachings. However, even after decades of proselytizing by SIL missionaries, there are still practicing shamans in some Waorani villages today. Although few Waorani claim to be shamans, what shamans do is something of much interest and concern in Toñampari. These concerns reveal specific ontological assumptions that underlie indigenous understandings of human and nonhuman agency.

Explaining the apparent decline of shamanism requires attention not only to missionary history and the specific role of shamans but also to the place of animals, spirits, and human enemies within a broader Waorani cosmos of alterity (High 2012a). Viveiros de Castro's (1998a) formulation of perspectivism or "perspectival multinaturalism" has had a major impact on anthropological understandings of Amazonian myth, cosmology, and shamanism. In a perspectival cosmology, humans, animals, and other beings share a universal "culture" or "spiritual unity" insofar as all beings see themselves as persons in the same way that human beings do (470). In this way, one's perspective is determined by the body rather than by cultural differences, leading Viveiros de Castro to contrast Western notions of "multiculturalism" to "multinaturalism" in indigenous America. In a cosmos where animals and spirits are attributed the consciousness and intentionality of humans, perspectivism is predicated on a relation of predation by which different beings struggle to assert their own perspective upon others.

While perspectivism is often taken to be an abstract cosmology that fundamentally challenges conventional Western notions of "nature" and "culture" (Turner 2009), it can also be understood in terms of culturally specific forms of moral evaluation that engage human and nonhuman perspectives (Londoño Sulkin 2005). One major concern in Waorani discussions of shamanism is the inherent danger of interacting with nonhuman beings, such as jaguar-spirits. Shamanism is dangerous because the act of adopting (or being overtaken by) the perspectives of spirits and animals is a transformational process also associated with assault sorcery or witchcraft. As a result, as in many other parts of Amazonia, shamanism and witchcraft are not understood as separate or independent processes (Hugh-Jones 1994; Fausto 2004; Whitehead and Wright 2004; Wright 2013). Clastres, for example, observed that a shaman occupies an inherently dangerous position between healing and potential violence: "The same powers that make him a doctor, that is, a man capable of bringing life, enable him to rule over death as well. For that reason, he is dangerous, disquieting; one is constantly mistrustful of him. As a matter of life and death, he is immediately made responsible for every extraordinary occurrence, and very often he is killed out of fear" (1989, 144). The dangers of interacting with nonhuman agencies help to explain the recent decline of Waorani shamanism, in which relations between humans and animals have an integral role. Jaguars are the quintessential predator animal in the Waorani cosmos and in shamanic practices. Shamans are described as people who develop a special kin relationship with jaguars through dreams in which a jaguar-spirit is "adopted" by a shaman (Rival 2002, 79). The jaguar-spirit subsequently visits the shaman and speaks through the voice of its human "father" during trances experienced by the shaman while dreaming.[9] As it temporarily inhabits the shaman's body, the jaguar-spirit tells its adopted father and his family where to find game animals. In the Waorani language, these shamans are called *meñera*, meaning "jaguar father/mother," and are sometimes referred to simply as *meñi* (jaguar).

In describing the process of becoming a shaman, Waorani often say that people do not themselves choose to become shamans. Those who suffer a near fatal illness or accident are said to be particularly vulnerable to becoming a shaman, especially if it was caused by witchcraft. In addition to *daikawo* (sickness) early in life, I have heard Waorani describe how narrowly escaping death later in life, such as surviving a plane crash or other serious accidents in the forest, may lead to a person becoming a shaman. In shamanism it is the jaguar-spirit who imposes its own perspective on an adoptive human father while dreaming, literally inhabiting and speaking through the shaman's body while he sleeps.[10] The relationship between shaman and jaguar-spirit is one of adoption because jaguar spirits are, like the most famous Waorani killers, seen as orphans. An orphan, someone who is alone without kin with whom to engage in proper social relations, is akin to a predator. Following a similar logic that revenge should be taken after the death of a kinsman, many of the most notorious killers in Waorani oral histories are described as orphans.[11] Since the moral "human" perspective is that of being prey surrounded by kin, the challenge for shamans, according to their peers, is to remain in a subordinate position in their relations with animal spirits. In contrast to the predatory agency of jaguars, shamans ideally demonstrate their human agency through being controlled by nonhuman beings, rather than by controlling them.[12]

Communication between animals and human beings is not restricted to shamanism. One man described to me how his father, upon experiencing an unexpected encounter with a jaguar in the forest, angrily insisted to the jaguar that he was not afraid, since he too was an orphan. Waorani people describe jaguars not only in terms of continuities with human perspective but also as having a particular kind of agency that is antithetical to human sociality. As Londoño Sulkin notes among the Muinane of Colombian Amazonia, jaguars and other animals are seen as "failures in moral sociality" to the extent that they create "immoral subjective states" (2005, 12). Jaguars are dangerous because they have no kin, and, like human "enemies" (kowori), they occupy a predatory position in relation to Waorani people.[13] Since being "prey" is part of what defines what it means to be a Waorani person, the subjectivity of jaguars and enemies is often expressed in contrast to the ideal of generosity and peaceful conviviality that Waorani people associate with their own sociality and life in a comunidad.

Sorcerers and Their Pets

Many Waorani today have misgivings about the close engagement with jaguar-spirits that shamanism entails and describe shamans as a dangerous obstacle to living in a comunidad. The ability of shamans to carry out assault sorcery is a major concern across Waorani households and villages. While there has been relatively little attention to the "dark" aspects of Amazonian shamanism in which shamans inflict harm on people (Whitehead and Wright 2004), during my fieldwork I was struck by how often Waorani people lamented, with much worry and frustration, the sicknesses, accidents, and deaths attributed to such practices. In some cases assault sorcery is described as a consequence of Waorani shamans attempting to control spirit-animals, thus inverting the expected direction of agency in relations between humans and nonhumans.

The question of who adopts or controls whom in the adoptive relationship between shamans and animal spirits is part of what makes shamanism dangerous.[14] In describing how shamans send animals to kill their enemies, my Waorani hosts compare the relationship between shamans and animals to a person having a domesticated pet. Whereas Waorani shamanism generally involves a jaguar-spirit inhabiting and speaking through the body of a shaman, in sorcery shamans are said to control their animal for the purpose of attacking people. In addition to jaguars, a shaman may engage the services of other animals, such as poisonous snakes and insects. While Waorani shamans are sometimes called *meñera*, in Toñampari they are more often referred to in Spanish as *brujo* or in the Waorani language as *iroi/iroinga* (male/female sorcerer).[15] The animal "pets" of shamans are seen to be endowed with special powers. The adopted jaguar of a shaman, for example, is said to be massive in size and able to glide long distances like a large forest bird.[16] When a shaman dies, the "orphaned" jaguar may become angry and prey on many people—much like orphaned Waorani men who in the past became famous warriors after avenging their kin.

Waorani shamanism presents a contrast to the shamanic dreams described among Amazonian groups like the Brazilian Parakanã, where a shaman is said to become dangerous to his kin when he surrenders his perspective to that of a jaguar, thus reversing the master/pet relationship (Fausto 2004). For Waorani people, it is the "master" or "predator" perspective itself that is antithetical to proper human sociality—a subject position associated with assault sorcery, enmity, and vengeful rage. It is for this reason that shamans should surrender to their jaguar-spirits rather than control them as pets.

Given the dangers of assault sorcery, it is no surprise that many Waorani do not generally see shamanism in a positive light. While few of my hosts claim to know much about the actual techniques of sorcery (High 2012b), some explain that a victim becomes sick when a shaman speaks badly of him or her after consuming the powerful hallucinogen *miyi* (ayahuasca). This may occur when the shaman has previously visited the home of a person he or she intends to kill. In these cases, the illness (*daikawo*) appears to be caused by the words themselves as the shaman/jaguar speaks or sings, announcing the victim's name. One man described to me how, in sorcery, the shaman sees a victim remotely "as if on a television or computer screen." In descriptions like these, it is the ability to see others, rather than being seen by them, that constitutes a position of power in shamanism.[17] In a similar way, Waorani people say that when encountering a jaguar in the forest, a person is safe if he or she sees the animal before it sees them.

Waorani explain that many revenge killings in the past were caused by sorcery. When children died of sickness, they were avenged by kin who attempted to kill the entire family of the suspected shaman. This was in part to prevent the possibility of counterattacks, but Waorani explain that other members of a shaman's household may also be directly responsible for sorcery. This is because other people who are present when the shaman is inhabited by his "jaguar-spirit" may speak to the spirit, evoking the names of people to kill. Waorani people speak literally about actual jaguars being sent by shamans to kill people. They also describe people becoming seriously ill as a result of the sorcery of these same shamans. Although they distinguish between being physically attacked by an animal and falling ill, these various misfortunes are attributed to the same predatory agency—often expressed metaphorically as being "eaten" by a jaguar.

In recent years Waorani have come to see shamans as a threat to the local ideal of living in a *comunidad*. Since virtually all major accidents, severe illnesses, and deaths are attributed to witchcraft, shamanism has led to serious tensions within this new concentration of former "enemy" groups. In this context Waorani reject shamanism locally not because of a declining confidence or belief in its power but because they take the consequences of shamanism so very seriously. As among the Parakanã described by Fausto (2004), the links between shamans, warfare, and jaguars make the shaman a "stigmatized" and "unfeasible figure" whose role is seldom publicly recognized (160). Among the Waorani this public recognition is rarely claimed but instead is attributed to specific people in cases of assault sorcery. In contrast to descriptions of assault sorcery as a practice by which indigenous Amazonian people challenge "modernity" (Whitehead 2002), Waorani people envision a comunidad where potentially dangerous shamanic practices are ideally absent. It is because of the dangers of dark shamanism that they denounce and discourage shamanic practices in hope of "living well."

Quichuas and Comunidad

While many people in Toñampari and other villages view Waorani shamans with suspicion and disdain, most cases of assault sorcery today are attributed to Quichua sorcerers. My hosts often explained to me that Quichuas attack them because they envy Waorani people "living well" on their vast and plentiful lands. Complaints about Quichua witchcraft seem only to have intensified since my first fieldwork in the late 1990s, at times culminating in outright paranoia and rage among families who have suffered a series of sorcery-related illnesses. While Waorani people often cite these attacks in their criticisms of Quichuas, their responses to sorcery also reveal how Waorani and Quichua shamanic practices are in some ways mutually implicated. Just as Waorani shamans are increasingly marginalized in local efforts to establish a comunidad, Quichuas have become the focal point in Waorani discussions of assault sorcery and shamanic curing.

In local understanding, Waorani and Quichua forms of sorcery are both distinct and related in important ways. Illness caused by Waorani shamanism is particularly dangerous because the victim must discover who is responsible for the attack and subsequently confront the sorcerer to be cured. Unless the victim's kin are able to discover the identity of the shaman, he or she faces almost certain death. When found, the implicated shaman can provide a cure by extracting a poisonous substance from the victim's body while shaking his or her hammock. If some of the violating substance remains in the victim's body after the curing, the victim is likely to become a shaman. This urgent need to approach the actual shaman who carried out the attack is one way that people in Toñampari distinguish between Waorani and Quichua forms of witchcraft. In cases attributed to Quichuas there is no need to confront the person responsible unless for the purpose of taking revenge.[18] The victim may instead pay another Quichua shaman to provide a cure or to diagnose who is responsible. In many if not most cases of sorcery, Waorani seek the help of Quichua shamans. The following situation that occurred during my fieldwork illustrates how Waorani and Quichua shamanism are mutually implicated in the ways people interpret and respond to sorcery.

One night I was awakened by some noise from the neighboring house, which sounded to me like a person vomiting. The next morning I was told that Yolanda, a young pregnant woman, had fallen ill after suffering a sorcery attack the night before. Her husband and other members of her household explained to me that she had been attacked by small, iridescent white creatures after going outside in the middle of the night. Yolanda described how these glowing white figures, which looked like animals, came from the forest and entered her body through the legs, causing pain in her limbs and a fever that left her virtually bedridden the following day.

Before long there was speculation about who was responsible for the attack. Yolanda's family attributed it to a family of Waorani shamans from a village several days walk to the east. They cited as evidence the fact that the sons of one of these shamans had recently visited Yolanda's village for a workshop sponsored by a foreign NGO, which was followed by an ëcme (communal feast). During the festivities a young man was injured in a fall while being chased by a group of people playfully attempting to smear *kaka* (red achiote dye) on his face—a common joking game among young people at these gatherings (see also Robarchek and Robarchek 1998). A week or so after Yolanda suffered the attack, her kin recalled how the son of one of the shamans had been involved in the incident at the party, and how this same man described his grandfather as having become a shaman as a result of being stranded in the forest for days after a tree fell on him. Yolanda's household suspected that the visitor had actually intended to harm local residents and that a shaman in his family was to blame for the sorcery attack on the pregnant woman. Since cases of Waorani sorcery can be attributed not only to a particular shaman but also to the shaman's whole family, it seemed plausible to my hosts that the visiting man was implicated.

Although some Waorani occasionally seek medical attention at the mission hospital in the town of Shell (near Puyo) for broken bones, malaria, and other illnesses, most say that the hospital can do little for victims of assault sorcery. In these cases Quichua shamans are said to be experts at identifying the source of witchcraft and in some cases can provide a cure. Soon after Yolanda's attack she traveled with her husband to see a Quichua shaman in Puyo. Upon their return, they described how the Quichua shaman confirmed their worries that a Waorani shaman was responsible. The shaman was unable to help further, they explained, since only the Waorani shaman who carried out the attack could cure her. Yolanda's husband explained to me the gravity of the situation: in order to prevent her dying, they would have to travel to another part of the territory to seek advice from a Waorani shaman and perhaps even visit the village where the accused sorcerer lived. As a result, Yolanda soon left to live with her parents in the village of Tiguino, some two days' walk to the north. She subsequently gave birth and returned to her husband a few weeks later, reportedly having been cured while away.

There are certain similarities between Waorani descriptions of Quichua and Waorani sorcery. In both cases it is said to be motivated by envy and is initiated by the shaman secretly from afar. However, sorcery accusations against Quichuas are far more common than those against Waorani shamans, even as people in Toñampari claim less knowledge of how Quichua shamans carry out these attacks. According to my Waorani hosts, a Quichua shaman may attack an enemy by casting a spell from afar or by placing a poisonous substance in the victim's drink. Much like accounts of Waorani sorcery, there is an emphasis on malevolent substances entering the victim's body. However, Waorani people claim little knowledge of how Quichua shamans carry out sorcery. They do, rather, have much to say about the suffering experienced by the victim, who may die without treatment.

Waorani people say that Quichuas are the true specialists in assault sorcery. I was often surprised during my fieldwork at the range of afflictions attributed to Quichua shamans, such as sickness, canoe accidents, and even suicide. Some Waorani described to me how they narrowly survived the fever and pain of a sorcery attack, and on several occasions I heard how a local man's canoe was mysteriously overturned in the river as a result of sorcery. While the man targeted by the shaman survived, one of his daughters drowned in the accident. Accounts like these indicate how, in indigenous understanding, witchcraft is a serious threat to people even beyond the intended target. In another case Quichua sorcery was blamed for the apparent suicide of a Waorani man in a nearby village. My hosts emphasized that he had been with Quichuas shortly before he died—the same Quichuas living just outside the Waorani reserve who are believed to envy Waorani lands. They explained that Quichua witchcraft can cause a person to behave in unusual ways that lead to death. Rather than having to locate the specific shaman who carried out the attack, victims of Quichua sorcery can approach any shaman for a cure. As in the case of Yolanda, Quichua shamans are also called on to deal with Waorani witchcraft, even if only to discover the origin of the illness. At the same time, there is a degree of hostility toward Quichua shamans, and sorcery accusations are one of the chief motivations for Waorani attacks against Quichua people.

The decline of Waorani shamanism and the increasing importance of Quichua shamans is part of a larger Waorani vision of growth and expansion in villages like Toñampari. For Waorani, the notion of comunidad implies an ongoing process of engaging with kowori and rival groups in new and productive ways. In order to live peacefully among them, it seems that engaging with jaguar-spirits poses too great a threat to the ideal of living in a comunidad. And yet, there are clear parallels between the dangerous agency attributed to jaguar-spirits and the "predatory" perspective attributed to Quichua people, and particularly their shamans. On more than one occasion my Waorani friends have proudly assured me that, in contrast to other villages, there are no sorcerers in Toñampari. The relative absence of shamans in Waorani communities today is part of a broader indigenous emphasis on avoiding conflicts that would threaten the current period of relatively peaceful interhousehold relations. And yet, as we have seen, the villages are still vulnerable to shamanic power. While Waorani jaguar-shamans remain a threat to the local ideal of "living well" in a comunidad, it is Quichuas who have come to be associated with the dangers of assault sorcery.

Shamanism and History in Western Amazonia

At first sight it may appear strange that Waorani people seek help from Quichua shamans—the same kowori who they accuse of witchcraft and frequently describe as morally inferior to themselves. However, if we elude the notion that the Waorani or any other indigenous Amazonian group constitutes a kind of naturally isolated social whole, the role of Quichuas in Waorani understandings of shamanism, like the interethnic marriages described in the previous chapter, can be seen as part of the ongoing intercultural dynamics of Western Amazonia. Rather than constituting the "acculturation" of a previously isolated group, Waorani-Quichua relations are part of an enduring regional system with deep historical roots (Reeve and High 2012, 156). In this way, shamanism reveals how interethnic relations in Amazonia have transformed in the context of colonial history and contemporary translocal processes.

Shamanic practices can be found in indigenous communities throughout much of Amazonian Ecuador and in parts of the Andes and coastal areas of Ecuador. While in popular imagination shamanism is often seen as emblematic of a primordial, pristine, or "authentic" indigenous culture, it is striking that in Western Amazonia it appears to flourish among indigenous people with most regular contacts with other indigenous groups and mestizos (Gow 1996). In much of Amazonia, shamans are seen to have privileged access to and knowledge of others, whether spirits, animals, or "enemies" (Taylor 1981; Viveiros de Castro 1992; Descola 1992; High 2012a). It is perhaps (at least in part) for this reason that some indigenous peoples closely associated with intercultural relations and processes of ethnogenesis since colonial times are those renowned for having the most powerful shamans in the region. In Amazonian Ecuador, it is Quichua-speaking people who generally have a longer history of direct social, economic, and spiritual ties with white people and indigenous groups previously classified as aucas (Taylor 1999). Often imagined as having a position between the most remote forest-dwelling indigenous people and mestizo culture, Quichuas are both feared and sought as the most powerful shamans in the region.

While white and mestizo people recognize Amazonian shamans for the potency of their assumed "wildness" and "primitive" knowledge (Salomon 1981; Taussig 1987), historically other indigenous groups have sought out Quichua shamans for their privileged access to and knowledge of white culture and manufactured goods (Taylor 1981; Descola 1993; Gow 1991, 1996). In his attempt to reconstruct a regional historical perspective, Gow argues that contemporary forms of shamanism, such as those involving the use of *ayahuasca*, may in fact have spread from the settlements and cities of "mixed blood" people toward the more remote forest-dwelling peoples. He notes that the indigenous groups most widely known for shamanism are precisely those who lived on colonial missionary reductions, where ayahuasca shamanism may have gained in following in response to the need to cure imported diseases that decimated these indigenous populations living in closer proximity to Europeans (1996, 107). This suggests that the shamanic traditions of Western Amazonia have likely transformed radically in the context of colonial history and particularly with regard to the desperate need to cope with diseases introduced by Europeans. Among the Waorani, for example, who are generally considered to be the most remote forest-dwelling group that survived into the twentieth century in Ecuador, shamanism is a far less prominent practice than it is among their Quichua neighbors.

This is not to suggest that Quichua shamanism is any less "authentic" or "indigenous" than shamanic traditions elsewhere in the world; rather, it should be considered in light of intercultural relations that have transformed over the past centuries. Nor does the relative absence of Waorani shamanism simply reflect a case of "acculturation" or culture loss in the face of missionaries and school education. It is striking that, while there are few shamans in most of their villages, most Waorani shamans today live in the areas most regularly visited by foreign tourist groups. As we have seen, Waorani people seek Quichua shamans both to cure illnesses associated with kowori people and to deal with sorcery attacks between Waorani. They are attracted to Quichua shamans not only for their renowned powers in dealing with nonhuman agents and distant peoples but also because Waorani shamans have a marginal place and negative connotation in Toñampari and other villages. Since shamans are just as likely to be accused of witchcraft as they are to be asked to give a cure, the role of shamans has become untenable in a context where the notion of comunidad is oriented toward avoiding potential conflicts that might disrupt the current period of relative peace. For those Waorani people committed to the idea of living in a comunidad, the presence of local shamans has simply become too dangerous. This is why most Waorani people see shamanism in a negative light, yet nevertheless they occasionally pay for the services of a Quichua shaman after suffering a sorcery attack.

Conclusion

This chapter has considered Waorani understandings of shamanism alongside what it means to them to live in a comunidad. In Toñampari an emphasis on avoiding direct confrontations between individuals and the general absence of Waorani shamans are part of local efforts to prevent a return to violence between rival groups. The changes that accompany this emerging notion of comunidad also reveal certain continuities in Waorani social organization and cosmology. Rather than evidencing the disappearance of indigenous culture in the face of outside pressure, the emergence of large villages, the decline of shamanism, and other key social changes reflect Waorani efforts to transform other people into kin and to create productive relations within their own vision of comunidad. Once we dismiss the common stereotype that extreme levels of violence are a defining aspect of Waorani society, we can better understand the value Waorani people themselves place on "living well" among an increasingly diverse group of neighbors. In the social world I have described, however, living in a comunidad involves maintaining a degree of household and personal autonomy at the same time that intercultural relations with kowori people are part of everyday life.

This is not to say that the Waorani have become a "peaceful" society, any more than previous generations should be defined solely by their violence. At times Waorani voice their concerns about how current conflicts and events may lead to a return to the violence that has such a strong presence in social memory. Like the elders who, after years of revenge killings and relative isolation, forged new social and economic links with Waorani and kowori neighbors at the mission settlement, my hosts in Toñampari embrace a similar process of intergroup alliance in their emphasis on comunidad. The transition from living in longhouses to village settlement reveals not only an enduring indigenous emphasis on individual and household autonomy but also key transformations embraced by Waorani people themselves.

CHAPTER 7

Victims and Warriors

Whether mourning the loss of kin, performing as "wild" Amazonian warriors, or describing Christian missionaries, Waorani ways of remembering violence evoke as much a sense of mutual experience as they do social and political divides. In all of the contexts described in this book, these memories reveal a specific cosmology and way of life through which Waorani people engage and come to understand relations that transcend the remote location of their villages. Just as shamans, kowori outsiders, and "uncontacted" people become targets of violence, so too are they remembered in certain contexts as kin. We have seen that, for many Waorani, violence not only leads to feelings of loss and anger but also to a certain "mutuality of being" (Sahlins 2011a) with people whose kin become victims of violence. In this way, even if an emphasis on avenging the death of a kinsman implies a potentially endless series of violent reprisals, Waorani perspectives on past violence also call for transforming relations of alterity and enmity into productive relations of kinship and marriage. It is precisely this transformation that many Waorani today describe as "civilization," a process that refers as much to the idealized conditions of contemporary villages and a proposed future for the Taromenani as it does missionization in the 1960s.

If I have succeeded in conveying a specifically Waorani way of being in the world, such a world should not be understood simply in terms of indigenous autonomy or a timeless cultural tradition. The lives of Waorani people, like people everywhere, are lived in part through ongoing social transformations and intercultural relations. Indigenous forms of social memory have an important bearing on the wider political and economic forces sweeping across Amazonia today, many of which are well beyond the direct control of people like the Waorani. In this context remembering is not just about establishing an accurate "history" that separates the past from the present or about distilling an image of what "authentic" Waorani culture may have looked like at a certain point in the past. Nor is Waorani memory centrally a question of "indigenous identity" in the simplified ways that indigenous peoples are often conceptualized and judged according to foreign expectations of cultural continuity and static tradition. Whether in embodied imagery of the colonial auca performed by Waorani youth in frontier towns or the biographies of specific people told by elders, the kinds of remembering I have described in this book have an orientation toward the future. In multiple and sometimes contradictory ways, these memories tell us something about what it means to be a Waorani person, what people aspire to be, and the kind of community they want to live in.

For Waorani people the past is a complex terrain of people and events that are idealized, lamented, and challenged according to changing social contexts. It may appear contradictory that the same people who emphasize what they describe as their "civilization" through missionary settlement also celebrate the autonomy and freedom of their ancestors in pre-contact times. Just as there are different ways of being Waorani, there are different ways of engaging the past in the present. While narratives of pre-contact autonomy and mission settlement tell different stories, they speak to equally important visions for a future that many Waorani hope to share. Just as having become "civilized" in the past is associated with new intergroup alliances and a period of growth and expansion, the emphasis on incorporating other people into contemporary villages and the desire to "civilize" uncontacted groups are part of this future orientation. The point here is that this kind of remembering, rather than expressing a generic notion of indigeneity rooted in "history" or "tradition," calls for a certain kind of relations in the present and in the future.

In describing my Waorani hosts, their stories, and their lives as I came to experience them over the course of several years, this book has centrally been an attempt to understand indigenous people in their contemporary context. Waorani people today face what sometimes appear to be insurmountable challenges, whether in negotiating with multinational oil companies, curing basic illnesses, or adapting to everyday life in urban spaces where they enter Ecuadorian society near the bottom of an entrenched national racial/spatial order (Rahier 1998). It is tempting to view contemporary Waorani experience through the lens of our own assumptions about "traditional" cultures struggling to come to terms with "modernity," whereby indigenous Amazonian people are destined to be assimilated or eliminated altogether by the march of modern progress. In this popular image rooted in Western social imagination, Waorani people are historical objects rather than people who have an active role in shaping the future of Amazonia. While the powerful social and economic interests that threaten the lands and way of life of the Waorani and other Amazonian peoples make such a teleological view compelling in some ways, I hope that my ethnography also challenges the model of "tradition" and "modernity" that informs conventional thinking about indigenous people.

It is precisely this tradition/modernity framework that appears to have misguided some of the best-known studies of violence in Amazonia. In Napoleon Chagnon's famous study of Yanomami warfare, for example, violence is presented not only as a timeless traditional practice but also as a primordial state of human nature. As violence is assumed to be part of a natural state of being for certain "tribal" peoples, we are tempted to read contemporary societies like the Yanomami and the Woarani in terms of either "traditional" violence or their acculturation in the face of modernity. Either way, such an approach eludes the weight and meaning of violence as it unfolds in the complexity of everyday social life and how violent practices relate to wider political and economic processes in the present. I hope to have shown the importance of thinking about violence as a contemporary concern in Amazonia rather than as an artifact of human evolution or colonialism. In locating Waorani understandings of violence in the context of social transformation, this book illustrates that violence in Amazonia is not simply a question of tradition, nor can it be explained exclusively as a result of externally driven processes associated with modernity.

The Waorani are no more "historical" than mestizo Ecuadorians or Europeans, and it is becoming increasingly clear that they are as much a part of the contemporary world as anyone else. Despite the ills of colonial history and the social and ecological crises in Amazonia today, the actions of indigenous people have important political consequences. In the space of just a few decades, they have gone from being seen by many as mere obstacles to development to being recognized as having a key political and economic presence on a world stage. Beyond the growing voice of indigenous peoples in debates about large-scale national development agendas, they have come to be seen by many as a valuable resource, whether as a reservoir of "indigenous knowledge" of plants of potential use in developing pharmaceuticals for a global market or as "eco-warriors" with key stakes in international debates about deforestation, conservation, and climate change. In this context the question is not whether they are part of a "modern" or "global" world but the extent to which people like the Waorani will be able to engage these processes on their own terms and to the benefit of their own communities in the future.

While the political activism of some Amazonian peoples has made impressive gains in recent decades, this activism coexists with popular Western ideas of indigeneity and "culture" that have long since been challenged by anthropologists. It is telling that they are often embraced more as symbols of national heritage and global environmentalism than they are as members of viable communities with their own agendas. As the public "warrior" performances I described in chapter 2 illustrate, Waorani engage creatively and productively with the kind of visual imagery that constitutes cultural authenticity in the eyes of outsiders. These encounters point to how such categories and images have become part of the politics and social imagination of Amazonian peoples themselves. Some critics, such as Adam Kuper, point out that in adopting "essentialist ideologies of culture and identity," indigenous peoples today assert their right to difference in the idiom of a "Western cultural theory" based on race and "primitive society" (2003, 395). While Kuper is concerned that indigenous rights posit privileged or even exclusive rights to minority groups at the expense of non-indigenous people, it is important to recognize that, in Amazonia as in other parts of the world, the indigenous movement is primarily a struggle against the discrimination and dispossession that groups like the Waorani have faced for centuries (Kenrick and Lewis 2004, 4). Put another way, it is about challenging the way certain people have been denied rights on the basis of cultural differences (Turner 2004, 265), regardless of how these differences are construed by more powerful groups.

It would be as misleading to deny the political importance of Waorani claims to difference on the basis of "culture" as it would be to dismiss their "warrior" performances at folklore festivals and protests as simply an artifact of colonial imagination. As Rita Ramos argues, to criticize indigenous people for drawing on essentialist notions of culture and indigeneity in this context "is to blame the conquered for the conqueror's bad language" (2003, 397). Whether we approach Waorani public expressions of difference in terms of colonial history or indigenous political activism, the forms of social memory I have described are much more than a metacultural practice in which Waorani people define and comment on their own "culture." Even as they adopt the language of their kowori neighbors and understand their symbolic place in Ecuadorian society, Waorani people do not see themselves as conquered. Nor is being an "indigenous people" or "nationality" the only or even the primary way in which they understand themselves to be different from other Ecuadorians. The concepts of difference that I have described in this book do not map easily onto the "identity politics" often associated with indigenous movements in Latin America. After decades of confrontation with oil companies and the Ecuadorian state, the Waorani have until recently been, and to some extent remain, relatively marginal to the national indigenous movement in Ecuador. Even as they engage in regional and national debates about indigenous issues through their own official political office, Waorani memory, sociality, and contemporary politics are not just about questions of what it means to be indigenous. I hope to have shown how they construe the relationship between past and present, self and other in ways that defy our own preconceptions about indigeneity, tradition, and modernity. Waorani politics are as much about Quichua shamans, conflicts between rival families, and challenging the actions of local indigenous leaders as they are about confrontations with oil companies and the state.

Yasuní-ITT and the Future of Amazonia

If Waorani ways of remembering are, as I suggest, as much about imagining the future as they are about recording past events, the question remains regarding what this future might look like. While it would be overly ambitious to make any serious predictions, many of the issues I have considered in this book have changed since I began my fieldwork and continue to change as I write these pages. This illustrates that any attempt at ethnography is at once more than simply a snapshot at a specific point in time and less than a comprehensive description of "Waorani culture" to be taken as a timeless authority. One could argue that this is in fact one of the enduring strengths of ethnography. While the stories and encounters I have described stretch across many years, recent events in Ecuador and in the world at large have immediate consequences for Waorani people. In this section I consider the implications of these ongoing issues, some of which have important bearing on questions I have raised about violence, memory, and intercultural relations in the previous chapters.

Over the past fifty years oil development has become part of everyday life for many Waorani and their encounters with kowori people. Historically, Ecuador's Amazonian region has been valued as a vast resource to be exploited by selling concessions to oil companies and by opening up the frontier to Ecuadorian colonists moving east in search of a better life. Expanding massively since the early 1970s, the oil industry today accounts for more than half of Ecuador's total export revenue and provides around a third of its tax revenue. As the imagined "wild Indians" of Amazonian Ecuador have at times asserted their presence by attacking oil camps and more recently by organizing politically to defend their lands, indigenous peoples have often been viewed as an obstacle to national development. The emergence of regional and national indigenous movements, along with the alliances they now forge with environmentalists across the globe, has radically altered the contemporary political landscape of Amazonia. In Ecuador, debates about environmental politics and indigenous rights have become an increasingly controversial theme since the election of President Rafael Correa in 2007. Correa's call for a "citizens' revolution" to establish a "socialism for the twenty-first century" has led to sweeping reforms in Ecuador. While the overall effect of this nationalist rhetoric will be the subject of much future debate, there has been a noticeable shift in the way the state has approached land, people, and natural resources in the Amazonian provinces. Seen conventionally as a source of potential wealth to be exploited by extractive industries, Amazonia has become part of a new national eco-political agenda that claims to situate ecology and indigenous people at the center of attempts to achieve an altogether new kind of development.

The creative potential and the limits of this emerging eco-political campaign became clear in the now failed joint proposal of Ecuador and the United Nations Development Program (UNDP) to prevent further oil development in the Yasuní National Park. One of the richest areas of biodiversity in the world, the Yasuní is home to several Waorani communities and includes vast expanses of forest inhabited by indigenous groups living in voluntary isolation.[1] In the "Ecuador Yasuní-ITT Trust Fund" initiative,[2] President Correa originally agreed to leave around 846 million barrels of oil underground if the international community compensated the government for at least half of the estimated revenues they would receive from extracting the oil. This in effect called for individuals and foreign governments to contribute around $3.6 billion over several years in exchange for certificates guaranteeing the Ecuadorian government would maintain the Yasuní oil reserves underground indefinitely. In proposing to invest the revenues in environmental restoration and conservation, renewable energy, scientific research, and social development, the Yasuní Initiative called for "a new cooperative model between developed and developing countries" (Yasuní-ITT 2010, 3).[3] Many also envisioned the initiative as a way for Ecuador and the international community to address climate change by preventing the emission of more than 400 million metric tons of carbon dioxide that would result from the burning of fossil fuels.

In marking a sea change in the way Ecuador assigns value to oil and biodiversity (Rival 2010b) Yasuní-ITT appeared to be part of a wider shift in social, political, and ecological thinking in a country whose new national constitution, approved by Correa's government in 2008 after a national vote, drew international attention for being the first country to establish the "rights of nature."[4] The Yasuní-ITT Initiative, which continues to have widespread support among Ecuadorians, emerged as a landmark proposal in framing environmental conservation and indigenous rights as part of a national interest. Many analysts and activists identified the initiative as a global model for environmental conservation that could benefit other biodiversity-rich countries that depend on environmentally destructive extractive economies. The Yasuní model directly addressed the problems of an export-led economy that has plummeted resource-rich developing countries like Ecuador into seemingly inescapable debt.

Discussions about the Yasuní Park have important implications for Waorani people, not least because some of them live within the boundaries of the park and claim much of it as their ancestral lands. While much of the Yasuní Initiative was framed in terms of promoting conservation, sustainability, and addressing historical economic inequalities between northern and southern countries, it also presented indigenous rights as part of a new model of development. Promotional materials, which made extensive use of photographs and videos of Waorani, emphasized "respect for the cultures" and "ancestral rights" of indigenous people living in the park. One of the specific goals stated in the proposal was to "allow the Tagaeri and Taromenani indigenous peoples to remain in voluntary isolation" (2010, 5). In this context the rights of indigenous people, like the "rights of nature," are understood to be part of a new regime of value oriented toward a sustainable future.

Despite the remarkable turn this initiative appears to have marked in Ecuador and internationally, it has not survived the Ecuadorian government's determination to maintain oil as the cornerstone of an otherwise fledgling national economy. On August 15, 2013, I joined three Waorani friends on a trip to the Plaza Grande in the city center of Quito, where we waited alongside a few hundred Ecuadorians in front of the national palace to hear President Correa's official address to the nation about the Yasuní Initiative. As many people had anticipated Correa's plans to abandon the initiative, there was a strong sense of protest in the audience even before Correa appeared on a widescreen television and announced his immediate plans to exploit the new Yasuní oil fields. Citing the lack of international financial support and the desperate need to alleviate poverty in Ecuador as reasons for abandoning the Yasuní Initiative, he described how new oil development would begin within weeks. Despite previous state-sponsored marketing campaigns warning of the fragility of the Yasuní and the need to protect it from further oil development, he now insisted that new oil drilling would affect less than one percent of the total area of the park and bring billions of dollars of revenue to the Ecuadorian state to develop the country.

Correa's controversial decision was not altogether surprising. Many suspected that he never actually intended to protect the Yasuní and instead used the initiative as a political tool to cultivate sympathy from environmentalists, allowing him to attribute responsibility for the ongoing destruction of Amazonian rainforest to the international community and foreign oil companies rather than the Ecuadorian state. As Correa noted in his speech, however, the failed Yasuní proposal has coincided with a wellspring of concern about environmental conservation in Ecuador, particularly with regard to Amazonia. While indigenous people across Ecuador have organized a number of mass protests against the state since the 1990s, debates about preserving the Yasuní Park have also become a source of key political debate and protest among mestizos in Quito and elsewhere in the country. Many of the protestors who came to hear Correa's speech were urban mestizos carrying placards demanding the protection of both the Yasuní and the indigenous peoples who live there. One of them was dressed as an indigenous Amazonian woman with a baby doll in her arms splashed with black oil. My Waorani friends, some of the few indigenous Amazonian people at the Plaza Grande that night, came dressed in street clothes and feathered crowns that caught the attention of other protestors. Before long they were busy giving interviews to news reporters about their thoughts on the Yasuní. Despite the anger they expressed about the prospect of further oil development on their ancestral lands, they appeared to be amused and keenly interested in the kind of solidarity they have come to expect more from foreigners than from other Ecuadorians.

FIGURE 19. Reporters interview a Waorani man at a protest in Quito against President Correa's decision to abandon the Yasuní-ITT Initiative

Just as the Waorani are celebrated in urban Amazonia and in the Yasuní campaign for their imagined warriorhood and closeness to nature, so-called "uncontacted" peoples like the Taromenani have become part of a wider narrative of conservation for what is assumed to be their "natural" or "pristine" state of isolation. This became particularly clear when a number of mestizo activists placed nude photographs of themselves posing and performing as Taromenani on Facebook as part of their campaign against oil development in the Yasuní. Like the Yasuní Park itself, indigenous peoples, and especially those living in voluntary isolation, constitute a specific symbolic value in national and global imaginations that to some extent delimits their place in the contemporary world. A global vision of environmental conservation and combating climate change, and the potential alliances it promotes between indigenous people and outsiders, holds a certain promise to benefit indigenous groups like the Waorani in the future. At the same

FIGURE 20. Oil roads and pipelines are part of everyday life for Waorani living in communities near the Tagaeri-Taromenani Untouchable Zone

time these alliances are inherently fragile because they are often based on misleading stereotypes about indigenous peoples that have characterized eco-politics in Amazonia in the past. As Conklin and Graham (1995) note, the "middle ground" between Western environmental activists and Amazonian peoples can collapse abruptly when the latter fail to live up to conservationist expectations.

Although being portrayed as "ecological" or "historical" people may bring certain advantages to the Waorani, such a symbolic politics may also limit how they and other indigenous communities are able to determine their own futures. It is one thing to accept the Waorani as traditional eco-warriors, the "noble savages" of our own imagination, and another thing altogether to recognize them as viable communities and individual citizens with diverse interests in the contemporary world. One question that remains is to what degree they can achieve this recognition when their ideas and practices betray the expectations of outsiders. How will foreign environmentalists, the UN or the Ecuadorian state react if, as has happened elsewhere in Amazonia, some Waorani decide to use their lands in ways that conflict with the current model of conservation? And what if, as many Waorani hope, the Taromenani or another "uncontacted" group decides to end their isolation and live among the Waorani or other Ecuadorians? This is partly a question of whether we can accept them when they don't conform to our own expectations of what indigenous Amazonian people should be like. Another question is how Waorani themselves will negotiate these contradictions in the future. While much remains to be seen, in this book I hope to have made at least a start at trying to understand how Waorani people engage with an intercultural dynamics in which they encounter not only new possibilities but also the stereotypes, prejudices, and power inequalities that have plagued this part of the world for centuries. At present, on the streets of frontier cities in Amazonian Ecuador the same Waorani adolescent who is accused of not being a "real Indian" for wearing jeans and a t-shirt can be turned away from a popular bar or restaurant for being an indigenous person. This is to say that although indigenous peoples have achieved a significant political presence that has to some extent challenged their historical position in Ecuadorian society, it is unclear whether the new social and ecological philosophy of initiatives like Yasuní-ITT would fundamentally alter the place of Waorani people in the national imagination.

Remembering the Taromenani

The presence of indigenous peoples living in voluntary isolation is no less important to my Waorani hosts than it is to proponents of the Yasuní Initiative. While the fate of the Taromenani is a pressing concern for Waorani people, their understandings of isolation, like their understandings of sociality and violence, present a certain contrast to the views of many conservationists and indigenous rights activists. Both in Ecuador and in the history of anthropology, indigenous peoples have often been presented as unified "communities," defined primarily by their assumed cohesion and mutual identification (Stasch 2009). For my Waorani hosts, being a Waorani person is indeed an important expression of self and other. In chapter 5 I described how they embrace living in a community that brings together families who were once relatively isolated. But as we have seen, particularly in the stories Waorani tell about past violence, they see themselves as anything but the "perfect unity of wills" by which communities have traditionally been conceptualized (Tönnies [1887] 1957, 37, in Stasch 2009, 7).[5] Like the disagreements Waorani elders describe in the past about attacking kowori intruders or taking revenge against rival groups, today there is considerable debate about how to deal with their "uncontacted" neighbors. For some, they are remembered as kin who should be drawn to live in villages among "civilized" Waorani. For others, they are dangerous enemies who must be killed to avenge kinsmen who were speared by Tagaeri or Taromenani in the past. Given the weight of violence in social memory and the Taromenani massacre in 2003, it is not altogether surprising that Waorani people today do not share a unified vision of these groups, much less a common strategy to deal with them. In this section I consider the possible implications of recent events that have plunged relations between Waorani and Taromenani people into further uncertainty.

In chapter 4 I described how, in the aftermath of the massacre in 2003, many Waorani feared revenge attacks by Taromenani survivors. Unfortunately, their predictions proved to be accurate. Several kowori loggers and Waorani have since been killed in attacks carried out by "uncontacted" people presumed to be Taromenani. Tensions culminated in March 2013, when an elderly Waorani couple were speared and killed near their home in Yarentaro, a village located along the oil road extending into the Yasuní Park in an area near the Tagaeri-Taromenani Untouchable Zone. The male elder who died reportedly had communicated with Taromenani on several occasions before the attack. It has been widely reported that the couple were killed after failing to provide sufficient pots, axes, and other manufactured goods demanded by Taromenani in previous encounters.[6] Some Waorani describe the attack as an act of revenge for the 2003 killings, while others suggest that the killings may have been in response to the poisoning of several Taromenani by items dropped near them by a helicopter. While much uncertainty remains about the recent violence and its causes, what is clear is that the victims' relatives wasted little time in mounting a search for the group responsible for the killings. Within weeks several Waorani from the surrounding area, heavily armed with guns, launched a revenge attack in which as many as thirty Taromenani were killed. Even as two young girls were abducted from the scene and continue to be held captive in a Waorani community, there has been little significant state intervention on behalf of the captives or their surviving relatives.[7] The situation of these girls is emblematic of the precarious position of "uncontacted" groups like the Taromenani in Ecuador, caught as they are between increasingly lethal frontier violence and the wider politics of isolation.

At the time of this writing, many questions remain about this latest series of killings. It is difficult, however, not to see certain parallels with the 2003 massacre, which was as revealing about Waorani understandings of violence as it was about intercultural processes and national development agendas in Amazonia. As with the 2003 Taromenani killings, Waorani people are divided in their views and their responses to these events, leading to renewed tensions between Waorani families and communities. The repeated statements of Waorani political leaders against state intervention mask what has become a potentially dangerous division between Waorani with regards to so-called "uncontacted" people. Many Waorani today speak of the need to protect their "uncontacted" neighbors from the onslaught of angry Waorani and the impact of extractive industries. For some, the fact that the captive girls speak a recognizable form of the Waorani language, alongside their status as kin of victims, confirms their identity as long-lost kin; for others the Taromenani are members of an "enemy" group they seek to eliminate in avenging their own deceased kin. But even for the Waorani killers, vengeance is not the only kind of relationship at stake with people living in voluntary isolation. As in Waorani accounts of spear-killings in the distant past and more recent dealings with kowori, it appears that the 2013 killings and abductions were carried out with a view to incorporating certain "enemies" into their homes and everyday lives. This is to say that these "uncontacted" people are also "potential affines" who, over time, may become familiar in the actualization of kinship.

Despite the legal recognition of the Untouchable Zone and ongoing debates about how to protect the rights of people living in "voluntary isolation," the Ecuadorian authorities and Waorani representatives appear to share the view that the Taromenani killings are an "indigenous issue," a "conflict between clans" to be handled by indigenous groups themselves rather than through state intervention. By casting the recent violence as a "clan conflict" and disavowing any connection between oil development and the recent killings, Correa's government embraces a popular image of "traditional" violence or "indigenous justice" that conveniently denies the state's responsibility for the current situation. Despite the many anthropological critiques of the idea that violence is part of the very nature of indigenous Amazonian people like the Waorani, these representations continue to have a certain political force. This is especially clear now in Ecuador, where such assumptions implicitly excuse and support the interests of extractive industries. Waorani politicians have appeared in news interviews to denounce oil companies and logging for contributing to current conflicts, at once calling for the government to bring these disruptive industries to a halt and insisting on Waorani autonomy in their own affairs. At the same time, international lawyers and activists point to the legal responsibility of the Ecuadorian state to protect people living in voluntary isolation. At the time of my writing, none of the Waorani men involved in the 2003 or 2013 attacks has been prosecuted,[8] and the impasse between indigenous rights and the politics of isolation can be seen in government inaction despite broad-based concerns about the fate of the Taromenani and other groups living in voluntary isolation.

If the recent killings point to the absence of a unified Waorani view of uncontacted groups, the current situation also makes abundantly clear that violence is more than just a question of memory, history, or "tradition." It is difficult to know just how closely the intensity of Waorani warfare prior to the 1960s was related to the dramatic social, economic, and epidemiological upheavals of colonialism and its aftermath in Amazonia. There should be no doubt, however, that the violence I have described is a contemporary practice that has significant bearing on not only the lives of Waorani people but also on other Ecuadorians who are part of the wider intercultural context of this violence. Rather than the disappearing trace of an exotic "lost tribe" or evidence of our deepest human nature, it reveals contemporary power relations in a region once invaded by European explorers in search of riches, then abandoned to its own fate, only to be revisited in recent decades by a new constellation of political and economic interests. I hope to have shown how my Waorani hosts engage with this process in terms of their own concepts, practices, and hopes for the future, even as this future depends on more than just their own actions. For better or worse, kowori have always been and continue to be among the other people through which Waorani conceive of their own way of life and experience its transformation. Like their seemingly enigmatic relations with the Taromenani, Waorani people see their relations with kowori outsiders as potentially destructive and productive. It is the transformation of these relations into kinship and comunidad that many Waorani convey in their memories of "civilization" and embrace as part of an uncertain future.

Afterword

Some of the recent events described in this book have continued to un-
fold in Ecuador. The most important of these is the arrest and imprison-
ment of seven Waorani men involved in the latest revenge attack against
the Taromenani. After many months during which the government was
criticized for delaying their investigation into the massacre of some thirty
Taromenani in March 2013, the following November national police entered
a Waorani village in the Yasuní National Park in a helicopter to make the
arrests. Along with the initial arrests, one of the two girls abducted in the
raid in March was taken into custody by government authorities. The men
are among sixteen Waorani accused of genocide by the Court of Justice of
Orellana Province, where they continue to be held in prison as a preven-
tive "security" measure. If convicted of the charge of genocide, they could
receive a prison sentence of up to twenty-five years.

For many observers concerned about the plight of a vulnerable, isolated
population, this response on the part of the government is simply too little
and too late. As we have seen in chapter 4, the gravity of the situation was
already evident after the 2003 massacre, when many Waorani recognized
the likelihood of further violence. There was a similar lack of response to
warnings that retaliation was imminent in 2013 after the killing of an elderly
Waorani couple in the Yasuní. And yet, Waorani are divided with regard to
what the state's role in response to the latest violence should be. During my

last trip to Ecuador in 2013, several Waorani people expressed to me their frustration about the lack of state intervention on behalf of the Taromenani and especially on behalf of the girls who were still held by their captors at the time. For others, even the belated arrests in the name of justice and human rights are an inappropriate application of mestizo laws to people for whom such laws are foreign. Relatives of the accused contend that the massacre was a legitimate act of retribution in their own culture and should be respected as such. Just as Waorani make appeals to the Ecuadorian authorities to respect their autonomy, lawyers and other commentators call for the state to recognize the latest massacre of the Taromenani as a form of "indigenous justice," arguing that revenge killings are necessary for restoring "equilibrium" in Waorani society (Aguirre 2014). As tenuous as such an argument might appear to people familiar with the history of intergroup violence in this part of the world, it has certain traction in a world where state institutions struggle to reconcile universal human rights with respect for cultural differences.

What should not be forgotten in this discussion is how an ever-expanding oil frontier in Ecuador continues to pressurize relations between Waorani people and groups living in voluntary isolation. For decades oil development has continued to push farther into areas where Amazonian people resist the occupation and destruction of their lands. Since president Correa's withdrawal from the Yasuní-ITT initiative in 2013 the drive for oil-based development has only continued and expanded, raising the likelihood of further conflicts between Waorani and outsiders in the future. Already, journalists and activists have reported the construction of new roads into the Yasuní Park to service oil production platforms, roads that appear to contradict the government's stated commitment to limit the impact of further oil development in the park (Hill 2014).

As in 2003, the current media focus on the Taromenani killings as a form of "tribal violence" or "indigenous justice" eludes the fact that these conflicts are as much about national and international economic agendas as they are about indigenous forms of revenge. While the power of oil reigns supreme, the Ecuadorian government appears to find the inconvenient presence of the Waorani and Taromenani increasingly difficult to ignore. Alongside the attention this situation has attracted internationally, a coalition of indigenous people and activist groups in Ecuador have collected the signatures of hundreds of thousands of Ecuadorians calling for a public referendum on Correa's decision to expand oil production farther into the

Yasuní National Park. Although the government has rejected many of the signatures as fraudulent, there is hope that national and global attention to environmental conservation and indigenous rights in Amazonia will make the growing public concern about these issues less easily ignored in the future.

Notes

Introduction

1. See, for example, Appadurai (1996); Whitehead (2002); Tsing (2005); and Meyer (2010).

2. Auca is a Quichua word that has been adopted into mainstream Ecuadorian Spanish, where it connotes "wild" forest-dwelling people.

3. Households today usually consist of parents and their unmarried children but sometimes include male affines who live with their wife's household for a period after marriage. In past times larger longhouses often incorporated more than one "nuclear" family based on siblingship (Rival 1996a). Chapter 4 considers how this household composition has changed considerably in the context of interethnic marriages with Quichuas.

4. ONHAE has since been replaced by a similar indigenous organization, NAWE, which stands for the Waorani Nationality of Ecuador. I use the spelling "Waorani" instead of the Spanish "Huaorani" in my writing in part to reflect this change and its increasing use by Woarani people.

5. In recent years anthropologists have adopted a historical approach to a wide range of themes, including indigenous warfare (Ferguson 1995), shamanism (Gow 1996), myth (Hill 1988), interethnic relations (Taylor 1999, 2007), and village spatial organization (Heckenberger 2005).

6. See, for example, Connerton (1989); Nora (1989); and Whitehouse (1996).

7. Robbins (2007) argues that a more general tendency in anthropology to emphasize cultural continuity has prevented us dealing with questions of change and rupture in the societies we study.

8. Despite the wide-ranging criticisms of Chagnon's work, his most recent book, *Noble Savages* (2013), reiterates and underscores his evolutionary approach to Ya-nomami warfare. The book, which is targeted at popular audiences, demonstrates that the traditional image of Amazonian warriorhood persists to some extent in anthropology and in Western imagination.

9. This focus on group solidarity and peaceful sociality can be seen as part of a wider "anthropology of peace" approach that questions the emphasis on violence in anthropological writing (see Sponsel and Gregor 1994; Gregor 1996; Howell and Willis 1989; Sponsel 2010).

10. Santos-Granero makes the important observation that a temporal perspective on Amazonian sociality reveals the inherent problem in describing any group as "violent" or "peaceful," arguing that "we should instead look at the social processes by which conviviality is constructed—and also destroyed" (2000, 269).

11. Studies of witchcraft and assault sorcery have also contributed to a renewed focus on violence in Amazonia (see, for example, Whitehead 2002; Whitehead and Wright 2004; High 2012a, 2012b).

12. Exceptions include Albert and Ramos's (2000) collection on the cosmological implications of contact between indigenous people and whites in Northern Amazonia, and Cepek's (2008, 2012) work on the connections between cosmology and political activism among the Cofán in Ecuador. Other examples include Bonilla (2005) and Kelly (2011).

13. As Clastres observed in indigenous South America, such an "acute sense of the absurd" should not be taken for a lack of underlying seriousness, as laughter is often a way people "[make] fun of their own fears" (1987, 130).

Chapter 1. Civilized Victims

1. See, for example, Oberem 1974; Reeve 1994; Uzendoski 2004; and Taylor 1999.

2. The vast missionary literature on the Woarani and the Tiweno mission includes: Wallis 1960, 1973; Elliot 1957, 1961; Kingsland 1980; Liefield 1990; and Saint 2005.

3. Rival (1993) describes a symbolic link between Waorani perceptions of growth in plants and trees and their understandings of past cycles of revenge, peace, and social expansion.

4. See also Wallis (1960) for an early missionary account of how a Waorani narrator interprets the thoughts and dreams of victims just before they died.

5. Both in these stories and in their everyday conversations, Waorani make extensive use of words that imitate sound qualities. Many of the hundreds of Waorani ideophones are accompanied by specific gestures that are central to communication and dialogue. Such extensive use of ideophones is not uncommon in Amazonia. Nuckolls (2010), for example, describes how, among Quechua speakers of Pastaza province in Amazonian Ecuador with whom Waorani intermarry, ideophones are at the core of communicative interactions between people and between humans and nonhumans. See also Uzendoski and Calapucha-Tapuy (2012).

6. In 1969 approximately sixteen Waorani died and several others were left severely disabled from a polio epidemic at the Tiweno mission settlement (Kimerling 1996, 179).

7. The film was produced by Every Tribe Entertainment and was shot in Panama, where most of the Waorani characters' roles were cast with local indigenous people.

8. Rival reported similar Waorani accounts of Dayuma's brother being fatally shot by Rachel's Saint's brother during the struggle (2002, 157).

9. This statement appeared on the "People of the Path" Web site: http://www .peopleofthepath.com/newpath-NEWS2.htm. It was signed by a well-known Waorani representative and political activist.

10. Despite the decline in the number of Waorani who identify themselves as Christian, there remains a handful of Waorani, mostly men, who became evangelical preachers during the mission period and continue to preach and read the Bible in Wao-terero.

11. Toña is a key figure in Waorani lore and was considered to be among the first Waorani to convert to Christianity.

12. Special thanks to Uboye Gaba for his help with the initial transcription and translation of this recording.

Chapter 2. Becoming Warriors

1. Price (2002) also describes how, in oral histories, forgetting is as important as remembering.

2. See Rival (1996a, 72–76) for a more extensive description of Moipa, his following, and their conflicts with kowori and other Waorani in the past.

3. In chapter 4 I discuss the history and importance this group has to Waorani people today.

4. Although to my knowledge there are no longer missionaries who reside permanently in Waorani villages, there are occasional visits from members of various evangelical and other denominations, especially in the larger villages.

5. In much of Amazonian Ecuador, the designation of "white" people has little to do with skin color but is instead a common identity among non-indigenous people of mixed (mestizo) descent who live in urban areas (Taylor 2007, 136). See Whitten and Whitten (2011) for an extensive historical and ethnographic analysis of how racial categories are used in Ecuador.

6. See Whitten (1976a) and Reeve (1993a) for more particular cases of this process of ethnogenesis.

7. See Whitten (1976a, 1978) for a closer description of how Jivaroan, Zaparoan, and other peoples merged to form Quichua-speaking ethnic groups.

8. Until recently the vast majority of schoolteachers employed to work in Toñampari and other Waorani villages were mestizos or indigenous people (primarily Quichuas and Shuar) from other parts of Amazonian Ecuador. Today, an increasing number of Waorani are taking up teaching and administrative roles in the schools.

9. See Overing and Passes (2000) for ethnographic examples of how peaceful sociality is idealized as an aesthetic of everyday conviviality in Amazonia.

10. See, for example, Turner 1995; Viveiros de Castro 1998a; Erikson 1999; Conklin 2001; and Vilaça 2005.

11. Connerton, among other social scientists, has described how memory is "habituated" in a range of ritual practices, bodily postures, movements, and pain.

12. See, for example, Conklin and Graham 1995; Conklin 1997; Prins 1997; and Jackson 1995.

13. This appears to be an example of Lévi-Strauss's (1966) characterization of "cold" societies projecting an image of continuity as historical transformations are incorporated into local institutions.

14. Oakdale (2004) describes how, in the context of village politics and urban ethnopolitics, narratives of past events involve generational strategies and conflicts between young and senior indigenous leaders.

Chapter 3. Like the Ancient Ones

1. However, a number of ethnographers have described aspects of gender antagonism and inequality in Amazonia (see Bamberger 1974; Gregor 1985; Murphy and Murphy 1974; Seymour-Smith 1991).

2. Waorani adults explain that, despite targeting specific men, these attacks sometimes involved killing entire families, either as a result of extreme anger or as a strategy to prevent potential counterattacks by survivors. In some cases surviving women and children were abducted and incorporated into the attacking group.

3. Interethnic marriages between Waorani and Quichua people are increasingly common and appear to be somewhat less stable than marriages between Waorani spouses. These marriages, most commonly between Waorani men and Quichua women, appear to evidence a shift from the "brideservice model" toward what Collier describes as the "equal bridewealth model" (1988, 71). Interethnic marriages generally involve a Waorani man and his family bringing money, food, or other gifts to a Quichua bride's household. In most cases, upon marriage the bride resides patrilocally with her Waorani in-laws.

4. Seymour-Smith (1991) describes how women's association with the internal reproduction of community and men's association with representing the group to outsiders is part of an ideology of male domination among Jivaroan groups.

5. Since Amazonian bodies are produced through conviviality and the collective consumption of similar substances (Vilaça 2005), it is no surprise that masculine agency is conceived as being created and enhanced by specific bodily processes. In some cases of warfare in Amazonia, for example, a killer is said to experience an infusion of the victim's blood into his stomach (Viveiros de Castro 1992), a substance that must be converted from external "enemy" potency into masculine agency through specific ritual practices (Conklin 2001). This work not only exemplifies how "predation" is a central idiom for relations of alterity in Amazonia (Viveiros

de Castro 1996) but also indicates that predatory relations involve specifically gendered practices that enhance the body's development.

6. The names *tageiri* and *taromenani* refer to the few highly nomadic groups living in the Waorani reserve who refuse village settlement and contact with non-Waorani people and Waorani who live in permanent settlements (Cabodevilla 1999). Many Waorani describe them as distant relatives with whom they lost contact during the mission period.

7. My discussion of "young men" refers to a broad category of Waorani males, including teenage students at village schools as well as married and unmarried men in their mid- to late twenties. What is central to this categorization is not exact age or marital status but rather the specific generational experiences of men who are compared to their elders and ancestors with regard to the hunting and warfare practices of the latter.

8. Several anthropologists have described how corporeal modifications and inscriptions mark subjectivity and social position in Amazonia (Santos Granero 2009; Turner 1995, 2009). Viveiros de Castro (2005) suggests that Amazonian cosmologies locate point of view and memory in the body.

9. Rival (2002) makes a similar observation regarding Waorani views on dietary changes leading to weaker bodies.

10. I sometimes heard these claims from sons of the same parents who on other occasions explained that they had never whipped their children.

11. Most of these English-language films are either dubbed in Spanish or have Spanish subtitles.

12. They also compared the tropical forest in the film to their own homeland (*monito ome*).

13. Oakdale (2005) also notes the increasing popularity of martial arts among the Kayabi, an indigenous group of the Brazilian Amazon.

14. Young people buy the videos and posters while on trips to the city.

15. Unlike other indigenous groups in Amazonian Ecuador who allow the manioc beer to sit and ferment for several days, Waorani women normally discard the remaining pulp within two days of mastication, resulting in a virtually nonalcoholic drink that is consumed relatively quickly.

16. This phenomenon is also related to the growing frequency of interethnic marriages between Waorani men and Quichua women, which generally requires a form of brideprice to be paid by the groom to his father-in-law in cash, meat, or manufactured goods. Some men say they work for oil companies specifically for this purpose.

17. The total Waorani population has increased from approximately five hundred in the 1960s (Yost 1981) to more than 2,500 today.

18. This is not to suggest that the experiences of Waorani women outside of their home communities are culturally or politically insignificant. Since the time of my primary fieldwork, the Waorani Women's Organization (AMWAE) has been estab-

lished in the regional capital, with the support of various NGOs and a U.S. Peace Corps volunteer. The organization has focused particularly on bringing together women from several communities to organize the production and sale of Waorani handicrafts in a city shop and abroad.

19. As Knauft has argued more generally in comparing shifting gender roles in Melanesia and Amazonia, these situations demonstrate "palpable tensions between customary and contemporary constructions of male worth" (1997, 240).

20. As Gutmann (1997, 402) warns, there is a tendency in academic and popular writing to assimilate all Latin American masculinities to a common narrative of sexist "machismo." My intention here is not to overgeneralize about Ecuadorian men but instead to highlight some of the key differences between Waorani and broader mestizo ways of being men in the frontier cities of eastern Ecuador. Many of the mestizo men and women in Ecuador's growing Amazonian cities have migrated from highland coastal regions of the country in the past two or three decades.

Chapter 4. Lost People and Distant Kin

1. See Cabodevilla (2004a) for a comparison between the objects recovered from the scene of the Taromenani attack and Waorani material culture. In addition to the spears discovered at the scene, there were also blowguns, a number of steel axes, machetes, and other manufactured goods there as well, indicating clearly that the group's relative isolation should not be mistaken for their ignorance of foreign people and technology.

2. The frontier village of Tiguino should not be mistaken for Tiweno, the village where the original evangelical mission was established.

3. I hope to make clear in this chapter that typical descriptions of the Taromenani and other indigenous groups as "uncontacted people" are misleading. Their relative isolation is the product of wider social, political, and economic processes involving other groups and the state, rather than a "natural" or primordial condition (Kirsch 1997). I use the terms "uncontacted" and "voluntary isolation" in reference to current discussions of the Taromenani in Ecuador while at the same time critically analyzing the assumptions often built into these categories.

4. See Cabodevilla (1999) for a detailed history of the Tagaeri and how they became isolated from other Waorani groups.

5. Ecuador's Executive Decree 552 was signed by President Jamil Mahuad in 1999, and the reserve was later renamed the Tagaeri-Taromenani Untouchable Zone (Zona Intangible Tagaeri-Taromenani). The official boundaries of the Untouchable Zone were only finalized in 2007, in part as a result of the 2003 killings (Rival 2010b, 5).

6. Rival (1996a) and Cabodevilla (2004a, 2004b) both describe the mythical qualities Waorani attribute to the Taromenani (sometimes spelled "Taromenane"), whether as contemporary neighbors or legendary people of the past.

7. See Stoll (1982) and Kimerling (1996) for a more detailed historical and political

commentary on the actions of the oil industry and its effect on Waorani communities in this area.

8. The Yasuní National Park, which covers nearly ten thousand square kilometers, is considered one of the richest areas of biodiversity in the world. Designated as a UNESCO biosphere reserve in 1989, it is also home to several Waorani communities and is a site of intensive oil production.

9. See Cabodevilla (2004b, 137–38) for a more extensive account of the history of conflicts between Waorani from Tiguino and the Tagaeri.

10. Cabodevilla (2004b, 38–39) provides an account of how some of the men involved described the attack.

11. Perhaps most impressive about this whole event was the speed with which even the most minor details of the killing appeared to spread in Toñampari and elsewhere. While some people spoke to me specifically about the massacre and its implications, I learned just as much about their views from conversations I overheard in the course of everyday life.

12. It is difficult to guess the precise number of people killed or injured in the attack. While the bodies of twelve victims were found at the scene (Cabodevilla 2004b, 29), some of those who escaped may have died later as a result of their injuries.

13. Some people were more eager to talk to me about the attack than others. Given the small scale of Waorani society, some Toñampari residents were close relatives of the men who carried out the attack, which likely influenced whether or not and how they spoke to me about it.

14. See, for example, Bashkow (2006) and Viveiros de Castro (2004).

15. See Bessire (2012, 468) for a more comprehensive review of how "uncontacted" or "primitive" societies have ceased to be a relevant object of anthropological study.

16. This is not to assume that such assertions of victimhood will not at some point be evoked to legitimate future revenge killings. As Robarchek and Robarchek (1998, 2005) have suggested, the notion of lost autonomy and victimhood are often the very basis of "rage" among the Waorani.

17 While we should be careful not to ignore certain aspects of relatedness that are in part determined by birth and descent (Lepri 2005), there is a noticeable emphasis on the processual or performative character of Amazonian kinship. See, for example, Gow 1991; Overing and Passes 2000; McCallum 2001; and Vilaça 2002.

18. Taylor (1993, 1996), Vilaça (2005), and Fausto and Heckenberger (2007) also contribute to discussions of how memory is central to considerations of kinship and the body in Amazonia.

19. For examples from Amazonia, see Taylor 1993; Whitehead 2002; and Whitehead and Wright 2004; for a related example from Melanesia, see Harrison 1993.

20. As Bloch (2013) notes, drawing on Astuti (2009), the explicit statements people make about kinship are best understood "not as ontological proposals for what is, but rather as declarations of what should be" (255).

21. Smith (2004) reports that, in the period leading up to the 2003 attack, the Taromenani were showing concrete signs of wanting to establish more direct contact with Waorani, building larger paths in the forest and allowing their houses to become more visible by clearing the area around them (89–90).

22. One exception is Howard's (2002) writing on the expeditions of Waiwai people in search of uncontacted "tribes" in northern Amazonia. Grotti (2007) and Grotti and Brightman (2010) also explore how Trio people in southern Suriname envision their forest-dwelling neighbors as "wild" people and attempt to undo their supposed "savagery" by nurturing or "taming" their bodies.

23. A few examples include Viveiros de Castro 1992; Taylor 1993, 2000; Fausto 2001, 2007; Vilaça 1993, 2010; and Rival 2002.

Chapter 5. Intimate Others

1. While Wao-Quichua marriages are common in villages in the western part of the Waorani reserve and those along the oil roads to the north and east, there are some villages with relatively few interethnic marriages.

2. Grefa's account suggests that there were significant cultural differences between Waorani groups at the time of her capture and that many Waorani raids were motivated by the desire to acquire manufactured goods (Cipolletti 2002).

3. There were also a small number of marriages between Waorani women and Quichua men on frontier plantations that received Waorani women, including Dayuma, who fled from violence between rival Waorani groups (Wallis 1960).

4. Whitten (2008) makes this argument specifically against the tendency among many scholars who appear to view historical ethnogenesis in Amazonian Ecuador as a process in which "the movement from one ethnic system to a new one" involves the "*loss of culture* from the donor" (24, emphasis in the original). It is clear from recent historical and ethnographic works, including this book, that any simple characterization of indigenous groups in terms of "culture loss," "acculturation," or "hybridization" has more to do with colonial imagination than the experiences of indigenous people.

5. Macdonald estimated there are forty thousand Napo Quichuas (1999, 9), and the official Web site of the Consejo de Desarrollo de las Nacionalidades y Pueblos del Ecuador (CODENPE) gives a conservative estimate of eighty thousand for the entire Quichua population of eastern Ecuador. More recently, Uzendoski and Whitten (forthcoming) give an updated figure of around 150,000.

6. Since the time of my initial fieldwork, heavy drinking has become increasingly common among adult men.

7. The problem of low teacher salaries in Ecuador was so severe during the course of my fieldwork that there was a national teachers' strike in 2003 that took months to resolve. As a result of such conditions, some teachers accept teaching jobs in remote parts of the Oriente with the specific aim of reducing their living costs by

relying partially on assistance from villagers (see Rival 1992 for an in-depth description of this process in Waorani communities).

8. Reeve (2002) notes that Quichuas from Curaray associate drinking alcohol and commercial activities with "colonos" (colonists) and not "real" Runa people. This suggests that such practices are a key reference point in processes of social "othering" in the region, rather than being an accurate depiction of any single indigenous group or community.

9. Unmarried teenage women may have been particularly uncomfortable answering my questions about potential Quichua spouses as a result of my status as a kowori man.

10. The sexual connotations of referring to someone of the opposite sex as *amigo* or *amiga* is not unique to the Waorani and is found elsewhere in Ecuador.

11. Riviere (1974) describes couvade practices, which are often seen as a form of "sympathetic pregnancy" among men, as "the set of ideas and related conventional behavior that intimately associates a man with the birth of his child" (425). See Rival (1998a) for a detailed ethnography of the Waorani couvade and its mutual implications for establishing consanguinity between men, women, and their children.

12. At the time of my fieldwork, there was only one woman (unmarried) who held a position within ONHAE.

13. In the late 1980s some Waorani men explained that they preferred Quichua brides as a result of the lack of potential Waorani wives nearby, since local women were seen as close relatives (Rival 1992). Rival describes how, after missionary settlement, the categories of *girinani* (kin) and *waomoni* (endogamous group) became confused such that villagers were at once seen as too closely related to marry and too far from the traditional endogamous nexus of potential cross-cousin spouses (1992, 135). Quichuas were seen as better educated and more "civilized," and thus a more attractive marriage option than a Waorani bride from a distant group (143). Quichua women were also valued as hardworking gardeners at a time when gardening was becoming an increasingly important part of subsistence in Waorani villages.

14. See Turner (1979) for an analysis of how parents are able to control their daughters and by extension their husbands in the context of matrilocal marriage.

15. Rival (2002) observes that this process of alliance and incorporation makes it very difficult to give clear definitions of kinship terms.

16. See Viveiros de Castro (1993, 1998b) for further discussion of the centrality of affinity as a generalized principle of Amazonian kinship.

17. Since Wao-Quichua marriages have spanned several generations, there are today some marriages in which one of the spouses is Quichua and the other "mixed" (Wao-Quichua).

18. In contrast, Rival (1992) suggests that "mixed" children are defined as Waorani only if they are given a proper Waorani name by a grandparent.

19. A few important examples include Overing 1983; Viveiros de Castro 1992; Fausto 2001, 2012; Descola 1992; Taylor 1993, 1996; and Vilaça 2010.

Chapter 6. Shamans and Enemies

1. See Ceron and Montalvo (1998) for an exhaustive study of 625 medicinal and other plant species identified and utilized by residents of a single Waorani village. Posey (1990) provides a general overview of indigenous knowledge of plants and their uses in Amazonia.

2. The question of how to reconcile the prominent value of personal autonomy with being part of a wider community or social hierarchy is an issue that resonates in many parts of Amazonia. Killick (2007), for example, examines indigenous political concerns that underlie personal autonomy and leadership among the Ashéninka of Peruvian Amazonia.

3. The word *minga* and the concept of collective work projects it represents are of Quichua origin and is practiced widely in the Andes.

4. Village presidents are elected periodically by adults at village meetings.

5. The parents of students are expected to provide game meat and garden produce for village schoolteachers.

6. Waorani understandings of comunidad are consistent with Robarchek and Robarchek's observation that "the new peacefulness is currently being sustained by the force of conscious social will" (1998, 161). Much like the notion of comunidad I describe here, they attributed the popularity of Christianity among the Waorani at the time of their fieldwork to this social goal of preventing the intense conflicts associated with the past.

7. It is worth noting that the victim in this case was a Quichua woman whose parents and siblings live far away in the Quichua town of Arajuno.

8. Yost (1981) described a similar Waorani concern about public participation in church services at the Tiweno mission, which was seen as part of a commitment not to spear one's neighbors.

9. Although Waorani say that women can become shamans, as far as I know there were no female shamans during my fieldwork. Rival (2002, 198) made a similar observation at the time of her fieldwork.

10. As Rival explains, "Waorani shamans do not take an active role in controlling their spirit helpers. On the contrary, they let the spirits possess them" (2005, 296).

11. This characterization of predatory jaguars and human killers as orphans illustrates how the predatory point of view cannot simply be assimilated to the kind of personhood appropriate to Waorani humanity (High 2012a).

12. Fausto (2008) describes how, in much of Amazonia, mastery constitutes a form of adoptive filiation in shamanism and other practices. He notes that "since we can never know who adopted who[m] and who controls who[m] . . . shamans and warriors must ensure that the subjectivity of their wild pets is preserved, which means that they can never become entirely tamed and domesticated" (343). In this way shamans are "forever on the verge of adopting the perspective of others contained within themselves" (343).

13. There are striking parallels between Waorani understandings of "orphan" jaguars and their descriptions of "uncontacted" Taromenani people. Both are defined in terms of their relative isolation from kin, a situation that appears to mark them out as having remarkable predatory powers.

14. Fausto describes humans and animals as being "immersed in a sociocosmic system in which the direction of predation and the production of kinship are in dispute" (2007, 500).

15. Shamans may also be referred to by the word for the animal they are associated with, which may explain the use of the term *meñera* for "jaguar-shaman," since the Wao word for jaguar is *meñi*.

16. These special jaguars cannot really die, as they are said merely to become smaller each time they are killed or that their spirits inhabit the bodies of other jaguars.

17. These accounts of sorcery appear to resonate with Viveiros de Castro's model of perspectivism, where different beings struggle to assert their humanity as a perceiving subject ("predator") rather than an object of perception ("prey"). Within this cosmic battle for perspective, people are at risk of being tricked or overpowered by nonhuman subjectivities that transform them into a prey-object (Viveiros de Castro 1998a, 483; Viveiros de Castro 2004; Lima 1999; Course 2010).

18. Given that accusations of witchcraft are often made against Quichua shamans living far away from the victim, the actual identity of the guilty shaman may not be known at all. In some cases, the witchcraft is associated with a whole Quichua village rather than a particular individual.

Chapter 7. Victims and Warriors

1. The Yasuní National Park, which originally consisted of nearly 1.5 million hectares, was reduced to 982,000 hectares in 1990 in order to facilitate oil development in oil Block 16. At that time the areas in the park where Waorani lived became part of the Waorani reserve and were opened up to intensive oil production, which continues in Block 16 today (Rival 2010a, 4).

2. Yasuní-ITT refers to the Ishpingo-Tambococha-Tipitini oil fields located in the Yasuní Park.

3. For full details of the Initiative see *Ecuador Yasuní-ITT Trust Fund: Terms of Reference* (2010).

4. The "rights of nature" are outlined in articles 71 through 74 in chapter 7 of Ecuador's 2008 National Constitution.

5. Stasch traces this historical tendency in anthropology and sociology to envision "community" as a unity or "communitarian oneness" to trends in late-nineteenth-century social thought, including Henry Maine's *Ancient Law* (1861) and Ferdinand Tönnies's concept of *Gemeinschaft*, a German word often translated as "community" (Stasch 2009, 7).

6. There are other possible explanations of the attack and why the particular couple was targeted. Cabodevilla (2013) describes how, based on previous encoun-

ters, the Taromenani may have held the male elder accountable for not preventing the building of noisy oil drilling sites and roads across their lands (60).

7. Cabodevilla (2013) provides an extensive account of the most recent attacks and the ongoing inaction of the Ecuadorian government in response to them.

8. The afterword of this book describes how, in late 2013, the national police arrested seven Waorani men, and one of the girls abducted in the recent killings was taken into the custody of government authorities.

Glossary

Dagengkai: drink made from the fruit of the chonta palm
Daikawo: sickness
Digintai: palm fiber bag
Durani: ancestors, "the ancient ones"
Durani baı: "like the ancient ones"
Durani onko: traditional Waorani longhouse
Eëme: feast involving multiple households, village party
Gercmara: pregnant woman
Geremempo: "baby father," a man who has made a woman pregnant
Girinani: extended kin, family
Iñinamai: to not know something (by not hearing)
Iroi: male sorcerer
Iroinga: female sorcerer
Kaka: achiote, a red dye use for body painting
Keë: masticated manioc mash used to make manioc beer
Kene: manioc root
Kengi: food
Kowori: outsiders, non-Waorani people, cannibals
Kowori bai: "like non-Waorani people"
Kowori onko: where the outsiders live, the city
Maeñika: forest fruit
Menki:brother-in-law, cross-cousin

Meñera: shaman, jaguar mother/father
Meñi: jaguar
Mine: unmasticated manioc mash used for specific dietary restrictions
Miyi: ayahuasca, a powerful hallucinogen
Monito ome: "our homeland"
Nanicabo: co-resident household group
Nanogue: married man
ñene onko: large house, communal building
Onko: house
Ononki: unjustified, unprovoked, in error or deceptive
Ore: white-lipped peccary
Pangi: to whip with a forest vine
Peneme: mashed mature plantain drink
Pii: anger, rage
Pikenani: elders
Tagaeri: "uncontacted" Waorani group, followers of Tagae
Taromenani: "uncontacted" people, mythological people with
    superhuman abilities
Teëmo: strong or hard
Tepe: manioc beer
Tiname: hard cane liquor, alcoholic spirits
Tiweno: Waorani village, location of the initial evangelical mission
Tiwino: Frontier Waorani village, located on the northern border of the
    Waorani territory south of the city of Coca.
Toñampari: Waorani village along the Curaray River, or "Toña's creek,"
    located near the site where five missionaries were killed in 1956
Waimo: beautiful
Wao: person
Waomoni: a closely related group of households
Waorani: people
Wao-terero: Waorani language
Waponi: good, pleasing
Waponi kiwimonipa: "we live well"
Warani: other Waorani people, non-kin, enemies
Wene: bad or evil, the devil
Wiwa: bad, ugly
Wiwi keranitapa: "they did badly"
Wiwi kiwinanipa:"they live badly"
Wori: deceased (suffix)
Yawe: toucan

Bibliography

Aguirre, Milagros. 2014. "Guerreros de la selva, presos tras matanza en pueblo huaorani," *El Universo*, March 9, 2014.

Albert, Bruce. 1989. "Yanomami 'Violence': Inclusive Fitness or Ethnographer's Representation?" *Current Anthropology* 30, no. 5: 637–40.

Albert, Bruce, and Alcida Rita Ramos. 2000. *Pacificando o branco: Cosmologias do contatono Norte-Amazônico*. São Paolo: Editora UNESP.

Appadurai, Arjun. 1996. *Modernity at Large: Cultural Dimensions of Globalization*. Minneapolis: University of Minnesota Press.

Argenti, Nicolas. 2007. *The Intestines of the State: Youth, Violence, and Related Histories in the Cameroon Grassfields*. Chicago: University of Chicago Press.

Argenti, Nicolas, and Katharina Schramm. 2009. *Remembering Violence: Anthropological Perspectives on Intergenerational Transmission*. Oxford: Berghahn.

Århem, Kaj. 1996. "The Cosmic Food Web: Human-Nature Relatedness in the Northwest Amazon." In Descola and Pálsson, *Nature and Society*, 185–209.

Astuti, Rita. 1995. *People of the Sea: Identity and Descent among the Vezo of Madagascar*. Cambridge: Cambridge University Press.

———. 1998. "'It's a Boy!,' 'It's a Girl!': Reflections on Sex and Gender in Madagascar and Beyond." In *Bodies and Persons: Comparative Perspectives from Africa and Melanesia*, edited by Michael Lambek and Andrew Strathern, 29–52. Cambridge: Cambridge University Press.

———. 2009. "Revealing and Obscuring Rivers's Pedigrees: Biological Inheritance and Kinship in Madagascar." In *Kinship and Beyond: The Genealogical*

Model Reconsidered, edited by James Leach and Sandra Bamford, 214–36. London: Berghahn.

Balée, William. 1995. "Historical Ecology of Amazonia." In *Indigenous Peoples and the Future of Amazonia: An Ecological Anthropology of an Endangered World*, edited by Leslie Sponsel, 97–106. Tucson: University of Arizona Press.

Bamberger, Joan. 1974. "The Myth of Matriarchy: Why Men Rule Primitive Society." In *Women, Culture, and Society*, edited by Michelle Rosaldo and Louise Lamphere, 263–80. Stanford, Calif.: Stanford University Press.

Bashkow, Ira. 2006. "A Neo-Boasian Conception of Cultural Boundaries." *American Anthropologist* 106, no. 3: 443–58.

Basso, Ellen. 1987. *In Favor of Deceit: A Study of Tricksters in an Amazonian Society.* Tucson: University of Arizona Press.

———. 1995. *The Last Cannibals: A South American Oral History.* Austin: University of Texas Press.

Basso, Keith. 1996. *Wisdom Sits in Places: Landscape and Language among the Western Apache.* Albuquerque: University of New Mexico Press.

Battaglia, Debbora. 1992. "The Body in the Gift: Memory and Forgetting in Sabari Mortuary Exchange." *American Ethnologist* 19, no. 1: 3–18.

Becker, Marc. 2008. *Indians and Leftists in the Making of Ecuador's Modern Indigenous Movement.* Durham, N.C.: Duke University Press.

Beckerman, Stephen, and James Yost. 2007. "Upper Amazonian Warfare." In *Latin American Indigenous Warfare and Ritual Violence*, edited by Richard J. Chacon and Rubén G. Mendoza, 142–79. Tucson: University of Arizona Press.

Belaunde, Luisa Elvira. 1992. "Gender, Commensality and the Community among the Airo-Pai of Western Amazonia (Secoya, Western-Tukanoan Speaking)." PhD diss., University of London.

———. 2000. "Epidemics, Psycho-Actives, and Evangelical Conversion among the Airo-Pai of Amazonian Peru." *Journal of Contemporary Religion* 15, no. 3: 349–59.

Berliner, David. 2005a. "The Abuses of Memory: Reflections on the Memory Boom in Anthropology." *Anthropological Quarterly* 78, no. 1: 197–211.

———. 2005b. "An 'Impossible' Transmission: Youth Religious Memories in Guinea-Conakry." *American Ethnologist* 32, no. 4: 576–92.

Bessire, Lucas. 2012. "The Politics of Isolation: Refused Relation as an Emerging Regime of Biolegitimacy." *Comparative Studies in Society and History* 54, no. 3: 467–98.

Bloch, Maurice. 1998. "Time, Narratives and the Multiplicity of Representations of the Past." Chapter 7 in *How We Think They Think: Anthropological Approaches to Cognition, Memory, and Literacy.* 100–113. Boulder, Colo.: Westview.

———. 2013. "What Kind of 'Is' Is Sahlins' 'Is'?" *Hau: Journal of Ethnographic Theory* 3, no. 2: 253–57.

Blomberg, Rolf. 1956. *The Naked Aucas: An Account of the Indians of Ecuador.* London: Allen and Unwin.

Bonilla, Oiara. 2005. "O bom patrão e o inimigo voraz: Predação e o comércio na cosmologia Pauamari." *Mana* 11:41–66.

Boster, James, James Yost, and Catherine Peeke. 2004. "Rage, Revenge, and Religion: Honest Signaling of Aggression and Nonaggression in Waorani Coalitional Violence." *Ethos* 31, no. 4: 471–94.

Bourdieu, Pierre. 2001. *Masculine Domination*. Stanford, Calif.: Stanford University Press.

Brandes, Stanley. 1980. *Metaphors of Masculinity: Sex and Status in Andalusian Folklore*. Philadelphia: University of Pennsylvania Press.

———. 2002. *Staying Sober in Mexico City*. Austin: University of Texas Press.

Briggs, Charles. 1993. "Personal Sentiments and Polyphonic Voices in Warao Women's Ritual Wailing: Music and Poetics in a Critical Collective Discourse." *American Anthropologist* 94, no. 4: 929–57.

Brown, Michael. 1993. "Facing the State, Facing the World: Amazonia's Native Leaders and the New Politics of Identity." *L'Homme* 33, nos. 126–128: 307–26.

Cabodevilla, Miguel Angel. 1999. *Los Huaorani en la historia del Oriente*. Quito: CICAME.

———. 2003. "Prólogo: Crónicas, quince años después." In *Crónica Huaorani*, edited by Alejandro Labaka, 7–10. Quito: CICAME.

———. 2004a. *El exterminio de los pueblos ocultos*. Quito: CICAME.

———. 2004b. "Comentarios sobre un ataque Wao." In Cabodevilla, Smith, and Rivas, *Tiempos de Guerra*, 15–30.

———. 2004c. "Tiempo de guerra." In Cabodevilla, Smith, and Rivas, *Tiempos de Guerra*, 47–66.

———. 2013. "La massacre . . . 'Qué nunca existió?'" In *Una tragedia ocultada*, edited by Miguel Angel Cabodevilla and Milagros Aguirre, 21–125. Quito: CICAME.

Cabodevilla, Miguel Angel, and Mikel Berraondo. 2005. *Pueblos no contactados ante el reto de los derechos humanos*. Quito: CICAME.

Cabodevilla, Miguel Angel, Randy Smith, and Alex Rivas. 2004. *Tiempos de guerra: Waorani contra Taromenane*. Quito: Abya-Yala.

Caiuby Novaes, Sylvia. 1997. *The Play of Mirrors: The Representation of Self as Mirrored in the Other*. Austin: University of Texas Press.

Carsten, Janet. 1997. *The Heat of the Hearth: The Process of Kinship in a Malay Fishing Community*. Oxford: Oxford University Press.

———. 2000. *Cultures of Relatedness*. Cambridge: Cambridge University Press.

———. 2013. "What Kinship Does—and How." *Hau: Journal of Ethnographic Theory* 3, no. 2: 245–51.

Cepek, Michael. 2008. "Bold Jaguars and Unsuspecting Monkeys: The Value of Fearlessness in Cofán Politics." *Journal of the Royal Anthropological Institute* 14, no. 2: 334–52.

———. 2012. *A Future for Amazonia: Randy Borman and Cofán Environmental Politics*. Austin: University of Texas Press.

Ceron, Carlos E., and Consuelo G. Montalvo. 1998. *Etnobotánica de los Huaorani de Quehueri-ono, Napo-Ecuador*. Quito: Abya-Yala.

Cervone, Emma, and Freddy Rivera, eds. 1999. *Ecuador racista: Imagenes e identidades*. Quito: FLACSO.

Chagnon, Napoleon. 1968. *Yanomamö: The Fierce People*. New York: Holt, Rinehart, and Winston.

———. 1988. "Life Histories, Blood Revenge and Warfare in a Tribal Population." *Science* 239:985–92.

———. 2013. *Noble Savages: My Life among Two Dangerous Tribes—the Yanomamo and the Anthropologists*. New York: Simon and Schuster.

Cipolletti, Maria Susana. 2002. "El testimonio de Joaquina Grefa, una cautiva Quichua entre los Huaorani (Ecuador, 1945)." *Journal de la Societé des Américanistes* 88:111–35.

Clastres, Pierre. 1987. *Society against the State: Essays in Political Anthropology*. New York: Zone.

Collier, Jane. 1988. *Marriage and Inequality in Classless Societies*. Stanford, Calif.: Stanford University Press.

Collier, Jane, and Michelle Rosaldo. 1981. "Politics and Gender in Simple Societies." In *Sexual Meanings: The Cultural Construction of Gender and Sexuality*, edited by Sherry B. Ortner and Harriett Whitehead, 275–329. Cambridge: Cambridge University Press.

Conklin, Beth. 1997. "Body Paint, Feathers, and VCRs: Aesthetics and Authenticity in Amazonian Activism." *American Ethnologist* 24, no. 4: 711–37.

———. 2001. "Women's Blood, Warrior's Blood, and the Conquest of Vitality in Amazonia." In Gregor and Tuzin, *Gender in Amazonia and Melanesia*, 141–74.

———. 2002. "Shamans versus Pirates in the Amazonian Treasure Chest." *American Ethnologist* 104, no. 4: 1050–61.

Conklin, Beth, and Laura Graham. 1995. "The Shifting Middle Ground: Amazonian Indians and Eco-Politics." *American Anthropologist* 97, no. 4: 695–710.

Connerton, Paul. 1989. *How Societies Remember*. Cambridge: Cambridge University Press.

Cornwall, Andrea, and Nancy Lindisfarne. 1994. "Dislocating Masculinity: Gender, Power and Anthropology." In *Dislocating Masculinity: Comparative Ethnographies*, edited by Andrea Cornwall and Nancy Lindisfarne, 11–47. London: Routledge.

Course, Magnus. 2007. "Death, Biography and the Mapuche Person." *Ethnos* 72, no. 1: 77–101.

———. 2010. "Of Words and Fog: Linguistic Relativity and Amerindian Ontology." *Anthropological Theory* 10, no. 3: 247–63.

Cruikshank, Julie. 1998. *The Social Life of Stories: Narrative and Knowledge in the Yukon Territory*. Lincoln: University of Nebraska Press.

de la Cadena, Marisol. 2000. *Indigenous Mestizos: The Politics of Race and Culture in Cuzco, Peru, 1919–1991*. Durham, N.C.: Duke University Press.

Denevan, William. 1976. "The Aboriginal Population of Amazonia." In *The Native Population of the Americas in 1492*, edited by William Denevan, 205–34. Madison: University of Wisconsin Press.

Descola, Philippe. 1992. "Societies of Nature and the Nature of Society." In *Conceptualizing Society*, edited by Adam Kuper, 107–26. London: Routledge.

———. 1993. *The Spears of Twilight: Life and Death in the Amazon Jungle*. London: Harper Collins.

———. 1994. *In the Society of Nature: A Native Ecology in Amazonia*. Cambridge: Cambridge University Press.

———. 2001. "The Genres of Gender: Local Models and Global Paradigms in the Comparison of Amazonia and Melanesia." In Gregor and Tuzin, *Gender in Amazonia and Melanesia*, 91–114.

Descola, Philippe, and Gisli Pálsson. 1996. *Nature and Society: Anthropological Perspectives*. London: Routledge.

Ecuador Yasuni Trust Fund: Terms of Reference. July 28, 2010.

Elliot, Elisabeth. 1957. *Through the Gates of Splendor*. New York: Harper.

———. 1961. *The Savage My Kinsman*. New York: Harper.

Erikson, Philippe. 1999. *El sello de los antepasados: Marcado del cuerpo y demarcación étnica entre los Matis de la Amazonía*. Quito: Abya-Yala.

Ewart, Elizabeth. 2013. *Space and Society in Central Brazil: A Panará Ethnography*. London: Bloomsbury.

———. 2003. "Lines and Circles: Images of Time in a Panará Village." *Journal of the Royal Anthropological Institute* 9, no. 2: 261–79.

Fausto, Carlos. 1999. "Of Enemies and Pets: Warfare and Shamanism in Amazonia." *American Ethnologist* 26, no. 4: 933–56.

———. 2001. *Inimigos fiéis: História, guerra e xamanismo na Amazônia*. São Paulo: Universidade de São Paulo.

———. 2004. "A Blend of Blood and Tobacco: Shamans and Jaguars among the Parakanã of Eastern Amazonia." In Whitehead and Wright, *In Darkness and Secrecy*, 157–78.

———. 2007. "Feasting on People: Eating Animals and Humans in Amazonia." *Current Anthropology* 48, no. 4: 497–530.

———. 2008. "Too Many Owners: Mastership and Ownership in Amazonia." *Mana* 14, no. 2: 328–66.

———. 2012. *Warfare and Shamanism in Amazonia*. Cambridge: Cambridge University Press.

Fausto, Carlos, and Michael Heckenberger. 2007. "Introduction: Indigenous History and the History of the 'Indians.'" In *Time and Memory in Indigenous Amazonia: Anthropological Perspectives*, edited by Carlos Fausto and Michael Heckenberger, 1–42. Tallahassee: University of Florida Press.

Ferguson, R. Brian. 1995. *Yanomami Warfare: A Political History*. Santa Fe, N.M.: SAR.

————. 1999. "A Savage Encounter: Western Contact and the Yanomami War Complex." In Ferguson and Whitehead, *War in the Tribal Zone*, 199–228.

Ferguson, R. Brian, and Neil Whitehead, eds. 1999. *War in the Tribal Zone: Expanding States and Indigenous Warfare.* Santa Fe, N.M.: SAR.

Fisher, William. 2001. "Age-Based Genders among the Kayapo." In Gregor and Donald Tuzin, *Gender in Amazonia and Melanesia*, 115–40.

Fogelson, Raymond. 1989. "The Ethnohistory of Events and Nonevents." *Ethnohistory* 36: 133–47.

Gewerz, Deborah, and Frederick Errington. 1996. "On PepsiCo and Piety in a Papua New Guinea 'Modernity.'" *American Ethnologist* 23, no. 3: 476–93.

"'Go Ye and Preach The Gospel'": Five Do and Die." 1956. *Life*, January 30: 10–19.

Gow, Peter. 1989. "The Perverse Child: Desire in a Native Amazonian Subsistence Economy." *Man, Journal of the Royal Anthropological Institute* (N.S.) 24:299–314.

————. 1991. *Of Mixed Blood: Kinship and History in Peruvian Amazonia.* Oxford: Oxford University Press.

————. 1993. "Gringos and Wild Indians: Images of History in Western Amazonian Cultures." *L'Homme* 33, nos. 126–128: 331–51.

————. 1996. "River People: Shamanism and History in Western Amazonia." In Thomas and Humphrey, *Shamanism, History, and the State*, 90–113.

————. 2000. "Helpless: The Affective Preconditions of Piro Social Life." In Overing and Passes, *Anthropology of Love and Anger*, 46–63.

————. 2001. *An Amazonian Myth and its History.* Oxford: Oxford University Press.

Graham, Laura. 1995. *Performing Dreams: Discourses of Immortality among the Xavante of Central Brazil.* Austin: University of Texas Press.

————. 2005. "Image and Instrumentality in a Xavante Politics of Existential Recognition: The Public Outreach Work of Eténhiritipa Pimental Barbosa." *American Ethnologist* 32, no. 4: 622–41.

Gregor, Thomas. 1985. *Anxious Pleasures: The Sexual Lives of an Amazonian People.* Chicago: University of Chicago Press.

————. 1996. *A Natural History of Peace.* Nashville, Tenn.: Vanderbilt University Press.

Gregor, Thomas, and Donald Tuzin. 2001. *Gender in Amazonia and Melanesia.* Berkeley: University of California Press.

Grotti, Vanessa E. 2007. "Nurturing the Other: Wellbeing, Social Body and Transformability in Northeastern Amazonia." PhD diss., University of Cambridge.

Grotti, Vanessa E., and Marc Brightman. 2010. "The Other's Other: Nurturing the Bodies of 'Wild' People among the Trio of Southern Suriname." *Etnofoor* 22, no. 2: 51–70.

Gutmann, Matthew C. 1996. *The Meanings of Macho: Being a Man in Mexico City.* Berkeley: University of California Press.

————. 1997. "Trafficking in Men: The Anthropology of Masculinity." *Annual Reviews of Anthropology* 26:385–409.

Halbwachs, Maurice. (1950) 1980. *The Collective Memory*. New York: Harper and Row.

Hanon, Jim, dir. 2006. *End of the Spear*. 111 mins. Every Tribe Entertainment. Studio City, Calif.

Harrison, Simon. 1993. *The Mask of War: Violence, Ritual, and the Self in Melanesia*. Manchester, Eng.: Manchester University Press.

Heckenberger, Michael. 2005. *The Ecology of Power: Culture, Place, and Personhood in the Southern Amazon, A.D. 1000–2000*. New York: Routledge.

Hendricks, Janet. 1993. *To Drink of Death: Narrative of a Shuar Warrior*. Tucson: University of Arizona Press.

High, Casey. 2006. "From Enemies to Affines: Conflict and Community among the Huaorani of Amazonian Ecuador." PhD diss. London School of Economics, University of London.

———. 2007. "Indigenous Organisations, Oil Development, and the Politics of Egalitarianism." *Cambridge Anthropology* 26, no. 2: 34–46.

———. 2008. "End of the Spear: Re-Imagining Amazonian Anthropology and History through Film." In *How Do We Know? Evidence, Ethnography and the Making of Anthropological Knowledge*, edited by Liana Chua, Casey High, and Timm Lau, 76–96. Newcastle: Cambridge Scholars.

———. 2009a. "Remembering the Auca: Violence and Generational Memory in Amazonian Ecuador." *Journal of the Royal Anthropological Institute* (N.S.) 15:719–36.

———. 2009b. "Victims and Martyrs: Converging Histories of Violence in Amazonian Anthropology and U.S. Cinema." *Anthropology and Humanism* 34, no. 1: 41–50.

———. 2010. "Warriors, Hunters, and Bruce Lee: Gendered Agency and the Transformation of Amazonian Masculinity." *American Ethnologist* 37, no. 4: 753–70.

———. 2012a. "Shamans, Animals, and Enemies: Locating the Human and Non-Human in an Amazonian Cosmos of Alterity." In *Animism in Rainforest and Tundra: Personhood, Animals, Plants and Things in Contemporary Amazonia and Siberia*, edited by Marc Brightman, Vanessa Grotti, and Olga Ulturgasheva, 130–45. Oxford: Berghahn.

———. 2012b. "Between Knowing and Being: Ignorance in Anthropology and Amazonian Shamanism." In *The Anthropology of Ignorance: An Ethnographic Approach*, edited by Casey High, Ann Kelly, and Jon Mair, 119–36. New York: Palgrave Macmillan.

Hill, David. 2014. "Ecuador: Oil Company Has Built 'Secret' Road Deep into Yasuni National Park," *Ecologist*, June 6, 2014.

Hill, Jonathan, ed. 1988. *Rethinking History and Myth: Indigenous South American Perspectives on the Past*. Urbana: University of Illinois Press.

———. 1996. "Introduction: Ethnogenesis in the Americas." In *History, Power, and Identity: Ethnogenesis in the Americas, 1492–1992*, edited by Jonathan Hill, 1–19. Iowa City: University of Iowa Press.

Hirsch, Eric, and Charles Stewart. 2005. "Introduction: Ethnographies of Historicity." *History and Anthropology* 16, no. 3: 261–74.

Hodgson, Dorothy L. 1999. "Once Intrepid Warriors": Modernity and the Production of Maasai Masculinities. *Ethnology* 38, no. 2: 121–50.

Howard, Catherine. 2002. "Wrought Identities: Waiwai Expeditions in Search of the Unseen "Tribes" of Northern Amazonia." PhD diss., University of Chicago.

Howell, Signe, and Roy Willis, eds. 1989. *Societies at Peace: Anthropological Perspectives.* London: Routledge.

Hugh-Jones, Stephen. 1994. "Shamans, Prophets, Priests, and Pastors." In Thomas and Humphrey, *Shamanism, History, and the State*, 32–75.

Jackson, Jean. 1995. "Culture, Genuine and Spurious: The Politics of Indianness in the Vaupes, Colombia." *American Ethnologist* 22, no. 1: 3–27.

Kelly, Jose. 2011. *State Healthcare and Yanomami Transformations.* Tucson: University of Arizona Press.

Kenrick, Justin, and Jerome Lewis. 2004. "Indigenous Peoples' Rights and the Politics of the Term 'Indigenous.'" *Anthropology Today* 20, no. 2: 4–9.

Killick, Evan. 2007. "Autonomy and Leadership: Political Formations among the Ashéninka of Peruvian Amazonia." *Ethnos* 72, no. 4: 461–82.

Kimerling, Judith. 1996. *El derecho del tambor: Derechos humanos y ambientales en los campos petroleros de la amazonia ecuatoriana.* Quito: Abya-Yala.

Kingsland, Rosemary. 1980. *A Saint among Savages.* London: Collins.

Kirsch, Stuart. 1997. "Lost Tribes: Indigenous People and the Social Imaginary." *Anthropology Quarterly* 70, no. 2: 58–67.

Klein, Harriett M., and Louisa R. Stark, eds. 1985. *South American Indian Languages: Retrospect and Prospect.* Austin: University of Texas Press.

Knauft, Bruce. 1997. "Gender Identity, Political Economy and Modernity in Melanesia and Amazonia." *Journal of the Royal Anthropological Institute* 3, no. 2: 233–59.

Kohn, Eduardo. 2013. *How Forests Think: Toward an Anthropology Beyond the Human.* Berkeley: University of California Press.

Kulick, Don, and Margaret Wilson. 1994. "Rambo's Wife Saves the Day: Subjugating the Gaze and Subverting the Narrative in a Papua New Guinea Swamp." *Visual Anthropology Review* 10, no. 2: 1–13.

Kuper. Adam. 2003. "The Return of the Native." *Current Anthropology* 44, no. 3: 389–402.

Lambek, Michael. 1996. "The Past Imperfect: Remembering as Moral Practice." In *Tense Past: Cultural Essays in Trauma and Memory*, edited by Paul Antze and Michael Lambek, 235–54. New York: Routledge.

———. 2011. "Kinship as Gift and Theft: Acts of Succession in Mayotte and Ancient Israel." *American Ethnologist* 38, no. 1: 2–16.

Lathrap, Donald W. 1970. *The Upper Amazon: Ancient Peoples and Places.* London: Thames and Hudson.

Lepri, Isabella. 2005. "The Meanings of Kinship among the Ese Ejja of Northern Bolivia." *Journal of the Royal Anthropological Institute* (N.S.) 11, no. 4: 703–24.

Lévi-Strauss, Claude. (1943) 1976. "The Social Use of Kinship Terms among Brazilian Indians." *American Anthropologist* 45:398–409.

————. 1966. *The Savage Mind*. Chicago: University of Chicago Press.

————. (1942) 1976. "Guerra e comércio entre os índios da América do Sul." In *Leituras de etnologia brasileira*, edited by Egon Schaden, 325–39. São Paulo: Nacional.

————. 1995. *The Story of Lynx*. Chicago: University of Chicago Press.

Liefeld, Olive F. 1990. *Unfolding Destinies: The Untold Story of Peter Fleming and the Auca Mission*. Grand Rapids, Mich.: Zondervan.

Lima, Tania Stolze. 1999. "The Two and Its Many: Reflections on Perspectivism in Tupi Cosmology." *Ethnos* 64, no. 1: 107–31.

Londoño Sulkin, Carlos. 2005. "Inhuman Beings: Morality and Perspectivism among Muinane People (Colombian Amazonia)." *Ethnos* 70, no. 1: 7–30.

Lutz, Catherine A., and Jane L. Collins. 1993. *Reading National Geographic*. Chicago: University of Chicago Press.

Macdonald, Theodore, Jr. 1981. "Indigenous Response to an Expanding Frontier: Jungle Quichua Economic Conversion." In Whitten, *Cultural Transformations*, 356–83.

————. 1999. *Ethnicity and Culture amidst New "Neighbors": The Runa of Ecuador's Amazon Region*. Needham Heights, Mass.: Allyn and Bacon.

McCallum, Cecilia. 2001. *Gender and Sociality in Amazonia: How Real People Are Made*. Oxford: Berg.

Meyer, Birgit. 2010. "'There Is a Spirit in That Image': Mass-Produced Jesus Pictures and Protestant-Pentecostal Animation in Ghana." *Comparative Studies in Society and History* 52, no. 1: 100–130.

Moore, Henrietta L. 1994. *A Passion for Difference: Essays in Anthropology and Gender*. Bloomington: Indiana University Press.

Muratorio, Blanca. 1991. *The Life and Times of Grandfather Alonzo: Culture and History in the Upper Amazon*. New Brunswick, N.J.: Rutgers University Press.

————. 1994. *Imágenes e imagineros: Representaciones de los indígenas ecuatorianos, siglos XIX y XX*. Quito: FLACSO.

Murphy, Yolanda, and Robert F. Murphy. 1974. *Women of the Forest*. New York: Columbia University Press.

Myers, Fred. 1988. "Locating Ethnographic Practice: Romance, Reality and Politics in the Outback." *American Ethnologist* 15, no. 4: 609–24.

Nora, Pierre. 1989. "Between Memory and History: Les lieux de memoire." *Representations* 26:7–24.

Nuckolls, Janis B. 2010. *Lessons from a Quechua Strongwoman: Ideophony, Dialogue, and Perspective*. Tucson: University of Arizona Press.

Oakdale, Suzanne. 2001. "History and Forgetting in an Indigenous Amazonian Community." *Ethnohistory* 48, no. 3: 381–401.

———. 2004. "The Culture-Conscious Brazilian Indian: Representing and Reworking Indianness in Kayabi Political Discourse." *American Ethnologist* 31, no. 1: 60–75.

———. 2005. *I Foresee My Life: The Ritual Performance of Autobiography in an Amazonian Community.* Lincoln: University of Nebraska Press.

Oberem, Udo. 1974. "Trade and Trade Goods in the Ecuadorian Montaña." In *Native South Americans*, edited by Patricia J. Lyon, 346–57. Boston: Little and Brown.

———. 1980. *Los Quijos: Historia de la transculturación de un grupo indígena en el Oriente ecuatoriano.* Otavalo: Instituto Otavaleño de Antropología.

Overing, Joanna. 1983. "Elementary Structures of Reciprocity: A Comparative Note on Guianese, Central Brazilian and North-West Amazon Socio-Political Thought." *Antropologica* nos. 59–62: 331–48.

———. 2000. "Conviviality and the Opening Up of Amazonian Anthropology." In Overing and Passes *Anthropology of Love and Anger*, 1–30.

Overing, Joanna, and Alan Passes, eds. 2000. *The Anthropology of Love and Anger: The Aesthetics of Conviviality in Native Amazonia.* London: Routledge.

Peeke, Catherine. 1973. *Preliminary Grammar of Auca.* Norman, Okla.: Summer Institute of Linguistics.

———. 1979. *El Idioma Huao: Gramatica pedagogica, tomo 1.* Cuadernos Etnolinguisticos no. 3. Quito: Instituto Linguistico de Verano.

Platt, Tristan. 1987. "Entre Ch'axwa y Muxsa: Para una historia del pensamiento politico Aymara." In *Tres reflexiones sobre el pensamiento andino*, edited by Therese Bouysse-Cassagne, Olivia Harris, Tristan Platt, and Veronica Cereceda, 61–132. La Paz: HISBOL.

Posey, Darrell. 1990. "Intellectual Property Rights and Just Compensation for Indigenous Knowledge." *Anthropology Today* 6, no. 4: 13–16.

Price, Richard. 2002. *First Time: The Historical Vision of an African American People.* Chicago: University of Chicago Press.

Prins, Harald. 1997. "Visual Media and the Primitivist Complex: Colonial Fantasies, Indigenous Imagination, and Advocacy in North America." In *Media Worlds: Anthropology on New Terrain*, edited by Faye Ginsburg, Lila Abu-Lughod and Brian Larkin, 58–74. Berkeley: University of California Press.

Rahier, Jean Muteba. 1998. "Blackness, the 'Racial'/Spatial Order, Migrations, and Miss Ecuador 1995–1996." *American Anthropologist* 100, no. 2: 421–30.

Ramos, Alcida Rita. 1987. "Reflecting on the Yanomami: Ethnographic Images and the Pursuit of the Exotic." *Cultural Anthropology* 2, no. 3: 284–304.

———. 1988. "Indian Voices: Contact Experienced and Expressed." In Hill, *Rethinking History and Myth*, 214–34.

———. 2003. "Comment on A. Kuper's article 'The Return of the Native.'" *Current Anthropology* 44, no. 3: 397–98.

Reeve, Mary-Elizabeth. 1988. "Cauchu Uras: Lowland Quichua Histories of the Amazon Rubber Boom," In Hill, *Rethinking History and Myth*, 19–34.

———. 1993a. "Regional Interaction in the Western Amazon: The Early Encounter and the Jesuit Years: 1538–1767." *Ethnohistory* 41:106–38.

———. 1993b. "Huaorani and Quichua on the Rio Curaray, Amazonian Ecuador: Shifting Visions of *Auca* in Interethnic Contact." In *Cosmology, Values and Inter-Ethnic Contact in South America*, edited by Terence Turner, 31–36. Bennington, Vt.: Bennington College, South American Indian Studies no. 2.

———. 1994. "Narratives of Catastrophe: The Zaparoan Experience in Amazonian Ecuador." *Bulletin de la Societe Suisse de Americanistes* nos. 57–58: 1 7–24.

———. 2002. *Los Quichuas del Curaray: El proceso de formación de la identidad.* Quito: Abya-Yala.

Reeve, Mary-Elizabeth, and Casey High. 2012. "Between Friends and Enemies: The Dynamics of Inter-Ethnic Relations in Amazonian Ecuador." *Ethnohistory* 59, no. 1: 141–62.

Richards, Paul. 1996. *Fighting for the Rain Forest: War, Youth and Resources in Sierra Leone.* Oxford: International African Institute.

Rival, Laura. 1991. "Huaorani y petróleo." In *Naufrago del mar verde: La resistencia de los Huaorani a una integración impuesta*, edited by Giovanna Tassi, 125–79. Quito: Abya-Yala.

———. 1992. "Social Transformations and the Impact of Formal Schooling on the Huaorani of Amazonian Ecuador." PhD thesis, London School of Economics, University of London.

———. 1993. "The Growth of Family Trees: Understanding Huaorani Perceptions of the Forest." *Man, Journal of the Royal Anthropological Institute* (N.S.) 28:635–52.

———. 1994. "Los indígenas Huaorani en la conciencia nacional: Alteridad representada y significada." In Muratorio, *Imágenes e Imagineros*, 253–92.

———. 1996a. *Hijos del sol, padres del jaguar: Los Huaorani de ayer y hoy.* Quito: Colleción Biblioteca Abya-Yala.

———. 1996b. "Blowpipes and Spears: The Social Significance of Huaorani Technological Choices." In Descola and Pálsson, *Nature and Society*, 145–64.

———. 1998a. "Androgenous Parents and Guest Children: The Huaorani Couvade." *Journal of the Royal Anthropological Institute* (N.S.) 4:619–42.

———. 1998b. "Prey at the Centre: Resistance and Marginality in Amazonia." In *Lilies of the Field: Marginal People Who Live for the Moment*, edited by Sophie Day, Akis Papataxiarchis, and Michael Stewart, 61–79. Boulder: Westview.

———. 2000. "Marginality with a Difference; or, How the Huaorani Preserve Their Sharing Relations and Naturalize Outside Powers." In *Hunters and Gatherers in the Modern World: Conflict, Resistance, and Self-Determination*, edited by Peter Schweitzer, Megan Biesele, and Robert Hitchcock, 244–62. New York: Berghan.

———. 2002. *Trekking through History: The Huaorani of Amazonian Ecuador.* New York: Columbia University Press.

————. 2005. "The Attachment of the Soul to the Body among the Huaorani of Amazonian Ecuador." *Ethnos* 70, no. 3: 285–310.

————. 2010a. "Ecuador's Yasuní-ITT Initiative: The Old and New Values of Petroleum." *Agricultural Economics* 70:358–65.

————. 2010b. "Planning Development Futures in the Ecuadorian Amazon: The Expanding Oil Frontier and the Yasuní-ITT Initiative." Available at http://www .sosyasuni.org/en/index.php?option=com_content&view=article&id=148:pl anning-development-futures-in-the-ecuadorian-amazon-the-expanding-oil -frontier-and-the-yasuni-itt-initiative&catid=1:news&Itemid=34 (accessed June 14, 2014).

Riviere, Peter. 1974. "The Couvade: A Problem Reborn." *Man, Journal of the Royal Anthropological Institute* 9, no. 3: 423–35.

Robarchek, Clayton, and Carole Robarchek. 1996. "The Aucas, the Cannibals, and the Missionaries: From Warfare to Peacefulness among the Waorani." In Gregor, *Natural History of Peace*, 189–212.

————. 1998. *Waorani: The Contexts of Violence and War*. Fort Worth, Tex.: Harcourt Brace College.

————. 2005. "Waorani Grief and the Witch-Killer's Rage: Worldview, Emotion, and Anthropological Explanation." *Ethos* 33, no. 2: 206–30.

Robbins, Joel. 2007. "Continuity Thinking and the Problem of Christian Culture: Belief, Time, and the Anthropology of Christianity." *Current Anthropology* 48, no.1: 5–38.

Roitman, Karem. 2009. *Race, Ethnicity, and Power in Ecuador: The Manipulation of Mestizaje*. Boulder: First Forum.

Roosevelt, Anna. (1994) 1997. "Amazonian Anthropology: Strategy for a New Synthesis." In *Amazonian Indians: From Prehistory to Present*, edited by Anna Roosevelt, 1–29. Tucson: University of Arizona Press.

Sahlins, Marshall. 1985. *Islands of History*. Chicago: University of Chicago Press.

————. 2011a. "What Kinship Is (Part One)." *Journal of the Royal Anthropological Institute* 17:2–19.

————. 2011b. "What Kinship Is (Part Two)." *Journal of the Royal Anthropological Institute* 17:227–42.

Saint, Steve. 2005. *End of the Spear*. Carol Stream, Ill.: Tyndale.

Salomon, Frank. 1981. "Killing the Yumbo: A Ritual Drama in Northern Quito." In Whitten, *Cultural Transformations*, 162–210.

Santos-Granero, Fernando. 1991. *The Power of Love: The Moral Use of Knowledge among the Amuesha of Central Peru*. London: Athlone.

————. 2000. "The Sisyphus Syndrome; or, The Struggle for Conviviality in Native Amazonia." In Overing and Passes, *Anthropology of Love and Anger*, 268–87.

————. 2009. *Vital Enemies: Slavery, Predation, and the Amerindian Political Economy of Life*. Austin: University of Texas Press.

Sawyer, Suzana. 2004. *Crude Chronicles: Indigenous Politics, Multinational Oil, and Neoliberalism in Ecuador*. Durham, N.C.: Duke University Press.

Schneider, David. 1984. *A Critique of the Study of Kinship*. Ann Arbor: University of Michigan Press.

Seymour-Smith, Charlotte. 1991. "Women Have No Affines and Men No Kin: The Politics of the Jivaroan Gender Relation." *Man, Journal of the Royal Anthropological Institute* (N.S.) 26, no. 4: 629–49.

Shaw, Rosalind. 2002. *Memories of the Slave Trade: Ritual and Historical Imagination in Sierra Leone*. Chicago: University of Chicago Press.

Smith, Randy. 2004. "La problemática territorial Taromenane." In Cabodevilla, Smith, and Rivas, *Tiempos de Guerra*, 83–131.

Sponsel, Leslie. 2010. "Into the Heart of Darkness: Rethinking the Canonical Ethnography of the Yanomamo." In *Nonkilling Societies*, edited by Joam Evans Pim, 197–240. Honolulu, Hawaii: Center for Global Nonkilling.

Sponsel, Leslie, and Thomas Gregor, eds. 1994. *The Anthropology of Peace and Non-Violence*. Boulder, Colo.: Cynne Rienner.

Stasch, Rupert. 2009. *Society of Others: Kinship and Mourning in a West Papuan Place*. Berkeley: University of California Press.

Stoll, David. 1982. *Fishers of Men or Founders of Empire? The Wycliffe Bible Translators in Latin America*. London: Zed.

Stoller, Paul. 1995. *Embodying Colonial Memories: Spirit Possession, Power, and the Hauka in West Africa*. New York: Routledge.

Taussig, Michael. 1984. "Culture of Terror—Space of Death: Roger Casement's Putumayo Report and the Explanation of Torture." *Comparative Studies in Society and History* 26, no. 1: 467–97.

———. 1987. *Shamanism, Colonialism, and the Wild Man: A Study in Terror and Healing*. Chicago: University of Chicago Press.

Taylor, Anne Christine. 1981. "God-Wealth: The Achuar and the Missions." In Whitten, *Cultural Transformations*, 647–76.

———. 1983. "The Marriage Alliance and its Structural Variations among Jivaroan Societies." *Social Science Information* 22, no. 3: 331–53.

———. 1993. "Remembering to Forget: Identity, Mourning and Memory among the Jívaro." *Man, Journal of the Royal Anthropological Institute* (N.S.) 28:653–78.

———. 1994. "Una categoria irreductible en el Conjunto de las naciones indigenas: Los Jivaro en las representaciones occidentales." In Muratorio, *Imágenes e imagineros*, 75–108.

———. 1996. "The Soul's Body and Its States: An Amazonian Perspective on the Nature of Being Human." *Journal of the Royal Anthropological Institute* 2, no. 2: 201–15.

———. 1999. "The Western Margins of Amazonia from the Early-Sixteenth to the Early-Nineteenth Century." In *The Cambridge History of the Native Peoples of the Americas*, vol. 3: South America, edited by Frank Salomon and Stuart B. Schwartz, 188–256. Cambridge: Cambridge University Press.

—. 2000. "Le sexe de la proie: Représentations Jivaro du lien de parenté." *L'Homme* 154–55:309–33.

—. 2007. "Sick of History: Contrasting Regimes of Historicity in the Upper Amazon." In *Time and Memory in Indigenous Amazonia: Anthropological Perspectives*, edited by Carlos Fausto and Michael Heckenberger), 133–68. Tallahassee: University of Florida Press.

Thomas, Nicholas, and Caroline Humphrey. 1996. *Shamanism, History, and the State*. Ann Arbor: University of Michigan Press.

Tidmarsh, Wilfred T., and Joaquina Grefa. 1945. Unarranged notes on the Aucas of the Nushino Basin. Quito: Archivo Histórico del Banco Central, col. 24, 1–8.

Tönnies, Ferdinand. (1887) 1957. *Community and Society*. Translated by Charles P. Loomis. East Lansing: Michigan State University Press.

Tsing, Anna. 2005. *Friction: An Ethnography of Global Connection*. Princeton, N.J.: Princeton University Press.

Turner, Terence. 1979. "Kinship, Household, and Community Structure among the Kayapó." In *Dialectical Societies: The Gê and Bororo of Central Brazil*, edited by David Maybury-Lewis, 179–217. Cambridge, Mass.: Harvard University Press.

—. 1980. "The Social Skin." In *Not Work Alone*, edited by Jeremy Cherfas and Roger Lewin, 112–40. Beverly Hills, Calif.: Sage.

—. 1988. "Ethno-ethnohistory: Myth and History in Native South American Representations of Contact with Western Society." In Hill, *Rethinking History and Myth*, 235–81.

—. 1991. "Representing, Resisting, Rethinking: Historical Transformations of Kayapo Culture and Anthropological Consciousness." In *Colonial Situations: Essays on the Contextualization of Ethnographic Knowledge*, edited by George Stocking, 285–313. Madison: University of Wisconsin Press.

—. 1993. "De cosmologia a história: Resistência, adaptação e consiência social entre os Kayapó." In Viveiros de Castro and Manuela Carneiro da Cunha, *Amazonia*, 43–66.

—. 1995. "Social Body and Embodied Subject: Bodiliness, Subjectivity, and Sociality among the Kayapó." *Cultural Anthropology* 10, no. 2: 143–70.

—. 2004. "Discussion: 'On Kuper's Return of the Native.'" *Current Anthropology* 45, no. 2: 264–65.

—. 2009. "The Crisis of Late Structuralism: Perspectivism and Animism; Rethinking Culture, Nature, Spirit, and Bodiliness." *Tipití* 7, no. 1: 3–42.

United Nations Human Rights Council. 2009. *Draft Guidelines on the Protection of Indigenous Peoples in Voluntary Isolation and in Initial Contact of the Amazon Basin and El Chaco*. Geneva: United Nations Document.

Urban, Greg. 2001. *Metaculture: How Culture Moves through the World*. Minneapolis: University of Minnesota Press.

Uzendoski, Michael A. 2004. "The Horizontal Archipelago: The Quijos/Upper Napo Regional System." *Ethnohistory* 51, no. 2: 317–57.

———. 2005. *The Napo Runa of Amazonian Ecuador*. Urbana: University of Illinois Press.

Uzendoski, Michael A., and Edith F. Calapucha-Tapuy. 2012. *The Ecology of the Spoken Word: Amazonian Storytelling and Shamanism among the Napo Runa*. Urbana: University of Illinois Press.

Uzendoski, Michael A., and Norman Whitten. Forthcoming. "From 'Acculturated Indians' to 'Dynamic Amazonian Quichua-Speaking Peoples.'" *Tipití*.

Vilaça, Aparecida. 1993. "O canibalismo funerario Pakaa-Nova: Uma etnografia." In Viveiros de Castro and Manuela Carneiro da Cunha, *Amazonia*, 285–310.

———. 1997. "Christians without Faith: Some Aspects of the Conversion of the Wari (Pakaa Nova)." *Ethnos* 62, no. 1–2: 201–15.

———. 2002. "Making Kin out of Others in Amazonia." *Journal of the Royal Anthropological Institute* 8:347–64.

———. 2005. "Chronically Unstable Bodies: Reflections on Amazonian Corporalities." *Journal of the Royal Anthropological Institute* 11, no. 3: 445–64.

———. 2010. *Strange Enemies: Agency and Scenes of Encounters in Amazonia*. Durham, N.C.: Duke University Press.

Viveiros de Castro, Eduardo. 1992. *From the Enemy's Point of View: Humanity and Divinity in an Amazonian Society*. Chicago: University of Chicago Press.

———. 1993. "Alguns aspectos da afinidade no dravidianato amazónico." In Viveiros de Castro and Manuela Carneiro da Cunha, *Amazonia*, 149–210.

———. 1996. "Images of Nature and Society in Amazonian Ethnology." *Annual Reviews of Anthropology* 25:179–200.

———. 1998a. "Cosmological Deixis and Amerindian Perspectivism." *Journal of the Royal Anthropological Institute* 4, no. 3: 469–88.

———. 1998b. "Dravidian and Related Kinship Systems." In *Transformations of Kinship*, edited by Maurice Godelier, Thomas Trautmann, and Franklin Tjon Sie Fat, 332–85. Washington, D.C.: Smithsonian Institution.

———. 2001. "GUT Feelings about Amazonia: Potential Affinity and the Construction of Sociality." In *Beyond the Visible and the Material: The Amerindianization of Society in the Work of Peter Rivière*, edited by Laura Rival and Neil Whitehead, 19–44. Oxford: Oxford University Press.

———. 2004. "Perspectival Anthropology and the Method of Controlled Equivocation." *Tipití* 2, no. 1: 3–22.

———. 2011. *The Inconstancy of the Indian Soul: The Encounter of Catholics and Cannibals in 16th Century Brazil*. Chicago: Prickly Paradigm.

Viveiros de Castro, Eduardo, and Manuela Carneiro da Cunha. 1993. *Amazonia: Etnologia e história*. São Paolo: FAPESP.

Viveiros Vigoya, Mara. 2004. "Contemporary Latin American Perspectives on

Masculinity." In *Changing Men and Masculinities in Latin America*, edited by Matthew Gutmann, 27–60. Durham, N.C.: Duke University Press.

Wade, Peter. 1994. "Man the Hunter: Gender and Violence in Music and Drinking Contexts in Colombia." In *Sex and Violence: Issues in Representation and Experience*, edited by Peter Gow and Penelope Harvey, 115–37. London: Routledge.

Wallis, Ethel. 1960. *The Dayuma Story: Life under Auca Spears*. New York: Harper and Brothers.

———. 1973. *Aucas Downriver*. New York: Harper and Row.

Warren, Kay, and Jean Jackson, eds. 2002. *Indigenous Movements, Self-Representation, and the State in Latin America*. Austin: University of Texas Press.

Whitehead, Neil. 1993. "Historical Discontinuity and Ethnic Transformation in Native Amazonia and Guayana." *L'Homme* 33, no. 28: 289–309.

———. 2002. *Dark Shamans: Kanaima and the Poetics of Violent Death*. Durham, N.C.: Duke University Press.

———. 2003. "Introduction." In *Histories and Historicities in Amazonia*, edited by Neil Whitehead, vii–xx. Lincoln: University of Nebraska Press.

Whitehead, Neil, and Robin Wright. 2004. *In Darkness and Secrecy: The Anthropology of Assault Sorcery and Witchcraft in Amazonia*. Durham, N.C.: Duke University Press.

Whitehouse, Harvey. 1996. "Rites of Terror: Emotion, Metaphor, and Memory in Melanesian Initiation Cults." *Journal of the Royal Anthropological Institute* 2, no. 4: 703–15.

Whitten, Norman, Jr. 1976a. *Sacha Runa: Ethnicity and Adaptation of Ecuadorian Jungle Quichua*. Urbana: University of Illinois Press.

———. 1976b. *Ecuadorian Ethnocide and Indigenous Ethnogenesis: Amazonian Resurgence amidst Andean Colonization*. Copenhagen: IWGIA Document 23.

———. 1978. *Amazonian Ecuador: An Ethnic Interface of Ecological, Social and Ideological Perspectives*. Copenhagen: IWGIA Document 34.

———. 1981a. "Afterword." In Whitten, *Cultural Transformations*, 776–97.

———. 1981b. *Cultural Transformations and Ethnicity in Modern Ecuador*. Urbana: University of Illinois Press.

———. 1988. "Commentary: Historical and Mythic Evocations of Chthonic Power in South America." In Hill, *Rethinking History and Myth*, 282–306.

———. 1996. "The Ecuadorian Levantamiento Indígena of 1990 and the Epitomizing Symbol of 1992: Reflections on Nationalism, Ethnic-Bloc Formation, and Racialist Ideologies." In *History, Power, and Identity: Ethnogenesis in the Americas*, edited by Jonathan Hill, 193–218. Iowa City: University of Iowa Press.

———. 1997. "Return of the Yumbo: The Indigenous Caminata from Amazonia to Andean Quito." *American Ethnologist* 24, no. 2: 355–91.

———. 2003. *Millennial Ecuador: Critical Essays on Cultural Transformations and Social Dynamics*. Iowa City: University of Iowa Press.

————. 2008. "Interculturality and the Indigenization of Modernity: A View from Amazonian Ecuador." *Tipití* 6, nos. 1–2: 3–36.

————. 2011a. "Ethnogenesis and Interculturality in the 'Forest of Canelos': The Wild and the Tame Revisited." In *Ethnicity in Ancient Amazonia: Reconstructing Past Identities from Archaeology, Linguistics, and Ethnohistory*, edited by Alf Hornborg and Jonathan Hill, 321–34. Boulder: University Press of Colorado.

————. 2011b. "Indigenous Modernity." In Whitten and Whitten, *Histories of the Present*, 165–85.

Whitten, Norman, and Dorothea Whitten. 2008. *Puyo Runa: Imagery and Power in Modern Amazonia*. Urbana: University of Illinois Press.

————. 2011. *Histories of the Present: People and Power in Ecuador*. Urbana: University of Illinois Press.

Whitten, Norman, Dorothea Whitten, and Alfonso Chango. 2008. "Return of the Yumbo: The Caminata from Amazonia to Andean Quito." In Whitten and Whitten, *Puyo Runa*, 200–230.

Wood, Michael. 2006. "Kamula Accounts of Rambo and the State of Papua New Guinea." *Oceania* 76, no. 1: 61–82.

Wright, Robin. 2013. *Mysteries of the Jaguar Shamans of the Northwest Amazon*. Lincoln: University of Nebraska Press.

Yost, James. 1981. "Twenty Years of Contact: The Mechanisms of Change in Wao (Auca) Culture." In Whitten, *Cultural Transformations*, 677–704.

Zeigler-Otero, Lawrence. 2004. *Resistance in an Amazonian Community: Huaorani Organizing Against the Global Economy*. New York: Berghahn.

Index

abduction: of girls from Taromenani, 178, 179, 181, 196n8; of Quichua man, 131; and slave raiders, 30; and Taromenani massacre, 106; of women, 37, 51, 82, 123, 188n2

abuse, spousal, 78, 94, 154–55

accidents: and assault sorcery, 158, 159, 162; and becoming a shaman, 157, 161

acculturation: and categorization of indigenous people, 71; and modernity, 169; and shamanism, 164–65; and social transformation, 56–57, 125; and Wao-Quichua relations, 145, 163

Achuar, 65, 122, 125

activism, indigenous, 7, 15, 71, 125, 169; and categorization of groups, 57; ecological, 170, 172, 174, 176; and imagery of indigenous people, 72, 170; and masculinity, 92; and national pluralism, 55; and oil development, 8, 53, 182–83; and Waorani solidarity, 8, 148

adversarial relationships, 71, 72, 73

affinity: and enemies, 7, 122, 139, 143–45, 146, 179; and intergroup relations, 141–43, 144–45; and kinship, 112, 143–45; and the "other," 141, 142, 144; potential, 141, 144; and use of term *brother-in-law*, 141, 143, 144

agency: and bodies, 79, 188n5; and cultural continuity, 11; and exteriority, 70, 76–77, 97; and gender, 76–78, 79, 89, 90, 93, 94; and generational change, 91–92, 93; and humans as cause of misfortune, 36, 39; and shamanism, 155, 156, 157, 158; and sociality, 93, 94; and urban indigenous politics, 94; and whipping, 80–81

alcohol: and education, 152; and *kowori*, 121, 126–28, 130; and masculinity, 95–96; and schoolteachers, 129, 151–53; and *tiname*, 126–28, 130; and Wao-Quichua relations, 127, 130, 143; and youth, 126–27, 128, 130. *See also* beer, manioc (*tepe*)

alterity, 3; in Amazonian anthropology, 77–78; and *auca* symbolism, 67; in indigenous cosmology, 13; and intercultural relations, 49; and kinship, 167; and politics of isolation, 110, 111, 114; and predation, 188n5; and social connection, 111, 118; and social memory, 74, 101; and uncontacted people, 118; and victimhood, 39, 40; and Wao-Quichua relations, 8, 122, 144, 147; and Waorani cosmology, 155; and Waorani narratives, 71, 72, 73; youth as managers of, 73

Amazonia: and anthropology, 7, 9, 185n5; and colonialism, 9, 30; and intercultural

Casey High is a lecturer in social anthropology at the University of Edinburgh. He is coeditor of *The Anthropology of Ignorance: An Ethnographic Approach.*

INTERPRETATIONS OF CULTURE IN THE NEW MILLENNIUM

The University of Illinois Press
is a founding member of the
Association of American University Presses.

Composed in 10.5/13 Minion
with Avenir display
by Jim Proefrock
at the University of Illinois Press
Manufactured by Cushing-Malloy, Inc.

University of Illinois Press
1325 South Oak Street
Champaign, IL 61820-6903
www.press.uillinois.edu